Face to Face with Asia

PIERRE MENDÈS FRANCE

Face to Face with Asia

Translated from the French by Susan Danon

Liveright · New York

Originally published in France in 1972 by Éditions Gallimard.

Copyright © 1974 by Liveright.
Liveright
386 Park Avenue South
New York, New York 10016
1.987654321
ISBN: 0-87140-567-9
Library of Congress Catalog Card Number: 72-97493

Designed by Mary M. Ahern
Manufactured in the United States of America

CONTENTS

PREFACE

At this time when the American edition of my book is about to be published, many events, all of them predictable, have taken place and have modified certain aspects of the problems of Asia.

When I was there, Tokyo was principally preoccupied with the rapid reestablishment of normal relations with China; Peking was awaiting Nixon's historic visit; New Delhi, with the war just over, was still under fierce tension vis-à-vis Pakistan and was facing very uncertain new economic problems. Nevertheless, prospects which have since become more clearly defined were already emerging everywhere. Their main development followed the establishment of direct contact between Peking and Washington—a contact which has proved to be gracious even though it has not yet adopted the classical form of diplomatic relations.

It was clear to everyone by the end of 1971 that we were approaching peace in Vietnam. I, in fact, never doubted that at least a partial agreement would be reached in the following months. It was even fairly obvious to most people that peace could have been concluded much earlier, since the conditions for this agreement, a few details excepted, had been practically met already. Nevertheless, this was still a preliminary stage.

Now that this problem has been settled—even if true peace and the construction of the future in Vietnam still, alas, have not been achieved—the fundamental problems can and must be broached. China, voted in by a strong majority, is now a member of the United Nations and already pulls her weight there. She now participates in international life, which has been profoundly modified by her very "presence." All these are important signs which make 1973 a turning point which will take its place in history. This transformation of the world situation has led the Soviet Union, Japan, and of course the United States to revise and adapt their policies. There are questions which can no longer be shelved. China finds herself facing new possibilities which are already emerging very clearly in commercial and economic affairs. In spite of her usual rigidity in the purely political field, she has not chosen to take a negative and destructive stand. China believes in and makes no attempt to hide her medium- and long-range policies, yet today she appears to be seeking the consolidation of peace. This does not surprise me, since it confirms what I have always expected.

The other countries must now support this resolve and consider it not only in their relations with China, but also in their relations with other countries throughout the world, especially in the Third World, in Asia and elsewhere.

I believe I was conscious of all this when I was there, and I took note of it in the following pages. Leafing through them, it seems to me that the large problems still appear basically and precisely the same now as they did then. Some things may seem to have changed outwardly, there may have been vicissitudes here and there, yet the heads of state were equally preoccupied by the development of the emerging nations, by their relations with the Soviet Union and with the United States, and by the transformed balance of power in the Pacific and, in a more general way, in the whole Asian world. The same worries, the same threats, the same aspirations, and the same impatience are with us today.

Consequently, the elements of information which I gathered on my journey and set down in this small book without pretension are still valid. If I were to retrace my steps tomorrow, I would undoubtedly witness other episodes and other incidents, I would undoubtedly collect a few other statements from different people. Nevertheless, I believe that, though the rest of the world knows and understands too little about these facts, the conclusions one can draw from them—and, what is more, the questions to which they give rise—are still as true and even as topical now as they were then, including their dramatic import.

That is why the value of these notes has not changed with time. Their only value is of fragmentary yet authentic impressions in which the reader will find implications that have lost none of their significance. We must not allow the complexity and magnitude of the events interacting across distant lands to make us forget their far-reaching consequences. These will be immense for the whole world as it undergoes profound change at the end of this twentieth century.

October 23, 1973

Thursday, 9th December 1971

Departure from Orly at one o'clock in cold but quite pleasant weather.

I felt a youthful excitement. My childhood dream was about to come true. I was going around the world!

It is curious that, because "the world is round," the direct route from Paris to Tokyo passes over the North Pole. We will fly very close to it. So many men have risked their lives to reach it and now every day dozens of planes fly over it.

I had one regret only: as it was dark I could see nothing. But would there have been anything worth seeing?

As I awoke, I saw that my watch, still at Paris time, showed midnight, yet day was dawning. We were flying over Alaska. Before us stretched a panorama of wasteland and ice, high mountains and snow sparkling in the early morning sun.

Soon we landed in Anchorage, to find an ultra-modern American-style airport in a desolate land. Equipment and gadgets found only in the most modern airports contrasted strangely with the completely wild state of nature. The weather was beautiful and the light magnificent.

As we took off, I gazed upon this unexpected agglomeration, lost in the far North. I was told that there are 250,000 Americans there, pilots and military men, but scarcely a single native.

I fell asleep after take-off, and when I woke up the stewardess told me that I had aged twenty-four hours. We had crossed the famous line that marks the change in date. Phileas Fogg gained a day by traveling the opposite way around the world. I had just lost as much and—even reasoning logically—it was a very difficult fact to accept.

Japan

Japan

Friday, 10th December

We arrived in Tokyo at five o'clock (local time). Some Japanese and French friends met us and took us into town. It is four miles from the airport to the town, but, because of the traffic, it takes three-quarters of an hour to cover the distance. We could see a panorama of highways, bridges, tunnels, railways, and subways intertwining, playing leap-frog, and encircling countless factories and super-modern buildings which were rather ugly in spite of their multi-colored neon lighting.

There is an overwhelming impression of swarming humanity, of saturation. The problem of overpopulation becomes obvious at a glance. After all, Japan has more than one hundred million inhabitants in a land much smaller than France, 80 percent of which is uninhabitable because of the terrain (mountains, rocks, etc.). It is understandable that several years ago the Japanese government began a birth-control campaign based largely on abortion. But such things are complex. They discovered that this would lead to a dangerous situation— the productive population of the country would decline— and so they were obliged to reconsider their plans. A friend accompanying me told me that, consequently, the birth rate has remained quite high, the most recent census of the towns showing an average family size of 3.75 persons (compared to more than 4 in 1965).

Still more congestion. My friends explained that the Japanese can no longer settle in the cities, where there is literally no more space. They are obliged to live in the rapidly developing suburbs. But the resulting traffic is mind-boggling.

The proportion of urban population (that in the towns and

immediate suburbs) to the total population is the highest in the world. An astonishing network of highways and other means of transportation result, with their inevitable environmental consequences: noise, pollution, and so on.

We were warmly welcomed at the French Embassy. It is in modern Japanese style and situated in a very prettily laid out park, quite unexpected in the middle of town. But above all I needed to sleep.

I slept for ten hours.

Saturday, 11th December

A tour of Tokyo with Mr. Suzuki and Mr. Giuglaris. Metal and concrete everywhere. In this land of earthquakes they have apparently developed dependable building techniques using concrete and steel. The result is incoherent and dehumanized. We seem to be passing through one hideous suburb after another, all intersected by overhead throughways running in all directions.

Because of the bombing, which destroyed almost everything, few old Japanese houses remain. There are a few Wilhelmian buildings from the period of German influence, which was especially strong under the Nazis. The robust, heavy, square Diet, for instance, reminds one of the triumphant Third Reich. Elsewhere, there are some traditional English red brick and yellow stone buildings. Nevertheless, it is American postwar architecture which dominates the scene. In some places you could almost believe you were on Park Avenue in New York. I am told, however, that these buildings are designed by eminent Japanese architects, who adapt foreign techniques to local needs and to the local spirit. My first impression is of a lack of imagination.

After the last war the Japanese missed their opportunity to rebuild a town in their own style, which would have reflected their own culture and could still have been compatible with modern requirements.

In the afternoon we continued the visit: large stores, stations, and so forth. From the thirty-ninth floor of a tower, we viewed the city: the same bustling scene of milling crowds and intense traffic. How would the city survive without this extraordinary system of highways, monorails, and subways!

Nevertheless, the people in the streets have smiling faces, and, although they appear to be very busy and hurried, they do not seem nervous or irritable.

Sunday, 12th December

Another morning spent sight-seeing: the Meiji Park, the No theater. And above all the cathedral, the most beautiful, most moving modern church I have ever seen; concrete springing up to the sky, soft light, serenity, and a profound silence.

On the way back we passed a procession of fifty or sixty people carrying red flags and large posters, which I, of course, was unable to read. We could hear the sound of a strange version of the "Marseillaise." These were strikers, marching to this hymn, preserving its revolutionary meaning.

I was invited to lunch with a diverse group of individuals: diplomats, journalists, jurists, and militants from pro-French organizations. Inevitably, our conversation centered on the important topics in the news: the situation created by the monetary crisis, the weakness of the dollar, the American balance of payments deficit, Nixon's decisions and their repercussions on international exchange rates. Whatever the outcome, Americans will henceforth be making a massive effort to readjust their balance of payments, which will hinder European and Japanese exports. If, as seems likely, the industrialized countries' net sales—exports minus imports—to the United States are reduced, there could be serious consequences, such as unemployment.

This situation will not immediately plunge Japan into a crisis; her exports amount to no more than 10 percent of her total production—a lower percentage than that of West Germany and England. However, more than a third of her foreign trade is with the United States; thus the threat is greater for her than it is for Europe. For certain industries that percentage exceeds two-thirds of exports. New buyers must be found for them. Where? In Europe? In the underdeveloped and the socialist countries? China, of course, comes to mind. In Japanese industrial circles there apparently is an inclination toward the normalization of relations between Tokyo and Peking in order to improve trade, which is already substantial.

But it is neither quick nor easy to replace the American market with those of China or Indonesia. Selling more to socialist and Third World countries poses some problems. Japan has specialized in manufactured products with an unusually large percentage of value added. This would explain why the Americans are her best customers. I believe that, if Japan has difficulties in exporting to the United States, she will try to increase her sales in Europe. We are likely to witness a major attempt to transfer Japanese exports—deprived of growth possibilities in the United States—to the Old World, especially since industrial prices are lower in Japan than in other producer countries: 10 percent less than in Germany, 20 percent less than in France. But in Europe, where similar articles are produced, this competition is not likely to be welcomed, as it is dangerous in view of Japan's competitive efficiency, based on high capacity and relatively low salaries.

Those with whom I spoke seemed conscious of the fear aroused by their commercial enterprises. They often speak about the success with which the Americans moved into Europe after the war, provoking relatively less reaction than the Japanese did in the United States and elsewhere. They would like to replace the Americans in Western Europe, avoiding, wherever possible, mistakes and exaggerations likely to generate extreme protests and resistance. They intend to invest capital and to buy European firms in preparation for their commercial offensive. Their government has already restructured the exchange-control regulations to encourage the investment of greater amounts of Japanese capital in western countries.

The first to be hit will be Great Britain, followed by Germany, Switzerland, France, and Italy. The entire problem should be examined collectively in Brussels. We were not capable of forming a united front to face the large problem of

American investments in Europe. I wonder if we will be more far-sighted about Japan's exports and the investments she is likely to make in the future.

What strikes me is the lack of initiative of our exporters toward Japan, which already has an important commercial surplus in Europe; this surplus, according to what I heard before leaving Paris, will be much higher in 1971 than it was in 1970.

I brought the conversation around to Japan's export possibilities in other markets, such as those of the socialist and underdeveloped countries. Here I met with a somewhat hesitant response. Would the type of merchandise Japan is used to exporting be suitable for these markets? The underdeveloped and socialist countries are mainly interested in equipment, transport materials, machines, and products of heavy industry which Japan has until now made in only very limited quantities, and which she herself finds it necessary to import from the United States. In order to be in a position, in the future, to meet the demands of this market, she will be obliged, to some extent, to change the nature of her foreign trade. This is never an easy task, as it entails changes which are often troublesome to undertake.

Moreover, the equipment others will buy from her will include a small proportion of labor and technology and a much larger proportion of raw materials and embodied energy. However, Japan lacks raw materials and sources of energy; her main advantage lies in selling hours of labor and what economists call "value added." Thus, in general, her foreign-trade prospects seem less profitable and more difficult to achieve than in the past.

In any case, Japan has a permanent problem linked to the very structure of the country: that of obtaining materials, as well as food products. Her own land does not produce the primary products essential to her. She has no colonial or post-colonial possessions, no oil concessions, no exploitation rights. She buys what she needs on the market, at market prices—a situation which can often be to her advantage, yet remains precarious and hazardous. In this manner she obtains petroleum at a better rate than most countries which own exploitation rights, but her supplies are continually uncertain, and this is one of her principal preoccupations. It inevitably affects her political attitude toward supplier countries: the United States on the one hand, the underdeveloped countries on the other, and probably China later on.

The Japanese point out that they have greatly increased the extent of their aid to the Third World. Japan is the second-largest supplier of aid to underdeveloped nations, immediately behind the United States. Her contribution is greater than that of France (and we must take into account that in France we classify as "aid" the sums of money devoted to our overseas territories and provinces, and they represent almost half the total). Japanese participation, therefore, is very high, and it seems likely that she will be obliged to increase it even further. But there is a direct connection, recognized by all those I questioned, between Japan's aid to underdeveloped countries and her search for raw materials. This is what gives special significance to Japan's interest in Formosa, Indonesia, South Vietnam, Thailand, Burma, and even in Latin America, where large Japanese firms come in search of basic products necessary to her economy. Apparently, here and there, where the memory of Japan's military presence is still alive, there have been difficulties with local protests.

Nevertheless, it is interesting to note that, according to the figures I was given, public or governmental aid remains fairly low and includes restrictive clauses for the beneficiary countries which aim at redirecting their commercial flow to Japan rather than their former mother-countries, toward which they continue to turn. Classical private investments, however, have grown considerably, which explains Japan's gratifying position (mentioned above) in the list of countries which trade actively today in the Third World. Not only are Japanese firms seeking basic products there, but they also are building factories and setting up distribution—and even export —networks for the resulting goods. This is causing anxiety in certain Japanese circles preoccupied by possible commercial rivalry between the manufactured products exported by Japan herself, and those identical products which will be made in the future on the shores of the Pacific by firms created with Japanese capital. (We witnessed the same kind of competition in Europe between American firms and companies created with American capital.)

Because of Japan's shortage of energy sources I was curious to know, and asked, what stage she had reached in the study of the possibilities of producing atomic energy. Japan does not have at her disposal any direct or secure supply of uranium; she is, at present, negotiating with France, the United States, and Canada. She is considering the installation of a certain number of power stations to be supplied by France and the United States primarily, and secondarily by a group consisting of Great Britain, Holland, and Germany. No one could give me further details.

We had a quiet dinner at the Residence and enjoyed the very agreeable hospitality of Ambassador and Madame de Guiringaud. The Ambassador drew an impressive picture of Japan's domestic and foreign political situation which he knows well, adding vivid descriptions of the main characters and forces at work in this country. How absurd to be staying here only ten days; unfortunately, I have no choice.

Monday, 13th December

A somewhat different luncheon from yesterday's. I was seated between Mr. Shigeo Horie, a former president of the Bank of Tokyo, and Mr. Satoshi Sumita, a former financial attaché in Paris and former Minister of Finance. Marie-Claire was placed beside Mr. Masayuki Yokoyama, an eminent Japanese jurist whose grandson is studying in Grenoble; the world is small indeed. Also present were professors, diplomats, and journalists, among whom were R. de Suzannet of *Figaro,* R. Guillain of *Le Monde,* Brisard of the A.F.P. (*Agence France Presse*), Giuglaris of *France-Soir* and of *Europe No 1;* the latter and Mr. Suzuki were partly responsible for my journey.

But chiefly I wanted to question the important Japanese people there. For them the resumption of relations with China is important, and to this end they must condemn Japan's past actions under the Middle Empire. But the Peking government is exacting. It insists on being recognized as the only legal government of China. So be it. It demands that Taiwan—formerly Formosa—be proclaimed a Chinese province without any reservations. So be it. It insists, as a prerequisite, upon Japan's unilaterally ending the treaty she signed with Chiang Kai-shek a few years ago under American pressure; that is a more delicate matter, as the Japanese have close economic relations with Taiwan. Some of those at the luncheon consider it almost impossible to terminate the cooperation treaty, at least at present.

In short, everyone (except, I am told, certain extreme right-wing factions, though these are few) hopes for an improvement in relations with China and for the end of the abnormal situation which has lasted twenty years. But the problems which normalization would cause bring to light certain nuances. The influential industrial circles would like to increase the volume of their business with China, although it is already fairly high. Japan, as a commercial partner of China, now represents about 20 percent of China's foreign trade. At the same time, neither the trade with Taiwan, nor the investments made there can be forgotten, for the economic progress of that large island has been considerable during the last few years, almost comparable to that of Japan. Such contradictory facts!

Nevertheless, even the head of the present Japanese government, representing the majority right-wing party, has expressed his desire to recognize the Peking government, going so far as to apologize publicly for Japan's past actions in China and for the suffering inflicted by Japanese militarism. But these declarations have not eased the situation, and Peking has several times made it clear that it refuses to negotiate with the political team in power.

In the meantime, countless delegations make their way to China where they have to hear—and sometimes make—

painful declarations; the Japanese government is the first to encourage these contacts, if only to maintain lucrative commercial relations through supposedly nongovernmental channels.

At the end of lunch I had a short conversation with Mr. Masayuki, a former ambassador and specialist in Vietnamese affairs. He does not seem optimistic about the chances for an early peace in Vietnam.

The same questions were brought up at dinner with Mr. Fujiyama, a deputy, a former Foreign Minister, and former Minister of Finance. He is the president of a league created to promote the improvement of relations between Peking and Tokyo, and he has recently been to China where he met Chou En-lai. Although a member of the Liberal-Democratic Party, at present in power, he believes that China's conditions, including the one concerning Taiwan, must be met. According to him, the departure of the Prime Minister, Mr. Sato, might make it possible to arrive at an acceptable arrangement. He speaks cautiously, but it is clear that he does not agree with the government and that in his opinion the possibility of a settlement is linked to a ministerial change. Furthermore, he hopes that Peking will not take advantage of the situation and try to take Taiwan by force, as he believes is possible.

Mr. Fujiyama remains moderate on the subject of the United States. He wonders if it is really necessary to end the Japanese-American security treaty; this treaty, he says, is not directed against Communist China, but against the Soviet Union, and the Chinese should agree to its being maintained. In return, the United States should reduce its military forces in the area, and in particular on Okinawa.

Will the Japanese be able to resist American pressure? Today, there is an important meeting in Honolulu between the American Treasury representatives and those of the Tokyo Ministry of Finance. The United States is putting forward a certain number of familiar requests and pressing in particular for the revaluation of the yen; but among other things, they are insisting on the opening of Japanese markets to their exports and on a new allocation of security expenses in the Far East. Japanese legislation today does indeed render it practically impossible for large foreign firms to settle in Japan. There are, of course, a few exceptions, the largest of which is I.B.M. But the controls, though slightly loosened in 1967, have remained tight enough to prevent the Americans from carving a considerable place for themselves in local industry, in contrast to what happened in Europe. The Japanese have built industrial establishments abroad and are determined to continue doing so in the future on an even larger scale, but they have not permitted other countries to reciprocate. They buy raw materials, technical processes, and know-how from abroad (Péchiney, for instance, sells them unfinished or semi-finished products, equipment, operational plants, and patents, but they have never succeeded in establishing themselves in Japan). The Americans wish to obtain what they call a liberalization—in other words the elimination of the protective system.

Of course, they run afoul of the resistance of the business community which is very powerful here. The Japanese economy is in effect dominated by extremely influential groups (the *zaibatsus*), conglomerates of banks, insurance companies, and industrial enterprises. More or less broken up by the American forces of occupation—much like the German trusts after the hostilities—they have regrouped, and their present power undoubtedly exceeds their former strength. The sales volume of one of the most important of them, Mitsubishi, corresponds to 10 percent of the national income.

Their activities in matters of public works, urban development, manufacture of military equipment, and so on, place them in close contact with the administration, political circles, and the government. Indeed, the state and heavy industry work side by side to aim for the same objectives and to reach the same ends (as shown by their political tactics vis-à-vis the developing countries). There is, therefore, a special connection between the ruling class and those responsible for the country's politics. The employers' associations form a general confederation, the *Keidanren,* where the most important and most influential financiers and managers can meet one another. Their ties with the government are not only very close but also are publicly acknowledged; this is also true of the Liberal-Democrats, the majority party up until now. Directors of large companies, high officials, and active members of the party in power all know one another well, having graduated from the same universities (one could almost say from the same university), and frequented the same clubs. So that any conflict occurring between a business group and the administration is solved within the ruling class itself.

When businessmen reach a certain age they turn to politics, while politicians often become managing directors. Business circles subsidize or finance political parties, movements (here they are called "clans"), or even leaders, and they make no attempt to hide this fact. Their financial contributions appear openly in their accounts and are published by the press.

There are inevitable economic consequences of this interpenetration of politics and business. They have no "Plan" as we understand it in France, yet the large firms and financial and banking groups structure the economy. An idea which is widely accepted, probably even by the masses, is that what is good for the trusts is good for Japan.

This afternoon I visited a Sony factory, a sizable corporation which has already spread abroad extensively and plans on doing so more and more. We were received by Mr. Morita, the managing director and, it appears, one of the most dynamic businessmen in Japan. His firm, starting from very little, today makes radios, television sets, video-cassettes, and calculators. He showed us several quite extraordinary experiments and demonstrations of the type of product he will be selling in the coming years. It was a very unusual demonstration, particularly of some kinds of television video-cassettes, the first of which are already being sold in Japan and will be available in Europe.

Sony exports more than one-third of its production to the United States. In spite of the shipping costs, customs duties, and the recently enforced 10 percent surtax, its sales are holding well. "Yet," says Mr. Morita, "our articles are a little more expensive than the American ones (about fifty dollars more for a television set), but they are of better quality and, in spite of the growing protectionist tendency in the United States, we expect to continue to increase our sales. Indeed, we are about to open a factory there to assemble television sets; we will send only from here those few parts which require the very delicate work at which we are unbeatable. We also plan to increase our sales in Europe considerably."

Mr. Morita's attitude led me to discuss with him the initiatives already taken by many branches of Japanese industry toward Europe, since these are sure to give rise to protests on the part of employers and employees alike. A young French diplomat with us told me that our industries should also take an interest in the Japanese market, where there are gaps to be filled. For instance, it appears that the Rossignol company thoroughly miscalculated the ski market in its export policy.

Visiting numerous workrooms, I was struck by the extremely intricate work performed on an assembly line, mostly by young girls between the ages of sixteen and twenty. They apparently work seven hours a day and earn a higher wage here than in other firms.

The salary range in Japan is much narrower than in Europe and the United States. Age is the basis for advancement. A young worker earns a relatively low wage which increases along with seniority. Women's wages are considerably lower than men's, partly because their work-spans are very short (often only until they are twenty-five or twenty-eight; there are practically no women over thirty-five still working). A worker in the same job all his life would see the level of his salary regularly rising and eventually reaching, at the end of his career, about four times what it was at the start. Added to this assurance of improvement in standard of living is a general wage increase. These are very important psychological factors in a country which until now has not known the problem of unemployment. In some factories there are young graduate engineers who earn less than many of the men working under them. They learn their professions on the job, wearing working clothes identical to those of the workers around them. They, of course, expect more rapid promotion, ultimately reaching higher salaries. But at the outset there reigns a kind of equality which is reflected in the behavior of all those involved.

In Japan, there are about 25 million households for a population of 105 million. Two hundred dollars is the average monthly family income. The development of production and of general prosperity is reflected in the increase in per capita income, which comes close to the Italian and Austrian level, and almost to the British level—though it is difficult to compare such dissimilar countries. But it is put to a very different use.

A large part of national income is channeled into industrial investment (the percentage is considerable, clearly above that of Western European countries, and accounts for Japan's high growth rate), supporting exports and the accumulation of monetary reserves. The individual, therefore, does not directly benefit from it. So that, considering the other aspect of the use of incomes, which is consumption, the average standard of living remains much inferior to that of the European countries.

Furthermore, individual consumption here has a very specific and original structure. The high proportion of family expenditure on such durable consumer goods as televisions and air conditioners can be explained by the strange method of payment based on bonuses. The actual wages are relatively low in comparison to American or European wages, but twice a year the workers receive a premium based upon the financial situation of the company, which consequently varies from firm to firm. It is always calculated in months, so workers receive three or four months' additional salary (seven, when they work for a prosperous company, and sometimes even ten). Evidently, the employers find this advantageous, since, in fact, a fraction of the total wage bill is deferred, which in the interval provides the companies with free and ample additional working capital with which to bolster their investments.

15

The benefit of this system to the workers is no less satisfactory, because it forces them to save, so that they spend a considerable share of their salaries and earnings not on daily consumption, but twice a year on buying durable goods such as electrical appliances. Advertising—which is very aggressive—constantly encourages them to do so; it is at the moment stressing the "three C's"—*car, cooler, color* (TV). The whole system replaces installment credit, widespread in the United States and Europe, but practically nonexistent here.

Instead of concentrating spending on food products, which could set off inflationary trends, the system directs a substantial part of salaries into a sector where technological progress and the increase in consumption allow a relative price stability. That explains why Japanese per capita consumption of television sets (they have a dozen channels here, two of which are state-owned), washing machines, textiles, and medical care is far above the average French, German, or English level, whereas meat consumption, for example, is below it.

Although salaries (including the bonus) remain 15 or 20 percent lower than those in Europe (this will actually be changed by the revaluation of the yen), Japan already has become the greatest consumer society in the world after the United States. She exhibits to an even greater extent than the U.S. the characteristics of the "New Industrial State," as John Kenneth Galbraith describes it.

In the last few years, her total production has increased by about 15 to 17 percent. Even if Japan is now entering a period of crisis (so much spoken of), her growth rate is likely to be superior to any in Europe. Thus, she will be able to undertake new investments, but the need to devote a part of her annual earnings to the improvement of living standards is beginning to be felt.

Indeed, the entire present situation is coming under discussion, and is, in fact, being contested by the union leaders, whom I would very much like to meet. But I am faced with an unexpected difficulty. Unlike the French unions, those here are not divided by profession, branch of industry, or activity. They are usually formed within the firm; each company has its union for all its personnel—workmen, technicians, white-collar workers. The result is a fragmentation of the trade union structure (wage demands may be tough, social movements and strikes may occur, yet these usually take place in individual firms). Nevertheless, I hope to have the opportunity of talking to trade union militants.

At any rate, it has already been agreed that I am to meet the leaders of all the political parties.

The first are the leaders of the Komeito, a left-wing party somewhat similar to the P.S.U. (*Parti Socialiste Unifié*). Originally intricately associated with Buddhism, it has long been dominated by this religious movement, and though it is becoming secularized, it is still strongly oriented toward and impregnated with moral preoccupations. (It is the "Clean Government Party.")

I met two of its leaders at half-past five: Mr. Junya Yano, deputy and secretary general, and Mr. Akira Kuroyanagi, senator for Tokyo. They at once voiced their dislike of the way in which the political life of the country is dominated by business and in which Japan is treated as an "economic animal"; according to them there is a need for a new kind of civilization better able to respect man and moral values. They condemn Japan's past unpardonable errors, for instance, vis-à-vis China. The nation must show "deep repentance" and "accept" humiliation and compromises to pay for its past attitude. Mr. Yano and Mr. Kuroyanagi disapprove of nuclear armament and violently denounce American policy in Vietnam. They naturally criticize the submissive attitude of Sato's government to the United States as having hindered in particular, they say, the essential need for better relations with China; in this matter they fully accept China's conditions concerning Taiwan and the plain and simple annulment of the Japanese-Formosan treaty.

But Japan's political life is dominated by the Liberal-Democratic Party, the right-wing movement now in power, whose leaders are Prime Minister Sato, Foreign Minister Fukuda, and, 17 though somewhat dissident, Mr. Fujiyama, whom I have already met. There are 301 Liberal-Democrats in the Diet; 90 deputies of the Socialist Party, which is the main opposition party; 30 from a so-called Social-Democrat group; 14 from the Communist Party and from the Komeito. These various opposition parties are on fairly bad terms.

Tuesday, 14th December

The newspaper *Daily Yomiuri*, which is the English edition of one of the most important Japanese papers, published this morning a six-column article under the title: "Who Really Won the Second World War in Asia?" signed by Robert Martin, an American specialist on Asian affairs. According to him, the war was really won by Japan and Chinese communism.

The Chinese Communists were weak before the war; they now occupy their entire national territory except for Formosa, and their worldwide influence is steadily growing.

As for the Japanese, what were their aims in 1935? They aspired to become the strongest power in Asia and to seize the natural resources and especially the oil of the states on the shores of the Pacific (starting with Indonesia). Finally, they wished to chase the Europeans from Asia. This is exactly what is happening today.

Japan is the third economic power in the world. She ranks first in naval construction; second in the automobile industry, electronic consumer goods, cameras, artificial and synthetic fibers; third in steel, glass, cement, and paper. She is nearing the Soviet Union's economic and industrial size and will soon overtake it. Her national income is around 200 billion dollars a year. Her foreign trade exceeds 34 billion dollars. Similar to what happened in Germany, Japan's military defeat, and especially the material destruction which preceded it, allowed her to reconstruct her industry; she started again from nothing, rid of the obsolete equipment which is still hindering the economy of many European countries. United States aid came quickly to support her efforts at recovery, and another positive factor was the opening of the American market. Better still, unlike most

18

industrial countries, the nation did not have to bear the burden of a large military budget; in Japan this represents only 1 percent of the national income, whereas in the United States it is around 10 percent. From 1960 to 1970 Japan devoted 10 billion dollars to military expenditure, whereas France, with half the population, spent 45 billion (not including nuclear armament).

There are other reasons for Japan's impressive expansion. First, there are the wages, which have long remained at an extremely low level, the submissiveness of the working people, and the infrequency of social conflicts. Then there is the rapidity with which the people adapted to new kinds of employment. In 1945, 45 percent of the work force was in agriculture, the remainder working mostly as artisans and in light industry; the rural exodus soon gained impetus, and today only 15 percent of the work force remains in agriculture.

Finally, we must take into account this extraordinary general intensity, this unanimous discipline in the service of productivity, both of which are demonstrated at every level of the social pyramid. Company directors act as feudal lords of the Old Regime, yet they are capable of making audacious, risky decisions and are prepared to accept the possible consequences. Any leader who has made an error, or who has failed, even though through no fault of his own, considers himself compelled to retire; anyone who is incompetent is eliminated, together with anyone who, after long conscientious service, seems unable to keep up with technological progress. Even the trade unions are loyal to the common task; the administrative staff gives freely of its time, sacrificing evenings and holidays when necessary. Everything is subordinated to production.

Nevertheless, I wonder if such a sudden evolution and such constraining efforts are not traumatic. It is an impression that has been growing on me during the last few days. Basically, the Japanese are hesitant, feel off balance, uncomfortable. I felt yesterday that the officials who had invited me expected me to give them an answer to their uncertainty.

Furthermore, the international monetary situation, reflecting their own uncertainties, has been troubling them considerably. Their very conversation proved it: like everyone here, they talked of nothing but the "dollar-shock." They must have been even more preoccupied this morning when they learned that the discussions in Honolulu between the United States and Japan more or less ended in a deadlock. Japan appears to have made a few concessions, but the general problem has not been solved. The commercial problems seem to have been discussed more fully than the strictly monetary aspects. I believe that in the coming months, commercial discussions will increasingly take priority over monetary questions of parities, devaluations, and revaluations which have especially held people's attention since last May. Indeed, the same thing is true of the bargaining which will be taking place between Western Europe (the Common Market and Great Britain) and the United States. Currency is only a superficial way of looking at things which attract everyone's attention. The upheavals in the world, above all, concern the economy. Will the governments ever understand this?

Returning to Japan's problems, it appears that the medium-sized companies are likely to suffer more severely than the larger companies from the consequences of the "dollar shock." The latter probably have greater resistance and resilience, and wider profit margins. The medium-sized businesses, on the other hand, are already facing real difficulties and their forecast for the coming year—according to a survey made by the Tokyo Chamber of Commerce—is pessimistic. A certain number of the small- and medium-sized companies are likely to disappear or be absorbed by the more powerful. This added concentration will affect economic power and, consequently, the general political outlook.

I have an appointment this morning with Mr. Iwaza, the managing director of the Fuji Bank, the largest investment bank in the country. The building is splendid, even sumptuous; his large, bright office is on the ninth floor; everything radiates power and organization.

Placing less emphasis on the economic side of the monetary

crisis than I could have wished, Mr. Iwaza stressed the intolerability of the absence of fixed rates and parities. In spite of the important commercial concessions that Japan made yesterday in Honolulu, there remain profound disagreements. He believes that Japan will be obliged to make new concessions which, it seems to me, he conceives only in the form of a further revaluation of the yen. In his opinion, it is in any case necessary for a rapid monetary agreement to be reached between Europe, the United States, and Japan. All the long-term problems (convertibility, general monetary reform, the position of the Third World), which would need two or three years to be settled, should be left for subsequent discussions. On the other hand, the revision of the parities and the establishment of new fixed rates are urgent, provided that they do not excessively threaten Japan's foreign trade.

The French government takes the opposite stand. It wishes to obtain assurances on the status of the dollar, the entire monetary reform, agricultural exchanges and prices, and the like, before the new parities are fixed. The Germans, having chosen to float the mark, and finding themselves at present in a somewhat false position, haven't the same possibilities for resistance, and are thus less well placed in the current discussions than the French. It is strange to see that France is in a more advantageous, more convenient position to negotiate than Germany or Japan, although her economic and monetary strength is inferior to theirs. I think that, had the French monetary policy been more realistic during the last few years and especially since last May, France's position today would be extremely strong. Unfortunately, because of her continual childish guerrilla-war against the pound sterling and the dollar, her campaign in favor of the gold standard, and her very heavy, self-imposed unproductive expenses, she is not really taken seriously in international financial debates.

In any case, the clear conclusion to be drawn from what Mr. Iwaza said is that in spite of their different interests, the United States, Japan, and Germany can now prepare to negotiate and eventually to agree on new monetary parities—

which, unfortunately, will not solve any of the pending problems and will undoubtedly be the prelude to future crises. Yet France, in my opinion, rightfully wishes to obtain exchange-rate guarantees before reaching a monetary agreement.

Whatever the outcome, Mr. Iwaza is adamant that the dollar can no longer serve as the international standard, as it has for the past thirty years. While keeping gold at the center of the system, he foresees an extension of special drawing rights (S.D.R.) in terms of gold. Personally, I doubt that gold can continue as the basis of the entire monetary mechanism, for it would have to remain theoretical, since no currency can in fact be exchanged for gold anymore, because there no longer is, nor can there be, any convertibility. The dollar, like the I.M.F. drawing rights, is defined in terms of gold, although no one can exchange dollars for gold. So what does this mean? We all debated the real value of the ruble, defined in terms of gold, yet inconvertible. The dollar and the S.D.R. are now in that same position.

Still more serious is the creation during the last three years of special drawing rights which consist of the injection of an additional ten billion dollars of purchasing power, at a time when the whole world is threatened by inflation. Instead of flooding the market, the opposite should have been done. Special drawing rights must not be arbitrarily created; they must be subject to precise regulations. I can see no solution other than to link the monetary organization directly to the economy, to production, and to the exchanges through a system monetizing stocks of basic products. Mr. Iwaza is naturally evasive on this subject.

I questioned him on the future plans of his bank in the international field. He described his present activities in the United States and in Germany. His bank does not yet have a branch in France. His son, however, is in France at the head of another Japanese bank.

Mr. Iwaza expects a considerable development of trade between Japan and Western Europe. Politely he stressed the role France could play in improving certain relationships, for instance, between Japan and China. But clearly France is not, in his opinion, as stable or interesting a factor as Germany in the economic world or in the development of business. Dusseldorf outweighs Paris.

Finally we discussed the fact that, like many others, Mr. Iwaza went on a pilgrimage to Peking a month ago. Actually he believes that one should entertain no illusions; he does not foresee any noticeable increase in Japanese exports to China in the very near future. The manager of the Fuji Bank discussed the question with Mr. Chou En-lai. The Prime Minister of Communist China reminded him that his government does not give priority to industry, but to improving food supplies for the Chinese; in short, to agriculture. He added that the Chinese wish to reach their objectives without any foreign aid, implying, however, that China might one day provide Japan with the raw materials she needs.

If a considerable increase of Japanese sales to China is improbable, why are Mr. Iwaza and his industrial and financial colleagues so impatient to renew relations with her that certain companies have already—in appearance or in fact?—liquidated large interests in Formosa so as not to appear on certain black lists? For Peking has already differentiated between "friendly" companies and the others.

All these questions were discussed again at a luncheon organized by the *Keizai Doyukai*, a very powerful employers' association. Present were directors of large companies who, according to the French Ambassador, are among "the fifty men who determine the country's policies." Indeed, some of them are the leaders of the large trusts which dominate Japan's economic and political life: Mr. Fuji, the vice-president of New Japan Steel, the largest Japanese metallurgical company, which by itself produces as much as the entire French steel industry; Mr. Nakajima, president of another steel company, which is in the Mitsubishi group; Mr. Mizukami, manager of the second largest import-export company in Japan; and directors of companies dealing in fertilizers, rubber, and the like. I thought that these gentlemen had invited me in order to question me on France and Europe, where they aim to increase their exports; as it turned out, however, I was able to question them freely and at length, and the conversation was most interesting. Naturally, we again spoke about China, since a certain number of them have either been or are planning to go there. Their business there is already considerable. For example, China purchases 250,000 tons of steel from Japan and even if China's own production, gauged at around twenty million tons, should expand, so will her future needs.

I asked the people I was talking with, since they were so interested in China, how they expected to be repaid for their developing sales. What could they buy there? Their answers were inconclusive. They mentioned certain agricultural products, vegetable oils (until now purchased mostly from the United States), coke (which Japan also buys there), and certain minerals. Nevertheless, these people think that China could develop exports in other countries, such as Southeast Asia. In particular she could sell textiles there, which would enable her to meet her trade deficit with Japan. This is not a definite solution. But these gentlemen insist that they are working, above all, on a long-term basis; ten or twenty years from now, the Chinese market will have become attractive. For the time being, they are merely preparing for the future— thus, the importance of normal political relations with China.

Those present were equally preoccupied by another question. During recent talks in Honolulu, the United States requested the suppression (or at least the relaxation) of the legal restrictions which impede large U.S. industrial investments in Japan. I had previously discussed this problem. The United States wishes to rectify its commercial balance with Japan and Europe, not only in order to reach equilibrium or gradually to pay off the dollar balances—that is to say her short-term debt throughout the world—but also to expand her foreign investments. This is quite illogical and I, myself, think that during the last few years the Americans have invested far too much throughout the world, only aggravating the imbalance of which we all are bearing the consequences. The present general situation, including the political and military disengagement that the Americans are carrying out a little bit everywhere, in Europe as well as in Asia, should lead also to a reconsideration or redirection of their foreign investment policies. Far from increasing their foreign investments on either continent, they should today be reducing them. I am not referring to the aid that they, like all rich countries, are expected to supply to the underdeveloped countries. On the industrialized continents they should be attempting to minimize, not increase American investments.

It is true that financial investments give rise to complex exchanges which are not always easy to understand. Thus, of the three or four billion dollars the Japanese have invested abroad, almost one billion has gone to the United States in compensation, to a certain extent, for the movements of American capital toward Japan. This type of investment—which includes, for instance, the projects mentioned by the director of the Sony Corporation—is not, in my opinion, the most desirable. The same could be said for the large Japanese investments in Australia. Although such operations can provide certain advantages in the early stages, I would not recommend their extension. Should Japanese capital be directed toward Malaya, Indonesia (where a great deal actually is being accomplished, particularly in the oil sector), toward India, Madagascar and —after the war is over—toward Vietnam, the result would be profitable both for the receiving and for the investing countries. Those regions are in dire need of development, and their populations lack employment and productive work. The arrival of Japanese capital would enable them simultaneously to exploit their natural resources which are as yet untouched, to provide the raw materials needed in Japan, and to achieve their own necessary national economic progress. It seems to me that the United Nations economic commissions and the other financial and monetary international institutions should be concerned about the idea of a reorientation of Japanese capital exports.

As I was hurrying to say good-bye after the luncheon in order to reach my next appointment, one of my hosts came up to tell me that he subscribes to *Courrier de la République;* I had not known that our small paper radiated all over the world and this gives me great pleasure!

I had a conversation next with Mr. Eki Sone, deputy and leader of the Social-Democratic Party, a small opposition party. He received me in a very large building next to the Diet in which the members of Parliament have their offices. As in the American Congress, each deputy has a spacious, comfortable office and the necessary personnel. Although Mr. Eki Sone represents a minor group, he has a large office with a well stocked library and another office where several people supplied with all necessary equipment work for him. The Assembly furnishes everything, all of which provides the members of Parliament with much better working conditions than those of their French counterparts.

Mr. Eki Sone speaks perfect French, having spent part of his career as a diplomat. He opened with the burning subject of China and criticized the Sato government for its former policies which discredited it in the eyes of the Chinese. He is not, however, ready to accept all China's conditions, in particular the one concerning the outright elimination of the treaty signed between Japan and Formosa. It would be possible to recognize Formosa as a Chinese province; but to fail to honor a signed treaty and to break it unilaterally as a prerequisite to any negotiations seems unacceptable to him. Here again, I noticed the desire to be on good terms with Peking, coupled with a certain dislike of having to give in to all its requirements.

The end of the day is to be devoted to the press. Ever since my arrival I have tried to ascertain what the newspapers are like, but, unfortunately, I am able to read only those printed in English. I can see that international problems, which are dealt with very seriously and competently, are considered to be very important and that much attention is given also to economic questions. I have the impression that the general public in

Japan is better informed, especially about economic affairs, than in Europe, particularly in France. The *Nihon Keizai,* a daily newspaper which deals exclusively with these questions, has a circulation of two million copies!

Three morning papers are published in English and what I most appreciate in them is the Anglo-Saxon technique of making a clear distinction for the reader between information and commentary.

We visited the *Asahi,* a newspaper which prints 9 million copies daily! The circulation here is the highest in the world. Even the boycotted, scarcely advertised Communist newspaper sells over 500,000 copies a day.

I revised the interview which is to be published in tomorrow morning's papers. The somewhat lengthy text has been reduced and, although correct, seems to me to have been weakened. I have often had the same trouble with French journalists!

In the meantime, the general manager was explaining how the newspaper functions to Marie-Claire. Advertising accounts for 55 percent and sales for 45 percent of revenue. Advertisers often attempt to influence the point of view expressed in articles. Subscriptions account for 98 percent of sales, which a European would find hard to conceive. The newspaper is delivered to the Japanese at home and paid for weekly or monthly. The newspaper's management organizes the distribution. In order to deliver the paper to subscribers early enough in the morning, the newspaper needs a large distribution force of people who supplement their normal earnings by working just two hours a day for the paper, in addition to people not otherwise employed, retired people, and even schoolchildren. In the town of Tokyo alone *Asahi* has a force of 65,000 distributors and one of the management's greatest preoccupations is what would happen if the distributors were to go on strike. Inasmuch as the job represents only a small part of their incomes, they could hold out indefinitely. It would be the end of the newspaper. This fear probably stimulated the Japanese press managers' recent plans to launch a new type of paper, produced in the home. An electronic machine, by wire or wireless, would make it possible for daily news to be relayed directly to subscribers' homes. Several experimental attempts have been made which demonstrate that this is technically feasible.

Wednesday, 15th December

Since my arrival I have noticed that the Japanese are extremely punctual. My audience with the Prime Minister, Eisaku Sato, was scheduled for 9:20 A.M. It started precisely at 9:20.

Mr. Sato, an impressive person who is a stalwart conservative, reminds me a little of Monsieur Pompidou. His eight years in office have been Japan's most successful expansionary period, which could explain the impression he exudes of power, confidence, and imperial style. He carries his seventy years very well. Nevertheless, he has announced that he will soon be retiring from office.

Using my projected trip to Peking as an excuse, he embarked at once on the Chinese problem; he would have preferred me to stop in Tokyo on my way back rather than on my way there so that he could hear my impressions; but that, he said, would have to wait for another time. The normalization of relations between Peking and Tokyo, according to him, depends on China's goodwill. It is true that Japan's former imperialist policies caused the Chinese much suffering and humiliation; but that belongs to the past. Today, his country wants peace and is not threatening anyone. There is no basis for accusing Japan of militarism; neither does she have an atomic bomb now, nor does she intend to have one in the future.

He takes a favorable and optimistic attitude toward China's future policies. He is convinced that the Chinese want peaceful coexistence and have respect for the right of self-determination of nations: "They are not imperialists and certainly do not plan to be aggressive." Praising Chou En-lai, he mentioned that "he does not come from a proletarian background." The Chinese Prime Minister can have no other intentions than "to consolidate the peace." For Taiwan an "acceptable solution,"

28

which Mr. Sato did not define, will have to be found. On the whole, the list of possibilities which he drew up was quite encouraging.

Mr. Sato became more cautious and somewhat evasive when I questioned him about possible solutions to the Vietnamese situation. He explained to me that he is not well informed on this subject and takes an interest in Cambodia only "because of spiritual and cultural affinities." Nevertheless, he believes that Japan must exploit the large margin of popularity which she enjoys in the three countries of former Indochina and even in North Vietnam. For the time being, Japan, under the auspices of the Red Cross, wishes to extend humanitarian aid, to all the suffering (this, in fact, tends to favor the South); she trades both with the North and the South in an effort not to commit herself. In fact, I believe she is taking advantage of the situation, as neutral countries close to war zones always have, by meeting the ever-increasing needs of those at war.

In short, Mr. Sato mentioned principally what he would have liked me to repeat in Peking. This impression was confirmed at the end of our conversation; he told me that I could inform the Chinese of Japan's good intentions at every social level and, above all, in government circles. I replied that, although I was on a private visit, my constant desire for peace everywhere in the world, made me consider it my duty, when questioned, to repeat anything that could contribute to reducing mistrust between nations.

The conversation, which was to have lasted forty minutes, continued an extra quarter of an hour, which apparently is very complimentary.

But in the afternoon there was a slight incident concerning the end of our discussion, which I had considered to be merely polite conversation. Shortly after I left, the official press agent broadcast an account of our conversation which stated specifically that Mr. Sato had asked me to transmit his wish for closer relations with them to the Chinese government. This may have been to show Mr. Sato's political opponents that he uses every opportunity to seek to make contact, but this publicity cast entirely the wrong light on our meeting and on my journey to Peking. I made use of a luncheon with the press to clear up the matter and explain that I have been given no such "mission."

Brisard, the representative of the A.F.P., presided over the luncheon. There were journalists from America, Australia, South Korea, Formosa, Sweden, and Germany. While drinks were being served, the noise of a crowd outside drew us all to the windows: people were parading in the street with red flags, shouts, slogans and cars carrying large posters. The strikers from a neighboring firm were demonstrating.

We went in to lunch. Before responding to their questions, I asked them about the Japanese press and they generally confirmed what we had learned the other day when we were received at the *Asahi.* But what puzzles me is how the "reactionary" newspapers, which do not have the means to pay for an inevitably costly distribution network, manage to expand. Their possibilities for growth are certainly limited. I imagine that many potential readers hesitate to attract attention by having certain newspapers, such as those of the extreme left, delivered at home. That is probably one of the reasons why this system cannot be adopted by those papers that carry a certain stigma.

But those present were becoming impatient to talk about the topics in the news. And I was to discover that they were demanding! A long discussion in English began which was devoted mainly to economic and monetary problems and to the talks between Pompidou and Nixon which ended last night in the Azores. This morning's newspapers, in fact, announced in large headlines that an agreement had been reached on exchange rates and parities. They reacted with optimism toward a situation which might be positive in itself, but is far from covering the true problems. Up until now the French government has maintained that commercial and economic affairs could not be separated and that it would be useless to fix new rates if a much wider settlement were not agreed upon. I found that position reasonable. What has happened to it now?

Besides, I reminded my hosts, parities have already been changed on various occasions over the last few years. This has not prevented the deterioration of the monetary system, speculative movements, the accumulation of useless dollar balances and, above all, alternating threats of inflation and higher prices and of unemployment and crisis—not to mention the dissatisfaction of the underdeveloped countries with a system which is unfavorable to them. Indeed, this morning, in the *Japan Times,* I read a very tough collective statement by some of those governments protesting that the monetary discussions take place among the ten richest powers in the world but neglect the others. It would be a mistake to ignore this protest.

We will have to follow closely the impending decisions concerning international trade, the new conditions fixed for exchanges (agricultural and industrial) and the working out of a reformed international monetary system. The latter should be capable of preventing the recurrence of the crises, the injustices, and the inequalities which prevailed in the past. I fear that the announced change in parities, with the momentary lull which will result on the exchange markets, will delay once again the more important but more difficult reforms constantly being postponed. In six months it will become clear that nothing has been achieved, and the same problems will arise once more.

In my long conversation with Mr. Ishibashi, deputy and secretary general of the Socialist Party, I found myself once again involved in a discussion of Japanese affairs which he, however, skillfully fitted into an international context with which he is clearly very familiar and which he mentioned several times. His ideas are often similar to those of the French left wing, particularly concerning the social situation in his country. He stressed the need to expand social security (which is very inadequate in Japan), to return to better relations with China, and for peace in Vietnam. His stand is radically anti-American, because of Vietnam and because of the excessive pressure the United States is exerting on matters of trade. He very much fears the much-requested liberalization of foreign trade and exchange-rate legislation as it would enable the Americans to sell and invest more in Japan.

As for Vietnam, the Socialist Party entirely accepts the N.L.F.'s conditions for peace. What is most urgent is for the Americans to evacuate the country entirely. In any case, if President Nixon in visiting Peking has the Vietnamese problem on his mind, he should know that it is up to the Vietnamese themselves to manage their own affairs, without any solution being imposed upon them from outside.

Finally, Japan "must maintain a neutral position and be on equally good terms with China, the Soviet Union, and the United States. Any bilateral treaty, such as the present one binding Japan to the United States, is dangerous." Mr. Ishibashi would like to see the signatures of Japan, the United States, China, and the Soviet Union on a treaty of general agreement on nonagression and security, with multilateral guarantees of their respective frontiers. I reminded him that between the two wars this was the formula used in the famous Locarno treaty. Unfortunately, for the time being, it is hard to see how the U.S.S.R. and China could subscribe to it, considering the nature of their relations and the Chinese attitude toward the Siberian frontier.

As matters stand, Mr. Ishibashi would hesitate to recommend ending the security treaty signed ten years ago by the United States and Japan, which is renewable annually. There would be the risk that Japan might find herself unsupported. This, in turn, could encourage the development of militarist tendencies. For under the pretext of defense, there would be a strong temptation to reconstruct a political-military system, which would be the end of the very young Japanese democracy. "Our history goes back two thousand years," Mr. Ishibashi said, "and we have only had a democracy for twenty years. Besides, it was imposed on us by the Americans when we capitulated! It is not yet well rooted in the country. That is why we are afraid of a revival of the old nationalist and militarist demons which have been so costly to us."

In all the conversations I have had, it has struck me that the Japanese have a guilt complex: they know what the Japanese imperialism between the two wars has cost, in suffering and sorrow, particularly to the Chinese. These memories, called up by the leaders in the country themselves, are immediately followed in official circles by the disavowal of any militarist resurgence. The army, they affirm, consists of no more than 260,000 men and this figure will not increase; the Constitution explicitly forbids Japan to participate in any war; she does not have the atomic bomb, and the like. All of which does not prevent the left wing from voicing its fears (which are also often mentioned in official Chinese propaganda).

The secretary-general of the Japanese Socialist Party would like to see his country adopt a systematically neutral policy, yet this change could be accomplished only by readjusting the balance of foreign trade. He is well aware of this fact. Today at least 30 percent of Japan's total exports go to the United States and, if intermediate markets are included, this figure reaches 50 percent. This is too much. According to Mr. Ishibashi, Japan's trade should be divided into thirds: the western, the socialist, and the underdeveloped countries. What is more important, the policy of "exports above all" should be abandoned. This slogan, which relegates social improvements to second place, has in any case today lost its justification, now that the world is undergoing a serious monetary crisis and the United States wishes to restrain imports. From now on, Japan must be assigned new goals—goals which he qualified as socialist: raising the standard of living, developing public facilities, fighting pollution, creating a genuine system of social security.

Japan certainly will continue to trade with the outside world, and the Socialist Party has its own opinion on this question. Should she export to the poor countries? Yes, but they have few resources and she will have to grant them long-term credits. To the socialist countries? Yes, but before doing so with China, her principal partner, there are political prerequisites. To the industrialized countries? Yes, but the international monetary difficulties will have to be overcome, so a request should be made for an international institution, such as the United Nations, to create a new currency which would be accepted in all member countries.

I pointed out that to sell on a long-term credit basis to the underdeveloped countries would not be a very good solution, as they are already in debt and many of them are forced to put aside 60 percent of their foreign currency reserves to meet their financial obligations which consist of amortization and interest.

As for the distribution of an international currency by the United Nations, I fear it might be dominated by political bias just as the special drawing rights have been, during the last three years. A solid, impartial, objective ruling must be made and imposed on everyone. Otherwise the decisions taken will once again favor the most powerful, which means the richest countries. This was another opportunity for me to explain my suggestions for monetary reform. I pointed out what advantages the project I was backing would bring to the underdeveloped countries (and later, indirectly to the industrialized countries). The secretary-general of the Socialist Party is very interested in all this.

Domestic politics. The Diet elections will probably take place in 1972. The Socialist Party expects to gain some seats. Nevertheless, it cannot hope to obtain the majority alone and will have to consider forming a coalition. With the Communist Party? Or with the Komeito and Social-Democratic parties? The best solution would be to bring together all the opposition parties and to include the trade unions, which at present are divided into four sections: *Sohyo, Domeï, Churitsurôren,* and *Shin-San-betsu.* Unfortunately, relations among these parties and sections are bad. The only way to overthrow the present majority would be to unite. But the Communists would not dream of forming an alliance with the Social-Democrats or the members of the Komeito—which they consider to be right wing or, more precisely, accomplices of the right-wing party in power. For the time being they therefore face a deadlock. But between now and the elections, the situation could become clearer.

In summary, this was a very intensive conversation with a pleasant, open, charming person.

Later I had an appointment with the Communist leaders, Mr. Nishizawa and Mr. Tatsuki, two of the seven permanent members of the Central Committee of the Japanese Communist Party. They began by declaring that they are in favor of presenting a common front in the interests of progress, that is to say, according to them, working in close association with the Socialist Party, but excluding the other more questionable parties. (I understand that this refers to the Komeito and to the Social-Democrats.) The stand of the opposition is more or less the same as in France: the union-of-the-left theme is supported by parties which do not attribute a common meaning to it.

The Communist Party claims 300,000 members and makes a considerable effort to increase its numbers, improve its contact with the masses, and penetrate all social levels, Mr. Keng Ji Miyamoto, its president, said: "You are as likely to find us in chess clubs as in fishermen's societies. We have to be everywhere."

Mr. Nishizawa, who is a remarkable man, gave a long, well-structured description of the domestic situation and the foreign affairs of his country. But his arguments always returned to international politics and to relations with the United States; according to Mr. Nishizawa, Japan's present difficulties (such as pollution, danger of unemployment, inadequate social legislation) are due to a government controlled by Japanese monopolies who in turn are associated with American interests. It is necessary for Japan to free herself from the influence of the United States and, in order to do so, she must end the so-called security treaty. Does this mean that she should turn to the Soviet Union or Communist China? No, the Communist Party only wishes to defend Japan's interests. That is why, for instance, it is hostile to the liberalizing measures which would enable American financial and industrial influence to expand still further.

Then Mr. Nishizawa spoke of the criticisms leveled at the Communist Party for its use of Parliament in its struggle; it does this in the hopes of "prevailing sometime in the next decade because we are realists. There can be no social-democracy without a parliamentary system—and we are not prepared to scorn any social reforms we can obtain in this way."

Then he commented on a recent declaration made by the president of his party on "the evolution in a highly industrialized country faced with the possibility of a complete impoverishment of its workers, which seems no longer to correspond to all that we see. Undoubtedly, the classical form of pauperism has disappeared, but a new style of dehumanization is developing, creating a highly frustrated working class, pollution of the environment, a housing crisis, and the like. The progressive forces must find solutions which recognize this new form of poverty and thus create a vista of social transformation."

In the last few days, I have heard it said that the Communist Party has always expressed a definite wish to remain independent, refusing in turn to condemn the Chinese Communist Party as requested by the Russians, and to take an aggressive position against the "revisionists" under pressure from the Chinese. This resistance, which is known to the Japanese public, has increased the Party's popularity. I mentioned this briefly and discreetly during our conversation and I felt that they were grateful to me for not trying to embarrass them by drawing too much attention to the differences between Peking and Moscow.

As we were leaving, they assured me that none of them has forgotten the part I played in ending the first Indochinese war and in reinstating peace. They hope a solution will soon be found in Vietnam in the same loyal and respectful spirit toward all nations as triumphed all too briefly in Geneva in 1954.

The day closed with a meeting with a militant trade union
36 ist. He described the action taken by his comrades and himself,

and I soon discovered that in this field things are very different here from what they are in Europe. Indeed, social conflicts are quite frequent but, when strikes take place, they nearly always affect only one firm, with its union and management opposing one another. As had already been explained to me, it is rare for discussions, negotiations, or strikes to affect an entire industry—as is the case in the United States, in the steel industry, for example, or in any other trade union. Neither do they have solidarity strikes. The workers' actions usually remain fragmented.

Conscious of this situation, certain employers try to stay on good terms with the unions in their firms, or with their union leaders. In my conversation with him Mr. Ishibashi actually underlined the fact that often relations were "too good" between certain employers and unions. Sometimes, the discussions between the employer and the militant unionists do result in a contract without the union ever giving up its independence. But it also does happen that union leaders are accused of having been bought by the management. They are not always free from the suspicion of corruption.

Thursday, 16th December

The headquarters of the *Sohyo,* the principal union center, is in a large four-story construction where countless offices are piled up. The building is full of activity. Noticing a bust of John F. Kennedy next to a portrait of Lenin, I said to Mr. Makoto Ichikawa, the president of the *Sohyo,* that this seemed to me to symbolize great openness of mind; he accepted the compliment with obvious pleasure.

Before answering my questions, my hosts made a point of saying that the Japanese workers have not forgotten what I once did to return peace to Indochina and to avoid a war which would have spread to the whole of Asia. This has been mentioned to me several times since my arrival in Japan. But I feel that these recollections of 1954 are warmer and obviously more sincere when they come from leftists and from the people. Probably because they are more responsive than the conservatives to a policy directed toward freeing colonies from the military domination and humiliation of colonialism.

Mr. Ichikawa described the concepts of his organization to me. I was struck by his knowledge of economic affairs and his wisdom and realism. There was no trace of prejudice or meanness in his manner of presenting the facts. He analyzed Japan's economic evolution, solidly supporting everything he said. He often branched into the political field in order to criticize the Japanese governments that have submitted so docilely to American wishes. As a protectionist, he is against the liberalization policy which the United States is trying to enforce.

There are four large trade unions. The *Sohyo* is often called the Japanese *C.G.T.*[1], as it is the most important union organization. It consists mostly of civil servants and people who work for the national administration, public services, and local agencies. It has special connections with the Socialist Party, but also joins the Communist Party in acting together on certain points of agreement like Okinawa, American bases, anti-nuclear policy, and pollution. Thus, in this way it openly politicizes its work and its demands.

The second center, the *Domei,* is more closely related to the private sector; this is where fragmentation along company lines is greatest. It often tends to encourage a spirit of conciliation between the employers and the workers, at least in Mr. Ichikawa's opinion; he blames the *Domei* for recognizing company unions. In any case, the *Domei* limits its action to wage claims which are often fragmented and it refuses to join in mass movements and political work.

The leaders of the *Sohyo* fear that there will soon be an unemployment crisis. It will be the first since the war. In the face of the danger, will the working class seek to maintain its basic, solid rights? Or will it give in to employers' demands? As the important report of the Tokyo Chamber of Commerce and Industry stresses (the one from which I quoted earlier), 1972 is sure to be a difficult year. Already, the steel, rubber, and preci-

[1] Major French union: *Confédération Générale du Travail.*

sion-instrument industries are experiencing difficulties and foresee a reduction in their sales. Several firms are announcing cuts in personnel. The medium-sized companies are the first to be affected, since they cannot hold out because of their narrow profit margins. The result will be a stronger concentration in large and very large business, and the unions know that their future actions will have to take these repercussions into account.

After my meeting with the *Sohyo* leaders, I visited Shinjuku, a new quarter of Tokyo. At the end of the war, private builders reconstructed this sector haphazardly, that is to say, with lamentable hygienic and safety conditions: no drainage, wooden houses, and clutter; very soon, the quarter became an actual sewer and, twenty-five years later, the decision had to be made simply to raze it to the ground. It was then decided to make—for the first time in Tokyo—a great experiment in urban development.

Through this reconstruction the Japanese tried to solve some of the capital's problems, of which there are plenty. Tokyo, which grew at random, is beginning to suffocate because of insufficient drinking water and housing, few public facilities, and the too narrow and dirty streets. Added to the twelve million inhabitants of the city are the commuters who come to work every day from the suburbs; there are traffic jams in the subways, in the streets, everywhere. The number of cars in Toyko has increased fivefold in the last ten years; there is proportionately less road surface there than in New York, London, or Paris. At Shinjuku, an attempt was made to overcome all these difficulties.

Although the work is far from complete, the contrast between this quarter and the rest of the town is striking. The general effect is of wide-open space. Surrounded by green stretches on straight boulevards, roads and sidewalks run side by side and cross while remaining separate. As for the buildings, they are architecturally similar to those on a New York avenue. But what is most striking is the plan for the entire sector: there will be shops, offices, company headquarters, entertainment, restaurants, and a huge railroad station, but scarcely any housing. Both sociologists and urban theorists criticize this type of plan which leads to thoroughly inhuman social segregation. There will be no children, no old people, or people who are not employed in the area. In the evening, once the offices are closed, Shinjuku, with the exception of a few nightclubs, will close down completely. Life there will be totally artificial, dehumanized (the same mistake is being made in Lyon in the Part-Dieu quarter).

It was Miss Honda who showed me around Shinjuku. She has been my interpreter since my arrival. She works in radio on programs beamed to the French-speaking countries (Vietnam, Laos, Cambodia, the Pacific islands, Pondichery, Madagascar, Djibouti . . .).

I questioned her about her life and her interests. As she lives outside Tokyo, she spends two hours a day on a commuter train. Life seems hard to her. It is true that her purchasing power, and that of the Japanese in general, has grown fairly regularly, as wages (including the bonuses) have increased slightly faster than prices. As a result, consumer behavior has changed; for example, less rice and more meat are purchased (yet the people have not to the same degree abandoned their habit of saving as insurance for old age). On this subject, the forms which savings take are interesting. They consist of liquid cash, bank or savings-bank deposits, or even old-age insurance; rarely are they in the form of stocks or bonds. This is also a well-known situation in our western countries, and it undoubtedly reflects a phenomenon of civilization. I discussed it the other day with Mr. Iwaza. People are no longer interested in the good old investments of our great-grandparents' day; they prefer more accessible liquid assets. This fact is particularly true in Japanese families of modest means, who keep more than half their savings in a liquid, quickly available form. On the other hand, higher-income families use a slightly higher proportion of their incomes to buy shares. But, even then the major part of their income is not directly invested.

The delicate question of whether to keep liquid assets or to make long-term investments exists in Japan as it does at home. Most of this conversion is carried out through the large banks, nearly all of which have connections with industrial groups, whose equipment or growth they finance.

Miss Honda interrupted my thoughts on this economic-monetary aspect of the utilization of incomes with a more human, more personal remark:

"Finally, and in spite of the increase in salaries and spending, I do not believe we are really happy."

"You have better quality clothes, domestic equipment (which means for a woman like you fewer and less tiring hours of work at home), more recreation. . . ."

"Yes, but is all this surplus really useful? We are made to buy numerous products, household utensils of all kinds, which we could easily do without. Do these objects which are forced on us by advertisements make us any happier?"

There is also the fact that Japanese consumers are not always willing to buy regardless of price. Their protective organizations are very powerful; in 1971, one of them asked its members to boycott a certain brand of color television set, which was being sold at too large a profit (moreover, intended to compensate for dumping the product on the export market). After several weeks the company in question was forced to give in, television set prices went down, and the managing director of the company apologized publicly to his clients . . . on television!

I am going by train to Kyoto. The station is vast, "functional," ultramodern. But how would I ever have found the right train without Miss Honda? Large, tightly packed crowds run in all directions, pouring out of the trains which are continuously arriving and rushing toward those that are about to leave. In this bustle, one cannot help thinking of the people who discuss the quality of life!

The famous Tokyo-Osaka line holds the world record for speed and number of travelers. The panorama is revealing: almost the entire coastal region through which the train rushes at 150 miles per hour is built up. Large- or medium-sized built-up areas, factories, highways, railroads. At long intervals some green patches with charming little traditional houses surrounded by very neat market gardens, stretches of water and beautiful trees. Not one square yard is wasted. But these glimpses are too few and far between, and the view is almost constantly urban.

I read the account of a conference Mr. Iwaza held last night. Without turning it into an issue for great political agitation or mobilizing action, Japan should patiently and modestly seek a reconciliation with China. Is he condemning the very active propaganda of certain left-wing circles? Or is he insinuating that Mr. Sato would be mistaken to stress his Chinese normalization policy? I cannot tell.

Then I read a long report that the *Sohyo* militants had given me on wages in Japan. Their documentation is very complete and competent on the general economic situation, methods of calculating wages, the standard of living, consumption, material and physical conditions of work, social laws, and the various categories neglected by the socioeconomic system. It includes statistics, detailed explanations of social or fiscal legislation, and the like. This conscientious, detailed, and extremely convincing piece of work is a credit to the research and documentation office of the center which initiated it. I wish that this kind of documentation were available to French militant workers and that their union organizations would publish such valuable reports often.

Friday, 17th December

Kyoto, once the capital and residence of the emperors until the nineteenth century, was not destroyed during the war. I remember reading a few years ago that the American military officers in charge of preparing the atomic bombing had at first chosen their objectives strictly from a technical point of view; Kyoto headed the ominous list. It was saved by the psychological warfare experts because of its past and the memories attached to it. Hiroshima and Nagasaki were then designated for the holocaust. As a result, unlike Tokyo, Kyoto still has quarters where there are old wooden houses, picturesque shops, mysterious little passageways. I was charmed by what I saw as we went up a labyrinth of little ascending alleys, with countless ingenious street-stalls along the way, leading to an old temple backed by a nearby hill.

Last night, when we arrived, I caught glimpses of strings of little streets, lit up by multicolored lanterns. Today, visiting the palaces and temples, I have particularly enjoyed the delicately tended gardens; Japanese gardeners care for trees with a refined knowledge of nature. Here and there we can see the entrances to mysterious and peaceful private estates and homes, which leave to our imagination the unfortunately inaccessible, but surely exquisite, interiors. All this makes for an impressive contrast to Tokyo.

In spite of its historic, even sacred, character, Kyoto is overrun with industrial installations. Large main arteries run through it with buildings, trams, cars, stores, neon lights, but the town is still full of mystery. It would be necessary to stay here a long time in order to penetrate it.

I read the newspapers. In the current discussions on how to solve the monetary and commercial problems, the Americans have expressed their wish to export cars, integrated circuits, computers, and the like to Japan more easily and more extensively in the future; they are at present prevented from doing so by exchange control and protectionist regulations on foreign trade. They also are asking for flexibility in the agricultural sector, where concern about elections seems very important for both sides. The United States wishes to sell products such as vegetable oils, citrus fruits, fruit juices, and beef to Japan; to each of these could be attached the name of the American state that must be gratified before the Presidential elections in November 1972. Only the Japanese farmers who themselves produce oranges, fruit juices, and beef feel directly threatened and are therefore violently protesting (and there are also soon to be elections in Japan!).

It appears that the Americans have made similar demands

on the Common Market countries to enable them to sell citrus fruits, vegetables, tobacco, and cereals more widely. This must have been included in the Azores talks. It will undoubtedly be a subject for discussion throughout 1972 and maybe even longer.

But the Americans above all wish to obtain something more from the Japanese: that famous liberalization of the laws and their applications which make it impossible for foreign firms to establish themselves in Japan.

During a dinner charmingly organized by Monsieur Yacovlevitch, the French Consul General in Osaka, we actually talked about one of the very rare companies which, under very special circumstances, has broken through the barrier. That is *Air Liquide,* the main French company in Japan, which has twenty-five plants. Second largest producer of oxygen and nitrogen in the country, it also makes equipment for the chemical industry which it sells either in Japan or in the other Southeast Asian countries. Eighty percent of the firm's stock belongs to the mother company and its president is French. At dinner, he explained the background of this exceptional situation. At the beginning of the century *Air Liquide* settled here with the support of the Japanese authorities, who needed its products. Having been seized during the war, the company benefited from the provisions of the peace treaty; that is how it stayed under French control. In its president's opinion this is an abnormal situation. He feels that Japanese stock ownership, as well as participation in the administration and management, will have to increase progressively.

I had a conversation with Father Meyraud, who also was present at the dinner. He has lived in Japan for twenty years and teaches in several universities in the Osaka, Kobe, and Kyoto regions. In spite of his affection for his students, he does not always feel sure that they understand him. It is difficult, even after having been here a long time, to communicate with the Japanese. "I have not noticed any nationalism or any xenophobia in my students," he said, "but they belong to a different world from ours, with a psychology and ideas which often separate us." Other Europeans have made similar remarks to me and have described their difficulties in forming genuine relationships with the Japanese. The latter are not hostile or disagreeable toward Europeans, as they sometimes are toward Americans. But the Japanese do not open up to strangers, to people different from themselves, who have a different style of life. A kind of psychological segregation makes real confidence and intimacy impossible. The Japanese do not, in front of foreigners, express their states of mind, their deep feelings, nor do they talk of their preoccupations, nor of their private lives. They merely exchange polite formulas and carry on professional discussions. These are two intellectual universes, two civilizations which cannot hope to fathom one another.

Nevertheless, European and particularly French culture is greatly appreciated here. Hundreds of students and even adults learn our language. It is unfortunate, as Monsieur Chaume, the director of the French Institute explained, that our cultural organizations have a serious handicap: the young people who have made the effort to learn French have no use for it once they leave the university; our commercial, technological, and maritime position is too weak (Osaka is a large port). Young women can find certain jobs requiring some knowledge of French (such as hostesses and secretaries) but there are no opportunities for young men. Why does France not make more of a commercial effort here? The hopes raised eighteen months ago by the presence of France at the Osaka exhibition, along with the visit of our Finance Minister and several manufacturers, have not been followed up. The Germans here, however, are active, dynamic, enterprising.

English is obviously the language most studied in Japanese schools. The Americans, strongly entrenched here for twenty-five years, with huge resources, benefit from the prestige and utility of the English language. Next in line is Spanish (because the Japanese travel a great deal in Latin America); it is used more than French. The Germans and Italians are making important cultural efforts but, even though they use considerable resources, they are not as effective as the French institutes.

The conversation naturally turned to education. The rate of school attendance in Japan is the highest in the world. Stress has been placed on education, it is true, for over one hundred years. Even at the beginning of the twentieth century, over half the children in the country were attending primary school. Today, all go to school until the age of sixteen and illiteracy has disappeared. This is undoubtedly the reason for Japan's effectiveness in industry and secondary and tertiary techniques.

I have always believed that the essential factor in development is the level of knowledge and general culture: the underdeveloped countries are those with a population which is incapable of carrying out the productive tasks of a modern economy, and those that lack the staff for carrying on the political, administrative, cultural, and industrial life of the country. Thus, the criterion for underdevelopment is above all a human criterion. That is why Israel has never been and is not an underdeveloped country. (I remember supporting this idea in a conference about fifteen years ago, where it was rather badly received by the Israelis, who very much wanted to benefit from the international campaign taking place in favor of the Third World.) In my opinion, Japan is in no way an underdeveloped country, even though the average standard of living of the Japanese has stayed relatively low. She has, among her ordinary population and her elite, men with modern training who are, therefore, capable of facing the economic difficulties and problems of our times.

How can Japanese education be described? I was given a report to read, published by the O.E.C.D. in 1970. Emphasis is placed on the selecting process rather than on developing the abilities of scholars and students, which would explain the rigorous maintenance of the examination system, which at all levels leads to intensive cramming. The relationships among students and teachers are based upon authority and coercion; there is no attempt at mutual consent, cooperation, and participation. In fact, this form of human relationship is not limited to education: it is apparent everywhere in Japanese society.

School attendance is compulsory at the primary level and for the first stage of secondary education. But, by now, over one-half the children in the country attend nursery schools. Many students continue their studies beyond the compulsory stage; more than 82 percent of those finishing the first stage enter the second. Over a quarter of these go on to higher studies. These are very high figures.

The aim of education at all levels is the preparation of numerous highly qualified technicians. They accept relatively low salaries at the start of their careers (within the wage framework I have already described), but they know that, because of their training, they will "climb" faster than the others and this for them creates the interest in and value of continuing their studies. This is a feeling shared by all the young people, at the secondary level as well as in the universities.

Education is free in all state schools, except for the universities. All schools and colleges are coeducational. Both schoolchildren and college students wear austere uniforms, like those worn in our schools in the nineteenth century. The Japanese say that this is to avoid class differentiation, to place all the children on an equal footing. It does contribute, however, a severe tone and an almost military discipline to the schools.

There are many private (fee-paying) schools and, as in the United States, this leads to important differences of quality and standard. Some schools or universities are not considered to be very good. Others have a brilliant reputation and parents, especially in the privileged classes, go to great lengths to have their children admitted there. Tokyo University, the ultimate in education, is the summit for any ambitious Japanese or for one with an ambitious family. The elite of the industrial, political, literary, or scientific fields pride themselves on having been educated there. A large majority of the students are sons of high officials—of industrial, banking, and business administrators. There are very few sons of farmers and no sons of workers.

On several occasions I have been told that the leftist movements of the last few years originated in Tokyo University.

Everyone seems to agree that—although very active at one time—they have recently subsided and are gradually disappearing. I have had the opportunity of talking to the representatives of all the political movements here except those of the left. As they are very divided and fragmented, it is difficult to know who would really represent them. In any case, the general opinion is that their influence has greatly diminished.

Saturday, 18th December

The press this morning is again talking about the restitution of the island of Okinawa by the Americans.[1] In itself this would be a great satisfaction to the Japanese, who would finally regain a territory and four million fellow-countrymen lost in the war. But the question is not so simple. Provision is being made for the United States to retain their more important military bases on the island, at least for the duration of the Vietnam War; and it even seems that it will be able to continue storing nuclear weapons there. Large segments of public opinion, and not only from the left-wing parties, are opposed to these agreements. Another complication is a clause in the signed settlement which orders preliminary consultation on the military use of Okinawa. When the American air force takes off from Okinawa to join in the fighting in Indochina, the American command must obtain Japanese consent. Up until now this clause has remained dormant, since the Japanese authorities could only with difficulty have controlled the bases, and probably preferred not to know what was happening there; in the future, this will no longer be possible, which promises lively debates among the public and in the Diet.

Furthermore, since the agreement announcing the restitution of Okinawa, all sorts of speculations have been developing about the fate of the other islands taken from Japan in 1945. At that time the Russians, for instance, annexed the Kuril Islands, which are neither demographically nor economically significant (they are mostly fisheries), but to which general Japanese public opinion attaches some importance. When Mr. Gromyko's proposed visit to Tokyo was recently announced in the press, it was understood by everyone that the Japanese would once again bring up this question. Strong Soviet resistance is expected, because Russia has as a principle never to return territories acquired after the last war (neither in Europe nor in Asia), and she has no intention of creating a precedent. There are rumors, however, that this time Mr. Gromyko may not be as intractable, in the hope of making a future Sino-Japanese dialogue more difficult.

Other former Japanese islands were, in fact, placed under the jurisdiction of Formosa; these are extremely important to Japan because the oil resources which are to be found within their territorial waters are among the richest in the world. Formosa flatly insisted that these islands were Chinese. Communist China, of course, has taken the same stand. This is an added complication for Tokyo, which finds itself opposed on this question both by Taipeh and Peking.

In any case, the imminent restitution of Okinawa by the Americans will give the Japanese a strong argument in their favor which they are sure to use to their best advantage against the Chinese, especially if the Russians have, in the meantime, agreed to make some concessions on the Kuril Islands.

Herman Kahn has written that by the end of the century the per capita national income will be higher in Japan than in any other country, including the United States. Other statisticians have affirmed that by 1975 her per capita gross national product will be greater than that of the Common Market countries. These forecasts are always questionable, as they presuppose that all other factors will remain unchanged, when, in fact, it is impossible to know if Japan's economic growth will continue at the same rate. What can be said is that in 1970 this rate once again surpassed all expectations.

Nevertheless, some economic or political mishaps are always possible along the way. First of all, the problem of the alienation of the individual in Japanese society, which has been sustained until now and seems to be more prevalent here than anywhere else, may suddenly erupt, with surprising consequences. Furthermore, the country is constantly faced with the problem of obtaining raw materials and sources of energy. What would happen if these were to stop arriving regularly?

Ninety percent of the oil consumed in Japan comes from the Middle East and passes through the Indian Ocean, which until now has been under Anglo-American control. The new presence in this ocean of a Russian fleet—which will continue to remain there, especially once the Suez Canal is reopened—and what may be of more consequence, the very active Chinese infiltration into the Persian Gulf, have created a situation which could cause anxiety. Japanese policy is attempting to secure other petroleum resources in Alaska, Canada, Indonesia, and Africa. Moreover, the steel industry is constantly preoccupied with obtaining enough iron ore and coal, vitally necessary to it; fifteen-year contracts have been made with Australia. The Japanese are seeking iron in India and Brazil; elsewhere, nickel, uranium, and the like.

This constant and anxious quest has political repercussions in Japan's sphere of influence. Before and during the Second World War, it was the "sphere of co-prosperity," based on military strength and directed primarily against the industrial and colonial powers and their allies: Great Britain, France, United States, Holland, Australia, and New Zealand. Today it is better to speak of a "zone of common interests," which would spread over most of Asia and all the states bordering the Pacific. The Chinese, who have not forgotten the recent past, cannot help being anxious about this. In their opinion, sooner or later, Japan's economic power will give rise to ambitions which will generate new conflicts.

To import basic products, Japan must export correspondingly. The Japanese are turning to Europe, now that the American market is becoming less accessible. That is the reason for the vigorous commercial campaigns launched in the direction of the Old World, which I already have mentioned. Europe is likely to oppose the "Japanese challenge" with stronger resistance than it did the American challenge in the past. This is the background of the negotiations that are very slowly developing between Japan and the European Economic Commission. A multilateral agreement will have to replace the former bilateral agreements which Japan had with the Benelux countries—with France, West Germany, and Italy. For both sides concerned, this will probably reduce restrictions on the sale of European goods in Japan and Japanese goods in Europe.

And Russia? The Japanese speak very little about her, yet they are developing significant trade with her. Japan is second to West Germany in exports to Russia and seems determined to improve her position further. That is why she has just signed contracts to build factories for the development of Siberia's natural resources, including petroleum; payment will be in the form of raw materials and naturally of oil. But this Japanese participation in the industrial development of Siberia provokes the Chinese; the latter consider that the Russians are occupying territories in northern Asia extorted from their weak emperors by the tsars through the so-called unequal treaties. Although China is not, for the time being, explicitly laying claim to this region, she undoubtedly expects the problem to arise one day. That is why Japan's presence in that area, even for purely economic reasons, can only displease her.

We visited the beautiful and moving site of Nara, with its palaces, temples, and gardens. We went by car, through an endless, hideous, chaotic suburb. No attempt has been made to protect the surroundings. Narrow roads: only one lane in each direction for an area with intense traffic. Pollution is so high that when we returned, Marie-Claire and I were covered with a blackish dust.

All this very active sector is in need of a huge effort in investment and collective facilities. The cost will be high and could deter, at least for a while, improvement in individual consumption and comfort.

In the evening, we went for a walk in the shopping area of Kyoto. The traffic there is worse than in Paris during the rush hour. We went into the camera shops to compare prices. They do not seem to be so much lower than French prices. (It is true that a heavy fiscal tax is included here.)

I was struck by the number of *pachenko* shops; it is an infernal popular game based on the same principle as the slot machine. The very small cash input and the attraction of large gains explain its popularity. After waiting in long queues, young boys and girls and also old women, housewives, pensioners—people of all sorts—play for hours in a kind of fascinated, drunken frenzy and end up numbed and impoverished.

Sunday, 19th December

The *Messageries Maritimes* has an agency in Osaka which receives at least a dozen French ships per month. It has about sixty employees and workers who have been on a determined strike for several weeks. The employees at the Chase Bank in Tokyo also are on strike. Some say that strikes have been particularly frequent lately in foreign companies, as though someone (but who?) wanted to annoy the foreigners, just as the Americans are trying to obtain the relaxation of government protectionism. Is there a political motive behind these social movements?

We left Kyoto for the Osaka airport. Forty miles along a good highway, passing through countryside covered with factories and building sites: here and there, one can still see carefully cultivated fields; for how much longer? In the meantime no available plot of land is left fallow. Plots of 40 or 50 square yards, shut in by buildings and the highway, are jealously looked after and constantly cultivated.

Osaka airport is similar to Orly or Chicago, perhaps larger. It is apparently already too small and is to be reserved for domestic lines and a more spacious airport built for international flights. But where will they find a large enough space on this territory eaten up by mountains, where every possible area has already been occupied?

The plane has taken off for its three-hour flight and I

should like to review my impressions on Japan in order to form an overall judgement. But how can I do this when French people, who have themselves lived in Japan for years find it difficult to see clearly and hesitate to answer the questions one is forced to ask?

Up until now the fact that Japan belonged to a diplomatic, military, monetary, and commercial world dominated by the United States was a stabilizing factor. But this Japanese-American relationship is inevitably going to relax. Today, Japan is not or no longer wishes to be a satellite. What direction will she take from now on? I have heard some of the French people I have spoken with predict either the best or the worst.

The worst is the old imperial, militarist temptation. Fortunately, the men governing Japanese society today have not forgotten the destruction and suffering that her imperial policy finally cost Japan. They remember the vast campaign which, having taken their country to the gates of India and Australia in 1943, collapsed totally and condemned her to atomic destruction. They have drawn their lesson from it. The military budget for 1971 is no more than 1 percent of the national budget. There is talk of increasing it in 1972, but it still would be proportionately much lower than that of our European countries. No, there is no longer a question of conquests. But the industrial expansion, the continuous search for raw materials and for food supplies and outlets, the importance given to profit; where can all this lead? The left-wing leaders worry a great deal and tend to agree with the Chinese propaganda on this question. For in Tokyo one can listen to the Peking radio. Some people even say that the Chinese speeches and declarations about the military danger from Japan are specifically aimed at disturbing Japanese public opinion, at turning it away from the American alliance, toward neutrality at first, in the hopes of making Japan, at a later stage, fall under China's influence. In any case, the Chinese denunciation of the Japanese military peril resembles the concerns mentioned by all those of the left with whom I have spoken during the last two weeks.

The last problem to arise if Japan were to rearm would be

53

the building of atomic and nuclear weapons. This is today very unlikely because of public opinion, which has remained very sensitive following the horrors of Hiroshima and which would object strongly to such a project. Nonetheless, a decision to equip the Japanese army with atomic weapons is not unthinkable, when one remembers the very advanced state of Japan's industrial development in the most modern sectors. Now the government is anxious to obtain fissionable raw materials, such as uranium, for civilian use, but a reconversion for military uses is always a possibility. Among those industrialized states which do not have nuclear weapons, Japan is the only one which today possesses the essential lift capacity; the Japanese space program, in fact, has a rocket capable of placing a stationary satellite in orbit; if Japan were to decide to make her own nuclear deterrent, she would thus immediately have a considerable advantage in this area over many other countries, maybe even over China.

For the time being, those responsible affirm that they will not embark on such a plan. Indeed, they do not even try to produce, in Japan, the traditional weapons that they need, preferring to buy them from abroad. The Western countries constantly maintain that military research is correlated with advances in very diverse economic areas, which is the reason for investing so much money in it; the Japanese experience contradicts this theory. There, research and applied science have always been oriented toward industrial requirements, particularly those of the leading industries and the exporters, and were never hindered by the need to divert resources for military use. And that has not done too badly for the Japanese economy!

My comments have taken me away from the questions I was thinking about: what are my conclusions on all I have seen? Marie-Claire, reading over my shoulder, says to me: "The Japanese are as ready for fascism as for communism." Perhaps, but it would neither be a fascism nor a communism of the kind we know. Japan will remain for a long time yet— maybe forever—a specific reality, something "apart."

For the time being, within the political framework of a classical democracy, the decisive influence of a limited number of men and interests prevails. It is no longer the traditional aristocracy or a military clan which dominates. Economic powers, businesses, and banks have taken their place. Yet, indisputably, a democratic system is what apparently functions here: freedom of the press, of speech, of behavior, of protest, freedom to strike, undoubtedly straight elections, as demonstrated by the parliamentary system in which opinions and parties oppose and confront each other. But it is likely to take a long time before the exterior forms of democracy result in changes in the actual power structure. Nevertheless, freedom is the source of transmission and development, and the value of the unfolding political experience must not be underestimated.

Some said to me that in the end what matters most is the dynamic economic and industrial expansion and the vast possibilities this opens for man and his development. Others told me that what counts most is the survival of ancestral psychological and sociological structures. And both opinions are doubtless justified. So what then?

When industrial development occurs slowly, progressively, the necessary psychological changes and adaptations can be made without too much difficulty. But if this expansion is sudden, explosive as in Japan, the evolution of behavior wavers. The history of humanity may never before have produced such a striking contrast. A hundred million men and women, still conditioned by time-honored traditions, have been carried along by an accelerated technological progress. What will be the outcome of this paradox? It is true that one can foresee the best or the worst. Will Japan in the twenty-first century know how to take advantage of the unique opportunity offered her by an unprecedented situation? We shall have the answers in the coming ten years.

Hong Kong

We arrived at Hong Kong International Airport at four o'clock. Like all the others it is, of course, ultramodern and functional. Yet, leaving it, one plunges directly into the Chinese town of Kowloon, which swarms with hundreds of thousands of inhabitants; practically no Europeans, however, live there. It consists essentially of horribly ugly flaking geometrical cubes, where 300,000 inhabitants per square mile crowd into an incredibly small space. It is one of the most demographically concentrated areas in the world, and gives the impression of a dirty hive.

The Consul General pointed out the terminal of the railroad which formerly extended into China, joined the Trans-Siberian line, and continued as far as Moscow. Now such a journey is out of the question. Travelers from Hong Kong to China must leave the train at the border a few miles from here and board another train which takes them to Canton and beyond.

When we reached the end of the Kowloon isthmus, a ferryboat took us to Hong Kong itself, which is an island. Living there, in the midst of a Chinese population which is much larger by far, are several tens of thousands of Europeans with their own houses, offices, administrations, and way of life. The center of town is like London, somewhat cross-bred with New York boldness.

The town was first built along the coast, but gradually took over the nearby mountain. Now there are buildings on the heights right up to the top of the rock.

The French Consul General's residence, which is halfway up, is a beautiful colonial Victorian house, old fashioned and pleasant.

We wandered around the shopping areas below and visited a Chinese department store which sells all sorts of articles from Communist China. Several similar shops of this kind do an extremely active business. Almost identical stores sell goods from Nationalist China!

We went up to the heights to look down over the bay. The view was magnificent. There were hundreds of different kinds of boats, a few British military vessels, two large American warships, countless cargoships, junks, and motorboats. It is very obvious that the town has grown out into the sea, gradually adding territory—so scarce and so valuable—and that this process is continuing.

In the evening, we dined in an exotic setting; the restaurant was on a boat. The style was Chinese and the Chinese food was excellent.

Everything is Chinese here, except for the 35,000 Westerners as well as the marks and reminders of the English presence and rule: the street names, the style of the official buildings, clubs, golf courses, banks, and the cricket grounds.

I am told that the entire Chinese population is fascinated by Communist China, not so much because of her Communist ideas as because of her widespread influence, prestige, international success, and, lastly, her power.

But, at least for the present, this does not create acute political tensions. Peking temporarily seems quite satisfied with the present state of affairs and uses it to best advantage. The proof is that most of the food supplies and a large proportion of the drinking water are provided by Communist China; she does not take advantage of this quasi-monopoly by charging excessive prices, for this would cause a wage increase which would be followed by increased export prices which, in turn, would upset the equilibrium of the entire Hong Kong economy. For the time being, at least, the Chinese are not prepared to kill the goose that lays the golden eggs.

The Communist Party is very influential, but does not generally create much trouble. It controls an increasing number of schools, a situation facilitated by the customary freedom of education here and by the lack of enough public schools in which to enroll all the children. It also runs some commercial enterprises, newspapers, and, in particular, a large daily paper, owned by a powerful figure, Mr. Fei Y-minh, whom I expect to meet tomorrow.

Monday, 20th December

Throughout history, Hong Kong has always been a warehouse: more precisely, a useful outlet from which Chinese goods could spread the world over and a well-equipped landing place for foreign goods on their way to China. That is why the entire colony is one vast free port, with practically no customs duties, very few trade restrictions, cheap harbor charges, and local money which is convertible to sterling, and thus, in fact, into any currency.

But Hong Kong has been playing a very different and diversified role during the past thirty years. Although the traditional commercial activities continue (and indeed flourish), the colony has become a rather important industrial center which imports raw materials, converts them into finished products, and reexports them. Hong Kong is no longer merely a port of transit but has become a manufacturing center. In twenty years the number of factories here has increased tenfold and the number of industrial workers eightfold. Paralleling this, a demographic explosion has taken place. In 1945 the population numbered 600,000. It has now reached four million.

It is clear that the survival of this structure in its present state depends at the same time on Communist China, on the continued serenity of the local population (how would it be affected by a crisis, by unemployment, by poverty?), and on the development of exports throughout the world. In short, it is a precarious situation.

Having arisen early, I read several speeches by the former and present governors of the colony that Monsieur de La Villesbrune had put aside for me. Their theme is that the English, here to serve the native population, would not stay by force or against its wishes. (Proof is that the troops here are only 7,000 to 8,000 strong, the police force consists of natives, and the freedom of the press is almost complete.) But their policy consists entirely of maintaining such a situation, a prosperity, or even an atmosphere, as makes their support desirable not only for the Chinese government which benefits from it, but also for the people here. Indeed, the latter are relatively peaceful and the Communist Party itself seems content with making moderate claims: they ask, for instance, for Chinese to become an official language along with English, for the number of schools to be increased, for salaries to be raised. They do not even demand a system of representation with universal suffrage. It is possible that the Chinese government is none too eager that a truly democratic experience should confirm, albeit temporarily, the population's inclination toward a colonial situation.

In the morning I went to the Chinese travel agency which serves more or less as a consulate. A young Chinese woman received me graciously and, obviously previously informed of my visit, arranged with care my departure for Thursday.

Afterward I met the directors of the Hong Kong branch of the Bank of Indochina. They are very interested in the monetary decisions taken in the last few days and the devaluation of the dollar, announced yesterday, which is causing them complex practical problems. They are impatient to know the new exchange rates, so as to know at last "on which foot to dance." As for the dollar, there is talk of an 8 percent devaluation.

They explained the colony's monetary system. The Peking government has established not only a sales organization for the local population here, but also, and above all, financial institutions. The first of these is a bank, the most powerful in Hong Kong, which handles most of Communist China's international transactions.

Chinese goods sold in Hong Kong for local consumption or for export to other parts of the world create receipts in Hong Kong dollars—practically a hard currency—and which, moreover, can pay for imports to the People's Republic.

These subjects came up again at lunchtime, when a group of

French people and natives of Hong Kong were gathered at Monsieur de La Villesbrune's house. Specifically, Mr. Peter Ho, the director of commerce and industry in the Hong Kong government, Mr. Kan, member of two of the colony's councils (the governor's advisory bodies), and several businessmen, such as Monsieur Lawrence Kadoorie, president of the *Alliance Française,* Monsieur Leouzon, the representative of Rhône-Poulenc in both Chinas, Korea, and Australia, as well as the Belgian Consul General and the French commercial advisor were present.

Some of them wish the Hong Kong dollar to follow the United States dollar inasmuch as 42 percent of Hong Kong's exports go to the United States and it is essential, in their opinion, to maintain the flow of commerce, even at the risk of causing an economic crisis with its social and political consequences. If tomorrow unemployment were to strike Hong Kong, its consequences would be unpredictable. The problems that would arise after a devaluation, however, cannot be ignored either, since to maintain their income the Chinese would then be forced to raise the prices of the goods they sell in Hong Kong, particularly food products. The cost of living would probably rise, and this would have social repercussions which would bring about an increase in manufacturing costs. That is why in some circles people would like the Hong Kong dollar to hold its position and its parity with the pound sterling, which to them appears quite natural, since it belongs to the sterling area. The decision will be made this afternoon at an important meeting which several of those present will attend. Some of them were noticeably uncertain.

From their discussions I was able to envisage the extraordinary confusion of monetary networks lacing Hong Kong, whose innermost workings they understand. The English are definitely masters at setting up mysterious and complex monetary mechanisms which they skillfully manipulate. One aspect of the system is the gold market which flourishes in Hong Kong. It is supplied by the entry of gold somewhat haphazardly regulated, but of which the British—at any rate—

are clearly well aware, and by some equally unorthodox exports to all the Southeast Asian, Indian Ocean, and Pacific countries.

The manufacturers are faced with more classic problems. They are anxious about the protectionist measures that have been taken for some years by the United States to defend itself against competition from products manufactured in Hong Kong; they, too, complain about the import restrictions that the British also have set up. They point out that, except for Japan, wages here are the highest in Asia, so that the prices of Hong Kong goods are no longer as competitive as formerly. I have my doubts about this since they must have greatly modernized their industries and achieved relatively high productivity (perhaps a little lower than in Japan). The advantages of long-standing relations which ensure Hong Kong a widespread commercial influence and an export effectiveness far superior to that of other Asian and Southeast Asian countries must also be taken into account.

Nevertheless, the competition between Japanese and Hong Kong industries, which is likely to become increasingly strong, has given rise to many questions. Everyone is impressed by Japan's productive development, her drive, her expansion in the entire region, and by the size of her investments in Australia, Southeast Asia, and Latin America.

Yet, as always, the conversation quickly returned to the exchange rates which have been fixed or are under discussion these last few days. In my opinion, not enough importance is given to the questions which are nevertheless predominant: the new bases for the monetary system, which eventually will have to be seriously discussed; the future of the underdeveloped countries, and so on. Indeed it is not surprising for businessmen and bankers to reason in this way; their objectives are their transaction balances and their profits. But the responsible authorities should have a different outlook; they seem to be making a grave mistake. The French had taken a reasonable stand, which Pompidou apparently renounced in the Azores. A simple revision of parities is no solution.

Among the problems to be solved someday is the existence

of dollar balances which amount to 60 billion dollars in short-term credits, with countless holders throughout the world—mainly central banks—that the United States will eventually have to pay in one form or another. The value of these balances has been reduced by 8 percent as of today because of the dollar devaluation and, from this point of view, I cannot understand why so many people are rejoicing. The United States owes us 8 percent less without having paid a cent. This devaluation was inevitable and necessary, but I cannot see that it is such a brilliant victory.

What is also shocking is the way in which all the recent discussions have taken place among the rich countries. The new rates have been or will be set by them, and them alone. The official statement published in Washington by the "Group of Ten" fixes the new parities, and even the bands of fluctuation for the future, and invites the other members of the International Monetary Fund urgently to get in touch with the Group to fix their consequent exchange rates; they are even told to avoid fixing rates favorable to themselves in commercial competition, in spite of the fact that the Ten themselves constantly revealed a similar underlying purpose in their recent negotiations. This procedure will create additional resentment in certain countries where the feeling will be that once again their affairs have been settled without their consent.

We had dinner with Mr. Fei Y-minh, a manufacturer and the owner of a large daily newspaper, whose connections with the Peking government are well known. Here he is active in political and commercial life, while there he is at the same time a member of the great assembly which periodically brings together the delegates of all the Chinese Maoists, those from abroad and from the People's Republic. Mr. Fei Y-minh never speaks of Communist China without saying "we."

Fluent and eloquent, he expresses himself in excellent French, very cleverly evading delicate questions. He began with courteous, flattering remarks about me: 1954 and the Geneva Agreement, Chou En-lai's appreciation of me, and so forth.

When he speaks of international questions, his manner is always undramatic with the "detachment" which the Chinese use when necessary. There is no trace of impatience.

—Taiwan? We shall see about it after Chiang Kai-shek's death; nobody else will have his authority and prestige and a solution will certainly be found then; it is essential for the Americans finally to withdraw; the Seventh Fleet has already been reduced to one or two ships and only seven to eight thousand American soldiers remain on the island; once they leave, everything will straighten out.

—Vietnam? The Americans will gradually reduce their forces to 50,000 men because Nixon can think only of the coming elections. He will have to continue withdrawing the American forces in Indochina; then it will be possible to form a coalition government in Saigon, followed by elections which will lay the foundation for a new political equilibrium. It will take another year or two, however, for the war to end.

—The Indo-Pakistani war? The difficulties have only just begun for India and also for the Soviet Union; "we" cannot accept what is happening and must watch how the situation unfolds.

—Japan? She will have to break her military pact with the United States; in every way American nuclear force on Japanese soil is unacceptable. Later we will be able to consider a nonaggression pact between Japan and China. But nothing is possible with Sato. Since he is expected to leave office next year, all this will be negotiated with his successor.

Nevertheless, Mr. Fei Y-minh several times expressed anxiety about an awakening of Japanese militarism. The Japanese produce one hundred million tons of steel a year and soon will be producing more. However great their internal consumption and power to export, their total production cannot be normally consumed; they are condemned to rearmament. Mr. Fei Yminh suggests a reduction in Japanese metallurgical production; he does not seem greatly disturbed by the possibility of consequent unemployment and social disturbances.

On Communist China's future foreign policies, a categorical and reiterated assertion: China has no expansionary or imperialist projects in view; she will never be a superpower with territorial ambitions. The only territories that she will one day regain are Hong Kong and Macao. She is in no hurry, but will wait for the right circumstances—in other words, for the most important and urgent problems to be settled. But, apart from Hong Kong and Macao, there is no question of China expanding and acquiring other territories. That never has been and never will be "our" policy.

Finally, Mr. Fei Y-minh declared that the meeting of the fourth Grand National Assembly is to be held in Peking next spring. This session was first announced for the beginning of 1971, then for the end of 1971, and now apparently it will not be held before the spring of 1972.[2] This shows that there are certain difficulties in political circles in Peking. Now this great assembly is particularly important because it must, among other things, elect, or rather reelect, the Prime Minister who in turn must present the assembly with a reshuffled cabinet. This reshuffling seems to be causing certain tensions or rivalries on a personal level and over general policies.

Returning to international politics, from all the opinions I gathered during that day in Hong Kong (from businessmen, financiers, diplomats, conservatives, or Maoists), together with those I heard last week in Japan, I can ascertain to what extent the United States' power is declining. The announcement of Nixon's visit to Peking, while perhaps courageous and skillful, already appeared as a symptom of a weakening in American authority and influence. The utter failure in the United Nations of the United States' resolution concerning the admission of China was another sign of weakening. The difficult monetary discussions between the United States and Japan have further modified and worsened the climate. Blunders made at the time of the Indo-Pakistani war have been harshly judged; there was the United States' indifference to the genocide in Bangladesh, the fact that they were openly making advances to the Pakistani government whose prestige in Asia was generally not very high, that they played the wrong horse when the war broke out, and that they then showed so much ill will toward India. All of this has been observed, judged, and resented in the entire Asian world.

The United States will have to bear the consequences of this for a long time. In any event, they will weigh on the future negotiations which it will conduct on the subject of Formosa and Vietnam.

Tuesday, 21st December

Ultimately, the Hong Kong dollar will not devalue and will remain pegged to the English pound. It is amusing to see that, in the press and elsewhere, there is talk of a revaluation of the local currency, because of the habit of using the American dollar as a reference point. In fact, it is the latter which has been devalued by 8 percent.

In any case, the decision taken here preserves the existing supply situation and consequently the standard of living of the population. But the devaluation of the American dollar will create difficulties for the Hong Kong exporters, since the United States is their most important market. The 10 percent surcharge on all imports established on August 15 by the United States will actually disappear, so that, for goods affected by it, the cancelled surcharge and the dollar devaluation will compensate one another. Nevertheless, compared to past years, exports from Hong Kong will still suffer by about 8 percent. There is one consolation: the Japanese, affected simultaneously by their own revaluation and by the American devaluation, will be struck even harder.

It is worthy of note that the decision not to change the parity of the Hong Kong currency was taken at the local level by the Governor, after discussions within the Executive and Advisory Councils. Considering the possible effects of any decision taken here on the volume of trade, the importance of Hong Kong's monetary balance in the sterling area, and the global stability of the pound, one must admire, once again, the broad decentralization of responsibility which has always characterized the British Empire. Thus, the rate of the Hong Kong dollar was decided upon solely on the basis of the interests of the colony, its economy, and its population. Of course, the Governor and his advisors are for the most part British civil servants or people under their authority. The fact remains that they exist in an atmosphere conditioned by the needs of the territory and its inhabitants. We had nothing comparable, unfortunately, at the time of the French Union. I can scarcely see the Governor of Djibouti or of the five settlements in India making decisions about their currency; not even the Resident in Morocco or the Governor General of Indochina. Paris made the decisions and often to the detriment of the colony. Of course, purely political measures were usually taken by the local French authorities (for example, the deposition of the Sultan of Morocco in 1953 or the savage repression in 1945 of the revolt in Madagascar). But on economic questions, it was Paris that decided on investments, exchange rates, foreign trade, and related matters, and in the most colonial spirit.

If Hong Kong had, through the years, been under the impression that everything was always finally decided in London and in the interests of Great Britain alone, there would be a different atmosphere here and a different type of relationship. Hong Kong might well no longer be a British colony. The fact is that, whatever its political bias, its ideological preferences or its attraction to the Chinese center of gravity, the population feels that it is well governed in its own best interest. This is a stability factor that even the Chinese are obliged to take into consideration. In fact, they will be able to take over the territory only when they are sure of providing its 4 million inhabitants with a state of affairs similar to the present one. Until then, they have no choice but to maintain the present situation, without even taking into account the advantages they can draw from it.

We left for Macao in a hydrofoil crossing the port and the bay. Everywhere, ships were loading and unloading, surrounded by a multitude of little coasting vessels or junks serving as ferries.

The journey takes an hour and a quarter and passes islands,

some of which are under British jurisdiction, others Chinese, and still others, Portuguese. This proximity is the cause of frequent incidents because these waters, which do not have precise limits, are constantly frequented by Chinese political refugees and all sorts of traffickers and smugglers.

Macao, a Portuguese colony since the sixteenth century, acquired splendor and wealth long before Hong Kong. But its grandeur belongs to a distant past. The town has gone to sleep. Today it looks poor and sad. The Mediterranean colonial style and the influence of Christianity still remain, but appear out-of-date, as though humiliated by Hong Kong's nearby proud prosperity.

There are 600,000 inhabitants, with a crushing Chinese majority and, naturally, they all are loyal to Communist China. There are many Eurasians, because of continuing intermarriage from generation to generation.

Their principal activities are tourism, sports, smuggling, the gold market, active trade, luxury or doubtful hotels, gambling dens, casinos, nightclubs, and many other things mentioned in undertones.

We paid a courtesy visit to the Portuguese Governor. In a vast palace which was once noble and rich, he presides with dignity over the decline of the ancient colony.

Unfortunately all reminders of the past, barracks, churches, theaters, and palaces are in an advanced state of ruin. Here and there a beautiful façade can sometimes be seen intact, but with nothing behind it.

In 1967 and 1968, Portuguese authority here was strongly shaken by a violent popular movement and incidents which resulted in bloodshed. Order was finally restored because Peking wished to avoid a total crisis. In the course of these events a curious figure emerged, Mr. Ho Yin; acting as intermediary, he acquired an authority on the island that has since never been questioned. He holds the same position here as Mr. Fei Y-minh does in Hong Kong. He and the Governor deal with any delicate problems, since the Governor is well aware that he is powerless without the former's agreement and support.

Mr. Ho Yin in the meantime devotes his time to avoiding acute difficulties and to spinning out a state of affairs, which benefits the local population and also, without a doubt, China, which uses Macao like a miniature Hong Kong. The latter probably is better for dubious activities than the large town which is still firmly under British control.

Here, as in Hong Kong, China assures the supply of food. But here she charges 20 percent less for fruits, vegetables, duck, and pork to enable Macao to maintain the lower level of prices and wages necessary for its survival. This differential in prices is perfectly realistic.

A fashionable joke about Macao among the French people of Hong Kong is that it formerly was Chinese territory, which became a Portuguese colony; now it is a Portuguese colony under a Chinese protectorate.

We visited Mr. Ho Yin in his offices which are in a bank and are protected by a strong team of bodyguards. He has large industrial interests here, which are in no way incompatible with the political role he plays. Welcoming us, he offered us his services to help us to visit Macao under the best possible circumstances. We thanked him very much, saying, however, that we were but simple tourists who had come to get acquainted with an interesting country and, knowing the very important role he plays in Macao, wished to meet him and to chat briefly with him.

It was raining hard and this somewhat spoiled the pleasure of the tour, which could otherwise have been lively and delightful. We took refuge for a moment in a casino where there were many ingenious games in all of which the odds were unfavorable to the players!

Both the Governor's and Mr. Ho Yin's secretaries saw us off on the hydrofoil; under their umbrellas they seemed quite at ease in their rather unorthodox situation.

Back in the port we found still more boats and activity than there had been in the morning. It is like being in the *Place de l'Opéra* at six o'clock in the evening, at the height of the rush hour.

At nightfall the town lights up. The largest building in the city center is the Bank of China which displays a huge neon sign that was translated for me: "Glory to President Mao." Next to it, scarcely less flamboyant, is the Hilton Hotel.

Passing through the bustling streets of the lower part of the town, we still have the feeling of being in London. Nothing is missing: the names of the streets, the parking meters, the cars with left-hand drive, the double-decker buses. There are also, however, a multitude of minibuses which seat fourteen people and seem to be in great demand. We should provide our own towns, like Paris and Grenoble, with similar minibuses, with their better service and maneuverability, along with our regular buses. Here I see them moving around in swarms (one a minute in the rush hours) and winding in and out of the congested traffic much more easily than the heavy coaches which encumber our streets. An aside: apparently the company that puts these little vehicles into circulation is Communist, from the boss down to the drivers and mechanics.

In the evening, we dined in Kowloon and wandered around; in the center of the town are brightly lit shops, attractive shop windows, cinemas, dense traffic, taxis, and so forth; there are packed crowds, window shopping or rushing to the cinemas, and restaurants (some luxurious, others much less so). We might have been in Times Square.

Wednesday, 22nd December, morning

At last this morning we have a rare spare moment which I am going to spend studying the morning newspapers and those of the last few days which have accumulated in my room. Much to my regret, they are indeed all in English.

Once again I am impressed by the quality, diversity, and substantiality of the information in the English press. These newspapers are meant for businessmen, high officials, even traveling salesmen or tourists. Nonetheless, the abundance and high quality of the economic information in them is striking. Although they cannot after all have a large readership, these newspapers provide me with a remarkable collection of information on the monetary crisis and the solutions recently decided upon, the equivalent of which I could not have found in the French daily papers. They not only cover the effects of recent events on the economy of Hong Kong and that of Japan, but also on the mark, the dollar, and the American economy. They also deal with decisions taken by the French government, with the future of United States' commercial relations with Asia, the Common Market, and Great Britain.

I would be very much interested to know what the Chinese-language newspapers publish on this subject. But I can only question the people I meet and they are able to give me only an insufficient, approximate idea.

The press, whether English or Chinese, obviously draws considerable revenue from the abundant advertising which is directly related to the colony's wealth and economic activity. Everything here rests on the prosperity and continuing success of this entire paradoxical enterprise.

How long will it last? For many more years seems to be the answer, considering the spectacular development of private and public investments: tenement buildings and ordinary housing, offices, factories, social centers, road networks, schools, hospitals, museums, and the extension of the port (by encroaching farther on the sea). The manufacturers or the administration decide on all these expenditures and inevitably must take into account the temporary character of their development, which could easily and at any moment be jeopardized by a political change or annexation by Communist China. The present precarious equilibrium also must enter into consideration when investments are evaluated. In private business businessmen must count on a short repayment period. I am told that they generally assume that the present situation will last for a minimum of four or five years, and they therefore intend to recover their investments in this length of time. Revenues beyond that date then become clear profit. As for public facilities, the local authorities, and over them the British government, must be banking on the fact that construction in the universal interest is strengthening and finally making the English presence more solid. In short, all this confirms the extraordinary profitability and productivity of investing capital here.

The British reasoning seems ratified by the presence of innumerable foreigners: Americans and Japanese, Germans and Belgians, people from Formosa. All are there. The French are too few, around 500 in all. They are with the *Alliance Française* (which in spite of everything has several thousand students), the *Messageries Maritimes,* and Air France. Every now and then, others come to bid for projects (recently a small barrage).

Nevertheless, apart from the English, who naturally hold the most important position, Japan is most likely to have an indirect influence on Hong Kong's future economic evolution. Traumatized by the recent monetary upheavals, Japan will be obliged to make a furious effort, if necessary by price-dumping and by striving to increase sales in Southeast Asia, in order to obtain in exchange a growing share of its primary products. She is in double competition and rivalry with Hong Kong, which has the same commercial structure and the same need for supplies and outlets.

What will future Japanese export prices be? There is a rumor that their selling prices will not be changed in spite of the strong upward revaluation of the yen. For the time being, Japanese goods in Hong Kong have not increased in price. This may be because the Christmas holidays are near. It is too early to judge, but it is certain that the Japanese shops will be closely watched during the next few weeks.

I well understand the measures taken yesterday by Giscard d'Estaing in the face of the new state of affairs. For months now his policy has consisted of limiting the flow into France of undesirable speculative capital. Now, he is expecting much of this capital to flow back to the United States. We will undoubtedly see some movement in that direction; not only Germany and Switzerland, but also Great Britain and France will be feeling the effects of all this. Those who speculated against the dollar will now reap the benefits, which explains the measures taken in Paris to come to the aid of banks and corporations which formerly held too many dollars and at present are in danger of a shortage. But this is likely to last only a very short while.

What is important for the future is the overall American balance of payments. I do not in the least believe the problem to have yet been solved. My friend Eddie Bernstein is said to have recently declared that an 11 percent dollar devaluation would be insufficient to improve permanently the American balance of payments. I believe he is right. This is sure to come up again soon.

In the meantime all the official declarations made in Europe and America are trying to create a feeling of optimism so that things will start off again "as usual."

But what will happen if the abnormal movement of capital to Europe continues? Will the Germans join a common organization to regulate the coming and going and vagabondage of liquid funds in search of refuge or speculation? If a European organization could finally be set up to supervise and guide unstable funds, which are the cause of so much disorder, it would be an important step toward the creation of a true Community (and much more effective than the readjustments of parities, which are now so fashionable).

In any case, the large problems concerning the international monetary mechanism remain unsolved and have, in fact, hardly been defined. The only decision the Ten have actually reached, and which in my opinion is not at all what is needed, is to widen the exchange bands. The former 1 percent maximum has now been stretched to reach 2.25 percent, which gives a possible variation of 4.5 percent in relation to the dollar and, at the most, of 9 percent among the other currencies. This is neither a solution, nor even a true reform; it could even be a new destabilizing factor.

What is the future of the dollar? For twenty years it has been the international standard. Today it finds itself in difficulty. As the currency of the most powerful economy in the world, it will continue to play an important role and will still be used for many international transactions. But psychologically and technically it is no longer the standard, the backbone of the entire monetary mechanism. What will the new system be? I very much doubt that the responsible principals as of now are ready to answer this question except by defending this or that short-term self-interest.

The last point I note today: yesterday's monetary agreements maintain a margin for appreciation of about 5 percent for the German mark in relation to the franc, as compared to the situation before the month of August. Commercially, the advantage from which we have benefited during the last three or four months is a minor one for us, but it is all the same quite considerable and will favor our exporters.

After having lunch in a huge Chinese restaurant, I went through the outer area of Kowloon, where factories and large apartment blocks are under construction. Often, one family lives in a single room, generally with a big terrace-balcony used also as a kitchen, where linen and multicolored clothes are constantly drying.

What are called the "new territories" stretch out from here, and cover some twenty kilometers. This is an area which the English rented from the Chinese for a hundred years—until 1997; Kowloon and Hong Kong island, on the other hand, are under British sovereignty, at least according to nineteenth-century treaties not recognized by the Chinese. These legal distinctions are not of great importance, because it is the entire structure which will or will not last depending on unpredictable circumstances and events.

The "new territories" consist of a rocky area with hills, mountains, ravines, and countless sea inlets and are scarcely inhabited. At the foot of the mountains there are a few fishing villages where there are traditional handicraft activities. We visited a small shopping quarter which slightly resembles the dirtiest streets of Marseilles or the most disagreeable souks in North Africa.

I received a phone call from Madame Haugen, the wife of a journalist who was captured in Cambodia a few months ago.

She has no news of him and fears the worst. I was told about this case before I left Paris and some journalists asked me to alert those on the spot who might have influence, such as Sihanouk—if I were to meet him—the government of the Chinese People's Republic, and the representatives of North Vietnam. I told Madame Haugen that I understood her anxiety and that I will speak of the matter to the people I am to meet. But I dared not give her too much hope; under the present conditions there it is difficult to obtain information about the fate of those who have been captured or wounded. It does not follow from this that the situation is any less awful. It is not the first time that journalists and press photographers have been wounded in the course of their work, but it is the first time that there has been no news of them for so long. Certain arrangements should be made analogous to, for example, the Geneva Conventions regarding prisoners of war, for instance; people who take such great professional risks have the right to better protection and their families have the right, at least, to news. This is something which I shall not forget next week in Peking.

This evening a Franco-Japanese agreement on the enrichment of uranium was announced. The French will build a plant for Japan. This is the result of earlier proposals we made not only to Japan, but also to Australia (the latter possesses important uranium reserves and France would gain a great deal from broad nuclear cooperation with her). It is unfortunate that this policy was not activated a long time ago; instead of concentrating on the military atom, we could have pushed forward much more rapidly by cooperating with the new or semideveloped countries which are without sources of energy. We now have much ground to cover if we are to catch up with other countries and above all with America.

Thursday, 23rd December

Departure from Hong Kong by car. We drove 25 kilometers on a road which crosses the peninsula parallel to the one

77

we took yesterday on our visit to the "new territories." On this side agriculture appears active and prosperous.

Cars, like the trains, are stopped at the border. Only freight trains which carry daily food supplies to Hong Kong may pass through: at least one hundred carriages a day carry pigs, chickens, ducks, fruit, and so forth. The trains smell of farms and fresh vegetables.

We took our leave of the Consul General who was so hospitable during our very pleasant stay in Hong Kong. He is not allowed to go any further.

China

A hundred or a hundred and fifty yards on foot and then a little bridge which marks the border. On the other side some young Chinese took charge of us, offering us an excellent meal while we were waiting to depart.

People were packed into the station like sardines. A thousand or two travelers were leaving Hong Kong to spend the next few days (national holidays in Hong Kong, but not in China) with their families in the Canton region; a joyous, impatient crowd of people, laden with countless parcels of various shapes and sizes, toys, presents, and food.

The train left at one o'clock. It moved slowly, and we were able to admire the prosperous, highly cultivated countryside: water everywhere and many gardens and terraces. The people in the fields were working in teams using rather rudimentary methods. We saw few agricultural machines and no tractors, but intense hand labor everywhere.

On the hills there were trees, hundreds of thousands of them, all relatively young, planted systematically during the last few years.

The trip was a chance for me to read a pile of cables from the A.F.P. One of them reports the conditions under which the election of Mr. Waldheim, the new Secretary General of the United Nations, took place. The Peking delegation's attitude on this occasion seems to me to be encouraging. China could have given in to demagoguery by supporting a candidate who was obviously inacceptable to one or another Western country and by outdoing the Russians. As it turns out, she seems to have preferred to play the game correctly and moderately. She voted twice against Mr. Waldheim, the Austrian candidate, but, knowing that a third negative vote would in fact constitute a veto, she then abstained, so that it was possible for Mr. Waldheim to be elected. Using in this way their right to abstain, the Chinese were effectively able to avoid participating in the designation of the new Secretary General without blocking the machinery in so doing. This flexibility is interesting to notice, since it could be a forecast of China's future behavior in the United Nations.

As for Mr. Waldheim, he declared that the admission of the divided countries to the United Nations would be the international organization's next important step. There is nothing new in this declaration as far as the two Germanys are concerned, for the principle of their entry into the United Nations is already more or less accepted; nonetheless, the door is being opened to both Vietnams and both Koreas. What do they think of this in Peking?

Here I am back in China after thirteen years. What changes will I find? The year which is about to end has been not only the one in which China entered the United Nations, but also has marked world recognition of the fact that discussions on any important international problem cannot be begun without Peking. The Indo-Pakistani war, the creation of Bangladesh, Japan's problems, the war in Vietnam, in short the upheaval of the entire continent, all have contributed to an enlargement of her role. And the healing of the crisis of the Cultural Revolution will now give to Chinese politics a new freedom of action.

The train drew slowly into the Canton station. We were somewhat formally yet perfectly cordially welcomed by some members of the Revolutionary Committee of Kuang-Tung and an official from the Foreign Ministry who is to accompany us to Peking.

We were taken to see a museum founded in memory of a military and revolutionary school organized by Mao Tse-tung in 1926. It has become a shrine to which many civilian and military visitors journey; everywhere there are portraits and statues of a very young Mao teaching the Revolution, discussing, convincing, persuading men around him, mostly young peasants. He appears much more of a teacher, even a preacher, than a revolutionary fighter. Pictures and diagrams show clearly the widespread influence of that school throughout China and the fact that it trained revolutionaries who spread out into many villages in all the Chinese provinces.

Rapidly touring the town we saw bicycles by the thousand. The houses looked depressing and badly kept up.

In the late afternoon we left Canton for Peking on a commercial airline in an old British-made plane. The flight took about four hours.

At Peking airport there was an important delegation waiting to meet me headed by Mr. Li Yao-wen, Vice Foreign Minister, and by the French Ambassador. Mr. Li Yao-wen drove me to the hotel in Peking. On the way he questioned me about Japan. I have a feeling that this subject will be brought up frequently.

The outside of the hotel, like the interior, has not changed since my last visit. I recognize the same spacious, overheated, old-fashioned rooms. This must have been where rich tourists and western businessmen stayed at the beginning of the century. It reminds me of Marienbad.

Friday, 24th December

In the morning Mr. Hu Shu-tu, Director of European Affairs at the Foreign Ministry, and Mr. Chou Chen-tung, an official from the same ministry, came to see me. They are responsible for organizing my stay and wanted to inquire what I would like to have fitted into the program. We agreed that I am to remain mostly in Peking and in Shanghai where there would be opportunities for interesting talks to take place. But very quickly Mr. Hu Shu-tu started asking me numerous questions on Japan and her former military demons.

In the streets of Peking there are old, gray, low houses side by side with modern buildings in the heavy Soviet style of the

Stalinist period. The streets are quite empty at this time of year. Few cars, but many bicycles. We also passed groups of young people walking in line; they are schoolchildren being taken out for exercise; those wearing red armbands are Red Guards.

On the whole, the general scene would be sad if it were not for the thousands and thousands of decorative young trees which beautify it.

But in the less important streets, one finds oneself in an animated crowd running from one shop to another. The shops are well stocked. The merchandise offered is abundant, especially in food products; it appears that the supply of food is no longer a problem. There are also the usual manufactured goods, such as bicycles and watches, which do not seem to be poor quality though they may be less refined, less exquisite than the Chinese goods sold outside the country, as in Hong Kong.

After lunch with the French Ambassador, Monsieur Étienne Manac'h, he and his wife came with us on our (traditional) visit to the Forbidden City. Thousands of Chinese go there each day to wonder at this astonishing vestige of the Middle Empire. I was told that the City was closed to the public during the Cultural Revolution because, since any reminder of the past was threatened, the government feared that leftists might destroy something there. Now like us, the Chinese visitors come to admire this extraordinary scene, and probably approve of what must be the considerable sums of money spent on its upkeep.

Dinner was with Vice Prime Minister Li Hsien-nien. Among the forty people or so present were the Vice Foreign Minister and the Vice Minister for Foreign Trade. A former commander in the army, Li Hsien-nien is one of the most important figures in the regime; goodlooking, with a direct expression, his style has remained strict and military. He is the closest person to Chou En-lai. Like all these veterans of the Long March who have overcome so many hazards, he shows great assurance, particularly since the political and economic successes of the last few years. The Chinese leaders never seem troubled by doubt. They have a fundamental confidence in the enterprise in which they are participating. Are there difficulties, rivalries, confrontations among them? Nothing comes through to the outside world. The internal political problems so much discussed throughout the world are not mentioned before a stranger. The diplomats stationed here never manage to gather any information from anyone to whom they speak. Nor do visitors.

Very quickly, as I had expected, my conversation with Li Hsien-nien turned to the subject of Japan. First he affirmed his friendship for the Japanese nation (which is not responsible for the crimes of its former leaders and which is destined to get along with the Chinese nation, if only because of geographical and cultural affinities), then the Vice Prime Minister said that Communist China has no confidence in Mr. Sato, who is too unstable and changeable; from listening to Mr. Li Hsien-nien, I have the feeling that the Japanese made a serious mistake at the time of the recent debates in the United Nations by co-signing the resolution in favor of Formosa's representation in spite of the entry of Communist China.

Soon, Li Hsien-nien referred to the "abnormal development" of Japan's economy the excess of which can lead only to rearmament and to a militarist rebirth which confirms, by the way, "information in the possession" of the Chinese government. He concedes Japan's need for "military forces for self defense," but I sense that this implies, with the exception of qualitative and quantitative limitations, the renunciation of the Japanese-American military pact and the liquidation of all the United States bases in Japan.

As for Nixon's visit to Peking, he was the one "to suggest it. We accepted, we could not refuse. We have no idea what may come of it, but China is prepared for any eventuality."

After dinner and after the traditional toasts, my host showed me around the Congress Hall where the dinner had taken place. It is a huge building with numerous rooms, the two largest of which can hold 7,000 and 10,000 people, respectively. With the exception of certain so-called commission rooms, the rooms are not very attractive. Each region has a room decorated in its own particular style. One is reserved for the "Chinese province" of Taiwan. It remains closed and will be furnished by the people who live on the island when it returns to the motherland.

On my way home, I thought about Mr. Li Hsien-nien's remarks about the "abnormal development" of Japan's industry. It is an expression I have already heard several times and I feel that I will hear it again. It is true that the Chinese are unpleasantly impressed, for example, by the fact that Japan produces 100 million tons of steel annually; they feel that this is unhealthy and can lead only to fearful consequences. As loyal Marxists, they are convinced that such production, if left unchecked, will force Japan to export widely and that in order to protect her exports, a positive military policy will become imperative. They see imperialism as the natural consequence of a so-called abnormal development of production. Some of them, like Mr. Fei Y-minh, therefore consider that Japanese production will have to be regulated and even limited. I have pointed out that, taking into account the age pyramid, such a policy could mean massive unemployment in Japan with easily imaginable consequences, but I have been unable to obtain a clear answer to this question. Although it worries the Chinese, it seems to me that they do not have a viable solution to offer.

Saturday, 25th December

We visited Tsing-hua University, the "new Socialist university" set up as a model for the whole country for methods and instructional research in science and technology. There is a similar institute for the study and advancement of agriculture.

Tsing-hua University was founded in 1911, after which it developed under American influence. In 1949 it was "liberated." Instruction there was then organized according to Soviet norms, which means that it trained men capable of organizing the workers and peasants. They explained to me that this was like the old feudal concept which trained the literate to govern the illiterate. It was harmful, since the students thought of themselves as an elite and began to despise the less educated social classes. The elderly intellectuals opposed all reforms.

The president of the Revolutionary Committee described this situation with indignation: as in many socialist countries, the universities in China, he said, had become "capitalist" again, in other words they were stagnant and isolated from the sociological environment, they instigated no change in the ruling classes. Furthermore, studies took far too long; young people spent eighteen years of their lives on school or university benches, without any contact with the outside world; they were "cut off from production and from the common people"; they despised their parents. The Cultural Revolution has changed all that, but not without difficulty; "it first had to engage in an armed struggle," which was long and violent.

In 1969 the university's Revolutionary Committee was formed. It consists of workers, peasants, teachers, university personnel and Red Guards. It "eliminated the bad elements." At Tsing-hua 2,600 teachers, that is to say the majority of them, immersed themselves again in peasant, working, or military communities "to receive a new education there. Now they can teach better." Some of those, who were "fatigued," were sent into retirement.

During that interval the university—like all the universities at the time of the Cultural Revolution—was closed, not only because of the tension which could be felt throughout the country and the restlessness which had come over young people, especially students, but also because the conflict was particularly acute between those who clung to the old university system and those who hoped to break up the structure and find new teaching methods. The old teaching methods based on the Soviet model had to be suppressed. Tsing-hua opened again only last year. There are, therefore, only first-year students here (2,800 altogether) while there is in fact room for 12,000 students. Many of the buildings are scarcely used and the campus is almost deserted.

Those in charge have published an account of the experiments undertaken at Tsing-hua; what emerges from it is that priority must be given to political education, that is "studying the thoughts of Chairman Mao." The link between theory and practice and between intellectual and manual work is also stressed. Institutes of higher education are obliged to work in close cooperation with farms, factories, workshops and the army.

The president of the Revolutionary Committee says: "Here we teach and at the same time we work in factories. This is true for students and teachers alike."

An old professor joined in : "I studied in the United States," he says, "and that influenced me for a long time. Without my even realizing it, my teaching was biased. I had theoretical knowledge but no practical ideas whatsoever; I even believed that theory is better than practice! I taught for forty years without ever knowing a worker or a peasant. Since the Cultural Revolution I have gone to factories five times for training. I saw that my knowledge was incomplete, if not incorrect, and I became more modest. Now some of my friends are workers. I no longer am one of those intellectuals who have no consideration for the workers' interests. Now the workers no longer call me 'Mister,' but 'comrade.' "

The aim of the university reform is to put "education at the service of the proletariat," in order to avoid a revival of the mandarin class. The professor must be a proletarian and a product of the "worker-peasant-soldier union." Students must be chosen on that same principle. They are required to have worked in a job for at least two years.

I asked how college students are chosen. They explained to me that periodically the university's Revolutionary Committee, following professional and educational criteria, decides to recruit a certain type of student. It then applies to the communes, army units, and factory committees, who present candidates "approved by the masses." They are selected by intermediary organizations (town or province Revolutionary Committees) which make the definitive choice based on several criteria, the first of which is political. Finally the future students "are chosen by the people" and by their selection organizations, which afterward supervise the students' work.

Students spend three years in one of Tsing-hua's eleven specialized faculties: among them electricity, computer science, and construction. Most of them have finished secondary studies besides two or three years of manual labor; they are about twenty years old and are very rarely married. The state pays for their room and board. Other older students who have had over five years of practical experience are "researchers": they try to find more effective technical methods, improvements, practical innovations, and more ingenious production procedures. They earn the same salary as they did when they were working at their trades. All of them regularly, for instance, during their holidays return to their original work units, that is, the factory, farm, or regiment which—once their studies are completed—they will rejoin permanently.

The new curriculum has demolished theoretical studies so as to give more time to applied work. Students in some departments, such as construction or hydraulics, spend half their time in factories. The university workshops which we visited produce spare parts or articles special-ordered by industries, and therefore contribute to the national economy. Some courses are given by factory workers.

A certain number of factories, in turn, have created universities of their own. For example, a computer-hardware plant connected with Tsing-hua, has set up a specialized university.

Studies have been cut short and simplified. Completely superfluous theories were being taught, says one of the professors. Now these are limited to what is really useful and necessary. For "by continuous practical experience the students are made to understand theoretical notions which used to be drummed into them in a purely abstract manner."

The relationship between students and professors also has changed. No more lectures are given and everyone participates in collective work. Education must be alive and must lead everyone—students, teachers and parents—"to participate actively."

I am under the impression that in reality matters are somewhat different from what I am being told. From several answers to my direct questions, it seems clear that the students have no effective role within the university's administration. It is, in fact, the Chinese Communist Party's Committee that formulates the general policy to be followed and settles all ideological problems; the Revolutionary Committee is the executive branch. The Party has supreme authority and the answer to my question on this subject was explicit: much more so, undoubtedly, than it would have been two or three years ago at the time when the power of the Revolutionary Committees was unquestioned. Now, the Party regulates everything in accordance with the state's needs in matters of scientific research, which explains, for example, the current studies on water recycling.

After this visit I had a discussion with Monsieur Riottot our cultural attaché. He says that he has noticed great progress in scientific and technological institutes like Tsing-hua, though less in the field of literature.

The Tsing-hua experiment is a practical one and probably what I have been told is not definitive; they are still feeling their way, looking for solutions. Predominant is the wish to bring about a mingling of all social levels and to avoid segregation of intellectuals and technicians from the people. I had already heard this concern discussed in 1958 when I was shown some experiments of another kind directed toward the same ends. This is possibly the most important and most difficult problem of our times. Particularly in a country where there are still many illiterate people and some with little education (in the adult population alone), anyone who has had a university education can easily feel "different" from and even superior to the others, and this state of mind can give rise to a new class. The children of the privileged of science and other disciplines will inevitably benefit from it; parents will transmit part of their experience and culture within the family circle and these young people will have an advantage even before they have begun their studies. This results in a kind of heredity within the social structure which is well known in the capitalist countries and indeed already noticeable in a number of socialist countries. About fifteen years ago when he was head of the Soviet government, Khrushchev complained in a famous speech about the proportion of university students who were the "sons of" (sons of officers, of high officials, of technicians, and the like). In China, they are attempting to avoid this stratification and that is why the experiments taking place there are so exciting.

Nevertheless, to avoid the risks I have just mentioned, they may possibly use methods which could reduce the effectiveness of their instruction. What of this method which imposes an interruption of at least two years between secondary school and university? Is it true that almost half a student's time can safely be devoted to practical work? Is the openly stated priority given to political criteria in the selection of students really admissable? Is it necessary to sacrifice pure research for applied research to such an extent? I am unable to decide in favor of either method but I am well aware of the seriousness of these questions for all those who are attempting to achieve a modern, more just civilization while advancing toward socialism. In a few years it will be interesting to see where China stands on this issue.

We returned to the hotel. During the two days I have been here, I have felt a curious sensation; I feel much more distant from Paris and the outside world than I did in either Tokyo or Hong Kong. It is hard to come by news other than the Chinese news bulletins in French and English which are provided for me. While in Japan and Hong Kong, I had the impression that, on political and economic issues, I was following world affairs closely, but here I cannot keep in touch and I feel very badly informed. This impression is a little disagreeable.

Tonight, Christmas is being celebrated in France and I am going to spend the evening with Chou En-lai. I found myself thinking back over our previous meetings which began in

1954 when he came to Geneva in the hope (and this is still my interpretation today) of bringing his country out of the isolation to which the western countries were trying to confine it. How much time has been wasted since then . . . but not for China; she is now sought after by everyone, almost courted, and in a few weeks President Nixon will be coming to knock at her door.

Chou En-lai has invited us to have dinner at seven o'clock at the Congress Palace, where we were last night. That is where he always receives guests. Apparently no diplomat has ever been able to call on him in his home or the office where he works, but always in similar anonymous, multifunctional places. The same thing applies to Mao Tse-tung, the location of whose Peking residence is hardly known (in fact, especially in the winter, he lives mostly in the south, because of the capital's very severe climate).

Chou En-lai gave us a cordial and smiling welcome. He has hardly aged at all. His skin is more wrinkled, his features more drawn, and he has lost a little weight. Yet his style remains the same: still very noble, refined and distinguished (dare I say aristocratic?). He has a curious manner of walking, which is almost silent and gives the impression of gliding over the carpet. I had already noticed this in Geneva and again in this very same place.

There is, however, a new assurance in his manner, a new sense of security, which is easily understandable when one bears in mind that for twenty-two years he has governed China, the largest and most populous country in the world, and that in the last few months he has carried off a series of spectacular successes at home and abroad.

As an opening gambit, he began: "What have you seen since your arrival in Peking?" I answered at random, mentioning Tsing-hua, and he began talking about the young people:

"It is a great problem for us, but also for all the other countries. There is dissatisfaction among the young. They feel that what they are taught at school is outdated, useless to them once they start living an active life. I believe there also are changes taking place in your country."

"Yes. Edgar Faure, whom you know, launched the first stage of reform in 1968, but many more will be needed. The young people—and not only students—feel a profound need for change and for adaptation to a new epoch which is sometimes difficult to define clearly, but obliges us to reflect and to scrutinize. That is a good thing."

"Here, studies used to last too long. We are reducing them. The young people however are in no position to judge whether other changes are needed; these must be conceived and put into effect by those who have experience."

What would the French Maoists think if they were to hear this?

I watched the Prime Minister with curiosity and, I admit, with admiration. He moves quickly, laughs readily, knows everything in detail, evidently reads many reports and files, and is gifted with an infallible memory. The conversation seemed to me more relaxed and free than that of the night before. We were fifteen at table instead of forty and in a smaller, less formal room. Chou En-lai remained with us for four and a half hours. And we talked, not only about the university. Fairly soon he came to foreign affairs.

Nothing escapes him in this field. Without the slightest hesitation he quotes figures and technical references on trends in the Japanese birthrate; the particular qualities of the steel produced in China, in Japan or in Europe; the situation in Latin America; what part England will be able to play in the Common Market; and similar topics. He did not seem to wish to concentrate the conversation on one particular subject and so it continued in extemporaneous confusion.

He is irritated, even exasperated by England's position on Taiwan and endlessly stresses what seems to him the equivocal attitude of Great Britain. This is the reason why diplomatic relations between that country and China are not at the level of an exchange of ambassadors, but only of chargés d'affaires. Comparing Great Britain's attitude to that of General de Gaulle, he praises the latter for having taken what, in his opinion, was an explicit position on Taiwan.

China will never surrender Taiwan, a Chinese province

which belongs to her. "We will wait the time it takes. After all, you waited forty-eight years for Alsace-Lorraine to be returned to you."

Taiwan continually kept reappearing in his conversation: apropos Nixon's visit to Peking, on normalization of relations with Japan, and criticizing Waldheim's recent speech recommending the representation at the United Nations of the "separated states" (Germany, Vietnam, Korea). Chou En-lai does not wish to discuss this, fearing that one day it could serve as a precedent for admitting Taiwan to the United Nations. "We do not wish such unacceptable situations to be endorsed in this way; we see a danger for others and for ourselves in such a move. Taiwan is our Alsace-Lorraine, never forget that." Where Germany is concerned, however, he accepts the proposition, because in that case the division is a consequence of World War II.

He has a truly Chinese perspective on every subject. Using this perspective, Chou En-lai takes his stand on all the problems we discussed. For instance, he knows China's traditional military forces would not now be able to win in the face of American or Soviet aggression; for this reason, he wants nuclear weapons and has chosen for China a deterrent policy for which De Gaulle pleaded in France.

I noticed in Chou En-lai, as I had in 1954 and in 1958, a strong persecution complex and a frustration, which are probably common to all the Chinese leaders. These feelings stem from past events and from the fact that China has remained completely isolated for many years. Chou En-lai, therefore, sees hostility and even threats almost everywhere: in Japan, in the United States, in India and, above all, in the Soviet Union.

Actually, for the time being he no longer fears United States aggression as he did in 1958. He feels that the American tide is retreating. On the other hand, he is haunted by "Russian social-imperialism." This is the point of view from which he judges recent events in India and in Bengal: the U.S.S.R., he says, wants to catch China in a vice; first there was the northern grip (a million Russian soldiers in Siberia, 300,000 others in Mongolia, missiles aimed at Chinese cities), now this is the southern grip (Bangladesh and India, future Russian military satellites, with bases for the Soviet fleet in the Indian Ocean). "This proves their aggressive intentions," he says in a hard and sarcastic tone.

For my part I cannot see what Russia would gain by attacking China; nor do I believe that India has such intentions. But it is clear that the Prime Minister is convinced of the contrary. "If they do not intend to fight a war, why all the display?" Although I have sometimes heard people say the opposite, I believe Chou En-lai to be sincere when he continuously affirms and repeats his fears of aggression.

All over Peking I have seen piles of sand and bricks, open trenches, and other such things. An underground town is being built, complete with supplies and first aid posts. Apparently the same is true in all Chinese cities. Civil-defense constructions are underway to shelter the population in the event of war and bombing. Such extensive undertakings cannot be simply for show. Officials, accordingly, therefore seem quite convinced that aggression is possible and that it could even be imminent.

Vietnam? Chou En-lai is firm about the fact that the Americans will have to leave (Kissinger may have understood it, he says, but it is less sure that Rogers did. What does Nixon think? We shall soon know.). Then the freed Vietnamese will organize themselves as they please. Will there be a unification? It is not so simple: The South has a puppet government; that of the North is entrenched. Once the South has a democratic leadership, it will be possible to think of reunification. That will give rise to difficult problems, because the government on one side is socialist and on the other, capitalist; Integration will require time and change. "It may take years."

In any case, the problem will not be settled by China herself, not even with the cooperation of the United States. It will be the Vietnamese who will do so and they alone. China supplies them with unconditional aid, no strings attached. Their political principles, their methods of waging war, and later of organizing the postwar period are their own affair. Nothing will be settled with Nixon without the participation of the Vietnamese; but if Nixon wishes it, the Chinese government "could act as an intermediary."

Cambodia? He praises Prince Sihanouk and goes on: "We have welcomed him here, but we are putting no pressure on him. He is free to do as he pleases and is totally independent. He is not faced with any of the problems De Gaulle experienced when, as a refugee in England during World War II, he had conflicts with his allies."

Once again the subject turned to Japan, about which the Prime Minister talks with a certain moderation, without hatred, but with mistrust. I told him about the strong tendency I noticed in Tokyo in favor of the normalization of relations and of finding a definition for a solution concerning Taiwan. This corresponds to deep popular feeling. "Oh, not only popular!" Chou En-lai exclaims, remembering with obvious pleasure the numerous visits to Peking of Japanese businessmen.

In fact, Japan is probably going to be obliged to reconsider her export policy for she will find it harder than in the past to sell her goods to the United States. Chou En-lai is well aware of the difficulties the Japanese are facing at this moment as a result, in his opinion, of their having given too much importance to their trade with the United States. They are reaping no reward; Japan is the first victim of the monetary and commercial policies adopted by the United States. That is Japan's misfortune, and may it be a lesson to her.

I pointed out that Japan is going to look for other outlets and that we have already experienced some Japanese commercial offensives in Europe, where those in the iron and steel industry, for instance, are complaining about the competition of Japanese steel exports.

Chou En-lai: "We also buy some from her."

I answered: "If you buy her steel, you will not hear the European steel manufacturers complain about it!"

Chou En-lai (laughing): "But the Japanese still lag behind the Europeans in certain kinds of special steel, particularly armorplate for ships."

He added that, in any case, Japanese steel production is much too large and is driving the country inevitably toward militarism. He would not, in fact, be hostile to an exclusively defensive Japanese rearmament. I have already heard this story; and once again the expression "self-defense forces" is used. Whatever happens, Japan must not take over the United States military position in Asia.

Chou En-lai does not in any way envisage a normalization of political relations as long as Mr. Sato's team is in power.

Another aside about China's nuclear force. According to Chou En-lai, it still is only in the "experimental" stage. China cannot, therefore, consider herself a nuclear power (according to French military sources, even though she is far behind the United States and the Soviet Union, she already has a certain number of operational devices). China is in no way a threat to peace as she has decided never to be the first to use the atomic bomb; that is a commitment which the "superpowers" have unfortunately not always made. Besides, the more countries with the atomic bomb, the less danger there is of war. The proof is that during the last twenty years two great powers had nuclear weapons at their disposal and no war has broken out between them; there only have been local wars between non-nuclear powers. This argument does not, however, entirely convince me.

We left the table, yet the discussion continued with the same liveliness. I told the Prime Minister that I shall soon be going to India. He reacted quickly: "You will hear unpleasant things about us there." I answered that misunderstandings and mistrust often arise between governments and nations and that it is necessary to try to surmount them. What has just taken place is the result of the Bengali people's rebellion against the abuses of the Pakistani government; did not twelve million unfortunate people flee to India to be protected from persecution? Chou En-lai is aware that there could have been a national problem in Bengal. But others could also arise elsewhere; to mention such minorities as the Sikhs, Tamouls, and Kashmiri. These are all scarcely veiled threats to the unity of India which is suspected of nurturing imperialist designs.

97

"The troubles in this region will continue. India has probably stirred up a fire in which she herself may be burned. It is curious that, out of three states ruled by women, two are imperialist: Israel and India."

"But has the international community fulfilled its obligations in both these two cases? Israel has been almost besieged for twenty years. India has been invaded by 12 million refugees. Yet nobody has batted an eyelid. Is it surprising that some acute crises have resulted? Neither the United Nations nor the great powers did their duty at the right time and sometimes went so far as to fan the flame."

Chou En-lai does not deny this.

The end of our conversation dealt mostly with demography and agriculture—subjects which always interest the Chinese. I mentioned various opinions I had gathered in Japan:

—Because of the progress in hygiene and medicine, there are more elderly people nowadays. More young people are needed in order to avoid a generally old population. After having strongly reduced their birthrate by a policy of drastic birth control, the Japanese realized that they were heading for a fall in terms of the ratio of the active population to the population of elderly and retired people. Once the danger of this imbalance became apparent, they revised their policy. It is correct to avoid both too rapid growth as well as an insufficient birthrate. This is a difficult adjustment to make.

Chou En-lai: "During the last few years, our demographic growth here in China has decreased. In fact we have worked in this direction. We always need to improve agricultural development. Before increasing the population, we must first think of giving our people enough to eat. That is why President Mao, referring to our national economy, stressed the fact that agriculture is the base, and industry the dominant factor."

Indeed, I am aware of China's important progress in agricultural production. I no longer hear of acute anxiety about food supplies as I did on my previous visit. This fundamental problem has been solved and Chou En-lai, who spoke so much about it to me a few years ago, is now completely reassured. In 1971, he says, 30 percent of China's arable land experienced disaster such as drought, floods, and insects. Well, in spite of it, production was higher than that of the previous year and even in excess of the country's needs. There will be no more famines like the ones that decimated the population in the past, for now production has improved and during the last twenty years a railroad network has been constructed so that every region can now be reached. If one region has a bad harvest, the people there will not starve to death as they would have formerly, since they will receive the necessary supplies from the other regions.

That is not all, he added. We are accumulating food reserves with which to be able to cope with serious situations, such as war. From our production we can even export rice, soya, and still other products to Vietnam, Ceylon, and Cuba. However, we import corn, as well as high quality seeds.

All this success does not alter the fact that agriculture continues to be regarded as of first priority in the construction of Socialist China. That always has been Mao's doctrine (and the cause of many doctrinal quarrels with the Russians over the last forty or fifty years).

Several times during the evening Chou En-lai spoke sorrowfully of General de Gaulle, and of the fact that death had prevented him from visiting China in 1972, as he had planned. I answered that such a visit would have added still more to his vision of vast historical perspectives and to his life which was already so full of great events.

At this point in the conversation, with a dart of malice and irony, Chou En-lai mentioned that as I belong to the opposition in France, he had wondered for an instant whether he could invite me with the Ambassador. The latter replied that fortunately there remain important points on which different French political movements, majority, and opposition, agree: China policy, Vietnam, and of course in the past, peace in Algeria. That is what makes it possible for neither of us to be in the least embarrassed at being there together.

When the time came for us to leave, Chou En-lai concluded:

"We have a glorious future ahead of us, but the road is still long and we shall encounter obstacles. In ten years you will return, but I will no longer be here to receive you."

He was moved, and I replied: "I very much hope to see you again, in the meantime, in Paris."

He answered, "I have already been in France, Paris in particular, in my youth."

This reminded me of some recollections he had mentioned to me a long time ago: "In Paris, you were acquainted with a *bistro* near the *Place de la Bastille,* where you used to hold clandestine meetings. I expect you to visit it and this time you will be able to go there openly."

He accompanied us out with his colleagues, shook our hands warmly and remained motionless, his arm raised in a friendly gesture, until our cars had passed through the great gate onto the avenue.

Sunday, 26th December

Last evening, Chou En-lai casually mentioned the talks that Bettencourt, Couve de Murville, and Peyrefitte have had in China during the last few months, and that Edgar Faure and Jacques Duhamel had before that. But neither he, nor Li Hsien-nien the night before, nor anyone else to whom I have spoken, has ever referred to Malraux and to his stay here two years ago. Why this silence? Whenever I have spoken of his coming here, I generally have been told: "Yes, he came with a letter from De Gaulle," as though a justification is needed for the fact that he was received. It is strange.

More comments on the meetings of the last few days: nobody obviously has discussed with me the Lin Piao affair. Nevertheless, those to whom I have spoken know very well that I have read countless articles on this subject in the western press. But it belongs to the category of things which do not concern foreigners and which it would not be suitable for the latter to mention.

When Pietro Nenni was in China, however, he questioned Chou En-lai, who is said to have answered: "We quite understand that the entire world is curious at a time when important things are happening here." That is all. Yet it is a great deal. For it confirms, on the one hand, that "important things" are happening (something which, before this statement, had not been officially acknowledged) and, on the other hand, that they are not unrelated to foreign politics (even if the main causes of the crisis were of a different nature).

In China, who talks about it? Where is it discussed? In the Party and at what level? Among the administrative staff? In the Army? Well-informed French people assure me that everyone here knows about the recent tensions and debates and that they are being discussed even at the lower levels of the Party. Apparently one can read between the lines in the newspapers and people understand or guess what is happening much better than it might seem.

The whole affair must be connected, more or less, to another problem—that of the succession—which is another subject no foreigner may mention. Nevertheless, Mao is getting old. When I see Chou En-lai, Li Hsien-nien, Huang Chen, Chang Hsi-jo—who fought side by side in the first struggles, and who, today, are dignitaries of the regime—I always ask myself what they are thinking about the inevitable time when their leader will die. How do they see things? What will happen? Who, from now on is the candidate who is staking his claims or, having been named, is consolidating his position?

Furthermore, the top position will not be the only vacant one. The men I have just named are themselves not young. They will have to be replaced in their present offices. It is true that I also have met representatives of the new generation— for instance, vice ministers who are generally between thirty and fifty years old. But it seems to me that between them and the first-team, the men of the Long March, there is a gap. How will the transfer of power take place between the founders of the Revolution and their successors—who have a different past and, therefore, a different psychology and other points of view? Some further indications may become apparent in the reshuffled government which is expected to result from the famous Congress, the National Assembly, the meeting of which is continually announced and always postponed. The fact that this meeting is constantly delayed confirms that the problem is not simple.

We spend Sunday as tourists. First a visit to the Great Wall, 50 or 60 miles from Peking, and then the tombs of the Ming emperors.

It is a pleasant outing at this season. In 1958 I came in the middle of summer in scorching heat. Today, however, the sky is cloudless blue and the sunshine is gentle.

The Wall of China is a classical, well-known sight. The historical, political, and military usefulness of the Wall, as well as its attraction for visitors, is understandable. The day China is open to tourists, hundreds of thousands of visitors will come here every year. For the time being there are mostly Chinese people from all over the country. We have, however, met an Iraqi delegation on a visit to Peking.

Then we go to see the Ming tombs. The tomb we are about to visit had been quite recently opened when I visited it in 1958. It was not open to the public and could be reached only through a kind of pit. The main entrance had not yet been cleared away; by now it has been arranged and the result is very artificial. Archeologists were then at work. I remember seeing the Emperor's sepulcher, that of his wife, and that of his concubine side by side; one of them was in very good condition, another had been worn away by time and termites. We could see the objects found in the crypt there: jewelry, textiles, censers, lamps which still held oil but must have been extinguished from lack of oxygen, and everyday objects. It was all disorderly but very moving. Today, everything has been solemnly straightened out and it has all at once become cold, almost glacial. The marble thrones, tables, vases, and so forth, have been placed symmetrically. I do not know whether that was their original position. All that is left today are three large red wooden boxes in the place of, or covering the coffins.

Most of the objects I had examined there have been brought to the surface and are exhibited in small nearby museums. There again they are beautifully displayed, but the result is artificial and typical of a museum—in other words, less touching, less human. Above them are paintings and sculptured scenes, and there are explanatory notices on the walls. These point out to visitors the political meaning given to this exhibition. They show, for instance, how many days of work or how much food the Emperor squandered on his own comfort, the decoration of his palaces, or the construction of his tomb; the stress is on what was brutally appropriated from the peasants; class revolts are given a modern significance. All this is probably the result of a somewhat biased interpretation of history; I do not believe that the peasant movements in the sixteenth, seventeenth, or eighteenth centuries had exactly the significance attributed to them in these pictures.

Nevertheless, I understand the necessity of presenting such remains of the past in terms which are comprehensible to everyone. I do not disagree with the didactic and explanatory principle; I simply find it here a little forced and a little rigid. The question is whether it is possible, in such circumstances, to be both truthful and subtle, objective and effective?

This evening we, together with other members of the French colony, have been invited by the Chinese to watch a private showing of a Japanese film which, in their opinion, reveals the nationalist and militarist propaganda which is developing in Japan. The film is good, and does indeed touch on political problems.

It tells the story of a young Japanese who in about 1930 was forced to enter a military school. He was strongly influenced by the instruction and training he received there and became a typical officer of the Imperial Army, ready to accept any sacrifice necessary for victory for his country. The training of the young men in military schools and units is harshly depicted. Inspired by the spirit in which he has been steeped in this way, the young officer fights in the war between his country and the United States. The ending is dramatic. All the main characters—in particular the hero—are finally killed.

A similar film shown in Europe would be considered antimilitarist and would probably provoke protests in armed-forces circles. The question, however, is the effect it could have on Asian and, more specifically, Japanese audiences. It would have been interesting to have seen it in Tokyo rather than in Peking, and to have observed the reactions of the Japanese youth of 1972.

Our hosts' strong wish to show us this film is proof that, in their opinion, it demonstrates the existence of militarist tendencies and motivations in Japan, even if the intention behind the film was in fact different. In their view, its only effect can be to heighten chauvinistic feelings. Indeed, they say that part of the Japanese press saw the same meanings in the film as they did. This is, therefore, something to think about.

French people are in a weak position to judge, as they do not know what the Japanese public's conclusions about the film would be. Yet those present tonight agree that a film of this kind could be shown in France without any difficulty and would provoke no nationalistic reaction or militarist sympathies.

Monday, 27th December

In the morning we visit some shops, where we intend to buy some souvenirs and characteristic objects, antiques if possible. I immediately recognize the small street to which I am taken. It is where I came with the same purpose thirteen years ago. At that time it was a bustling street with countless little shops, a collection of odds and ends, like a flea market, but where one could sometimes discover amusing or curious articles. I am no specialist in Chinese antiques and I am not sure that I chose correctly then; yet I felt that what I had taken back was generally fairly attractive and pleasant.

The street has become very clean, but it is deserted. The shops are closed, some of them empty, and some of them converted into living quarters, workshops, or depots. The fronts of many of them are hidden by large wooden shutters or by low brick walls. Old shops, which were nationalized even then, have now been closed down. All one can find now are three or four shops with signs in English, obviously there for tourists, which sell commonplace goods that one can buy in the Galeries Lafayette or on the Rue de Rivoli. The selection is very uninteresting and, after buying a few small things, we return, feeling disappointed.

We are invited to lunch today by Prince Sihanouk who has set up the exiled Cambodian government in Peking. It is in a large building, which was once the French Embassy, but which was seized by the Chinese at the time of the Revolution and never returned.

Prince Sihanouk, a lively, picturesque, aggressive character received us, with his wife, who is of French origin.

They gave us a Khmer lunch, which is a culinary style I had never tried before, different from Chinese but equally delicious.

Our host quickly embarked on political subjects and described the situation in his country. The coup d'etat which forced him into exile (he was on a trip abroad at the time), he says, has placed a team of military men in power who are completely isolated from the people and incapable of exercising any real authority over the masses, especially in the rural areas. If the regime had not been upheld by the South Vietnamese troops and especially by the American Air Force, it would have collapsed long ago. The Khmer forces, which have rebelled against the present government and General Lon Nol, already occupy 80 percent of the territory. We are not trying, says the Prince, to take Phnom Penh. There is no point in causing the death of many people and in destroying our capital, since it will fall "like a ripe fruit" the day we decide to enter it, probably during the next dry season (that is to say in October–November 1972). Lon Nol holds a certain number of towns, Phnom Penh and the great port of Sihanoukville in particular, but his army is unable to insure safe transit between these towns. The underground fighters, masters of the entire situation, will undoubtedly be victorious—especially since the events of last autumn in Laos and Cambodia.

Sihanouk believes that most of the military operations will take place in these two countries. If the Americans have not already completely evacuated Indochina by then, this will be where they and their hangers-on will meet with defeat. It may take time, but the outcome is certain, the American defeat is assured and the Prince is perfectly confident that he will soon re-enter his capital. I believe he talked a few months ago about retiring from political life once he had participated in the national struggle; now this is out of the question: he seems certain that soon again he will be at the head of his country.

But how will this come about? Two different forces are engaged in the national struggle: the "Sihanoukists" (this is the word used by the Prince) and the Communists. We are criticized, he says, for accepting North Vietnamese support. "Indeed we do. Why not? As far as I know, General Leclerc did not refuse American aid to chase the Germans out of Paris."

Sihanoukists and Communists are allies in this battle. They have agreed that the national life after the liberation will be based on principles of liberty, of respect for the rights of man, and of democracy.

Nevertheless, later in the conversation Sihanouk made no attempt to hide the fact that he has several times had difficulties with "his Communists," some of whom at times tried to control and dominate him. (It is clear that he is not very much attracted by communism, especially the strict type.) But he never let them have their way; he reminded his allies of the pact they had signed. Now they are keeping to the rules of the game. What is certain, at least in my opinion, is that the Communists are there on the battlefield and are organizing themselves for the future, while Sihanouk's influence from Peking can only be distant and indirect. He referred several times to his return to Cambodia; he says, however, that the general feeling is that it is best for him to remain in Peking for the time being.

He is constantly having talks with the Chinese authorities and has complete confidence in Chou En-lai. He believes the Chinese will always be "correct" with him and will never do anything, either to hinder his action before the liberation or to prevent him from reassuming his position as head of the Cambodian state afterward.

We spoke about Nixon's visit to Peking. Sihanouk has for some time now noticed a definite change in the Chinese attitude toward matters concerning the United States. He says the wind has changed, and that there is no longer the same bitter criticism. The meeting will be extremely important. One could fear lest the Chinese and Americans together might make decisions about the problems of the former French Indochinese countries and confront them with a *fait accompli.* We are now, Sihanouk says, completely reassured. Chou En-lai has affirmed that he will not decide on anything without us; matters concerning the Indochinese countries must be negotiated directly with them; Chou En-lai will leave no doubt in Nixon's mind on this matter.

Nor will a rigged solution in Indochina be accepted in exchange for an American renunciation of Taiwan. Sihanouk says that Chou En-lai has assured him that he will take the following stand with the Americans: "Our basic position on Taiwan is unshakable, but we can wait; there is no hurry. On the other hand, the conflict in Vietnam must be rapidly ended and the Americans must leave."

He returned to Cambodian policy after liberation. Somewhat contradicting himself, he let it be understood that while he would be the head of state, in fact the Communists would be governing. But, he added, they will be obliged to consider some national and human realities because the Cambodian peasant is not ready for communism. "We will have some sort of moderate, intermediate socialism. The Communists themselves will reach a similar formula, for it conforms with the national character."

What will relations be among the former Indochinese states? They must not fall under the power of just one of them (he is obviously thinking of the Democratic Republic of Vietnam in Hanoi). The consequent disequilibrium would not be desirable for anyone. "I discussed this with Chou En-lai, who agrees with me. The former Indochinese states should remain quite independent and the Chinese will help to insure this."

He is indeed still somewhat anxious about this question. Today, North Vietnam is the logistic center of the war, for it is there that the distribution of arms takes place (except for the Khmer forces whose supplies come directly from China). Won't the North Vietnamese and perhaps also the Russians later misuse the present system, which can create an imbalance that is to their advantage? "North Vietnam will fulfill her commitments. That is why we had a meeting near Canton a year ago of the leaders of North Vietnam, of the N.L.F., of the Pathet Lao, and of the Khmer resistance. We decided that from now on we would meet regularly, so as eventually to form a sort of association or federation on an equal footing. . . . The next meeting will be in Hanoi in February, about the same time as Nixon's visit to Peking. We will stay there a few days, wait for the results of the Peking discussions, and then publish a joint declaration on our conclusions as free governments. Chou En-lai fully approves of this decision."

Sihanouk went on to say that he believes the United States political situation will become difficult as the result of changes likely to take place in Thailand and Burma. The members of the Thai government today obey American orders; they are, however, watching the course of events and are sure to change sides when the time comes: "They are extremely shrewd and we can trust them; as soon as in their judgment the circumstances are ripe, they will be perfectly capable of turning around and doing what is necessary." And besides, in the north of Thailand there are areas completely beyond government control which have a large population of Laotian origin. They share the ideals of the people of Northern Laos and are in touch with North Vietnam; the entire country is in an upheaval.

I was curious to hear what he would say about Burma, where I planned to be in two weeks. He says that "The Ne Win regime in Burma is on fairly good terms with the Americans. But after some hesitation, it decided to resume relations with Communist China. Ne Win even came to Peking where he was well received. He also is aware of the turning tide and, when the time comes, he will know how to avoid the very serious consequences the American departure could bring to his country. Indeed, also in Burma, particularly in the North, there are uncontrolled regions where there are both underground fighters more or less under China's influence and remnants of Chiang Kai-shek's army, which no one, neither the Chinese, the Thais, the Americans, nor the Burmese have been able to dominate."

Before taking leave I spoke to my host about the shocked reaction in international press circles over the disappearance in Cambodia of eighteen French and foreign journalists and of three members of a French organization similar to the Peace Corps. There has been no news whatsoever of them for nearly two years. He is aware of this situation and tells me that he has informed the Khmer troops of the information he has received. They answered that they could find no trace of those who have disappeared. Some of the people captured might possibly have been in the hands of the North Vietnamese. Sihanouk therefore contacted the Hanoi government, but could obtain no precise information from them. He added very frankly: "When most of our peasants see a white man, they presume him to be an American and, therefore, an enemy. Some of the journalists who have disappeared may well have been victims of violent popular action; this would not be surprising in a period of such agitation, considering the feelings of my countrymen toward the Americans." He promised me that he would start a new search in the country itself. But, as I feared all along, I will not have reassuring news to take back to the French journalists' families, nor to send to Madame Haugen in Hong Kong.

Sihanouk and his wife accompanied us to the porch and once again invited us to pay them a visit in Phnom Penh once they have returned there (for they have no doubt that this will happen soon).

Before dinner there was a concert of Chinese music. I am no

specialist on the subject, nor am I capable of judging the quality of the music played for us tonight. Yet I appreciated the fullness and exaltation of the symphonic works which all are dedicated to the Chinese epic and, in particular, to the national fight against Japan. The hall was packed and the young audience (many of whom wore uniforms) was enraptured by the warmth and emotion which flowed from a concerto dedicated to the Yellow River. The music continually expressed patriotic and revolutionary themes. The announcer on the stage was holding the Little Red Book in his hand.

This is the first time since my arrival in China that I have seen it brandished. The only other copies I have noticed have been in libraries or among the propaganda distributed free to visitors. Apparently the effigies, portraits, and statues of Mao in the streets and public places have noticeably diminished in number as compared with two or three years ago. All this is connected with the changes taking place and the tensions which perhaps still exist within the Party. It would be interesting to find out more about this. . . . The reason given for the further postponement of the solemn meeting of the National Congress is that certain provincial Party Committees have not yet been reconstituted and, therefore, cannot send their delegates. Nobody knows when these sessions will take place. This is an awkward situation, as the Congress is to be the framework for certain changes as well as a relaxation of government structure, all of which should make it possible for new men to reach high positions. It could be the start of the succession, but that seems to be blocked for the time being.

A similar difficulty I heard about concerns the adjustment of relations between the Party and the Army. Six months ago, 60 percent of the Party's regional secretarial jobs were held by military men. At present the situation is gradually being modified and military power is decreasing. The Party is strengthening itself, becoming more independent, and is once again progressively taking over; this will take time, as there is a certain amount of resistance.

What nobody questions is Chou En-lai's growing influence.

He was not one of the principal Party figures a few years ago. Although he was indeed responsible for China's government, he was not one of the leaders within the actual Party. His power has grown continuously, especially since Lin Piao was dismissed; his authority and prestige are now undisputed, particularly in matters of foreign policy.

I take note of a French cable which says: "According to the American State Department, since last year the People's Republic of China has been providing more aid to the Third World than the Soviet Union." The Americans are decidedly flattering the Chinese!

In spite of the services of the A.F.P. and a few French newspapers which arrive with considerable delay, I still feel cut off and far away. News does not pierce the Bamboo Curtain. What is the state of monetary affairs these days?

Nevertheless, I hear that the Russians are expanding their new policy of talks with Japan. Gromyko's coming visit was announced while I was in Tokyo. Now, I hear that Kosygin also will be going to Japan next year. Moreover, a Soviet mission led by the First Vice Minister of Foreign Trade will also be going there to negotiate the exploitation of certain petroleum reserves in Siberia. I had heard about this earlier; the Chinese are grinding their teeth.

Tuesday, 28th December

Every day I go to the post office in the hotel to send off letters and post cards. This morning the woman in charge insists on showing me a series of commemorative stamps that the Chinese Postal Service has issued for the centenary of the Paris *Commune*. I am touched by this homage to old revolutionary and patriotic Paris.

We are going to visit a so-called medical-instruments factory (since that was its original purpose). We are welcomed by the presidents of the Revolutionary Committees from the factory and the street. Since the Cultural Revolution organizations called Revolutionary Committees have been established in all centers of collective life (for instance, town halls, factories, schools, hospitals, and communes). From groups of activists who led the Cultural Revolution and purified the old institutions, they developed into administrative and management establishments. The Revolutionary Committees are organized in a hierarchy; in a way, they fit into one another, so that the Revolutionary Committee of this factory is under the control of the street committee which, in turn, is under the control of the district committee, and so on.

The factory was founded in 1959, a period of general improvisation, especially in industry, which actually tended to handicrafts everywhere. It was a question of producing a few medical instruments as best they could with the small means at their disposal. Apparently this particular factory was created by the women of the district. Sometimes by taking and repairing machinery thrown out by other larger establishments, sometimes by making the most of very simple methods, and often with a great deal of ingenuity and courage they gradually built up this enterprise which now employs 360 people. Most of the women founders had no professional or specialized knowledge; they tell us that they learned technique through practice: "Practice comes first." I had already heard this at Tsing-hua.

The buildings are stark and dilapidated. There are a dozen workshops, or rather workrooms, which were not originally intended for this purpose and are therefore uncomfortable and inconvenient. Women make up 80 percent of the work force. Most are between thirty and fifty years old and have no technical training; 10 percent of them, however, trained in other factories where they learned to use certain machines.

In the first rooms the work is very simple and purely manual; their tools are rudimentary and sometimes include old, obsolete machines. A little further on, however, there are presses and lathes like those we had in France thirty or forty years ago. Still a little further on, and quite unexpectedly, there is some very modern equipment which includes, for example, machines with photo-electric controls similar to those I saw in Japan.

They explained to me that there are planning organizations which determine the needs of industry at regular intervals and pass on orders to the production units capable of accomplishing particular tasks. That is the way in which this factory is periodically assigned a work program. The factory receives the necessary machinery or machine parts in one way or another. Some of the very refined machines we see here have been sent to them in this way during the last few years. At the same time, some of the workers are sent away to learn how to use them. This is how the training and retraining of suitable personnel is accomplished. On the other hand, there has been no modernization or even adaptation of work which can be done by the old methods.

It is clear that under these circumstances a large part of the factory work force continues to work with rudimentary methods and tools, under what are sometimes unhealthy and dangerous conditions. Their output can only be mediocre. An enterprise such as this nevertheless insures a certain volume of production and its contribution is not negligible even if, by force of circumstances, it often is of questionable quality. In an economy where labor is abundant—almost unlimited—it is better to make use of it in this way than to consign it to unemployment. Yet this limits the rise in the general standard of living, especially as salaries in this factory are scarcely differentiated: the unqualified workers, whose productivity is low and who use the most primitive methods, earn approximately as much as the other better trained workers who, using modern equipment, have a much higher output. Nevertheless, even if we in the European industrialized countries sinned in one way, are not the Chinese carrying things to an extreme in the other?

All the workers in this factory live in the immediate neighborhood. The system of local enterprises insures that men and women are employed close to home so that they do not have far to go, can continually remain in their familiar environment, and have as work-friends their neighbors whose children go to school with theirs. However, it also results in a subordination of the worker to the enterprise and in a segregation which has its human, social, and political drawbacks. Work is based on subcontracts, so that the kind of production undertaken by an enterprise changes periodically. Thus this factory, which was originally created to manufacture medical instruments, today produces hardly anything of that kind (with the exception of a few metal medicine cabinets and some sterilizing units). It has been converted to produce entirely different goods which vary from one Plan to another, and sometimes even more frequently. The workers are therefore expected to adapt, to convert, to learn new trades. This is not unhealthy psychologically—on the contrary. Nevertheless, it demands what is sometimes a painful effort for mature men, not to mention the elderly. It may explain my impression that in the first most backward and old-fashioned workrooms the workers were forty or fifty years old or more, whereas, further on, the electronic machines were controlled mainly by young women of twenty or twenty-five.

Marie-Claire asked what was arranged for the workers' children. Apparently they are looked after in a neighboring daynursery or creche. Could we see it? We were immediately invited there and arrived ten minutes later. One thing is clear: this visit was not on the program. We asked for it quite unexpectedly and it can, therefore, not have been "prepared."

The buildings are dilapidated and their façade is sad. But everything is very clean. The children look healthy and all are warmly dressed, no colds, no coughs, no runny noses or spotty faces. Seemingly not in the least intimidated, they smile and welcome us without any constraint. In one room the smaller ones are asleep under warm covers. The kitchen is basic but does not smell.

One thing, however, is astonishing: the discipline. These three- to five-year-old children return to their places without any disorder or delay. They sit with their hands behind their backs; at a signal they take up their picture books or their building games; at another signal they sing a hymn to Mao. They applauded us when we came in, waved "hello" nicely without any shyness, but with a little too much unanimity.

When I return to the hotel, I discover some French newspapers which unfortunately are a few days old. They discuss the monetary situation. The great optimism which was apparent after the Pompidou-Nixon meeting in the Azores and later, after the conference of the Ten in Washington, does not seem to have survived. The Europeans seem embarrassed, faced with a situation which has given rise to delicate problems. It has not been enough to modify the exchange rates; the basic difficulties remain and have even become more specific.

"The recent decisions in Washington will oblige European firms to make a serious effort," is what Monsieur Raymond Barre, Vice-President of the Commission at Brussels, is supposed to have said. He apparently regrets that the United States, which is trying to improve its balance of trade, has not taken steps to moderate its capital exports. That seems obvious to me, but so far nothing serious of this kind has been planned either by the Americans or by the Europeans.

Nevertheless, Europe clearly does not lack foreign exchange as well as other means of putting pressure on the United States, at a time when the latter is making a great many demands. Yet it very much seems as though America has obtained, or is about to obtain, large concessions from the Europeans—in my opinion not always legitimate. The dollar devaluation constantly called for by the French government is not an end in itself: the French press saw it as a glorious victory but—even though, as I believe, the measure was necessary—it carries with it no positive advantage for us. In return we now are faced with very pressing American demands some of which are going to provoke serious reactions; the grain question, for instance. It is certainly right to try to improve the health of world markets for basic agricultural products; I have long believed in the necessity of accumulating stocks in order to stabilize markets and prices. But why limit the operation to grains and make the Europeans bear the brunt of the whole matter? The only explanation possible is that the proposed measures are favorable to American interests and, with elections coming up, to the Republican administration! What we should really be seeking is the cooperation of every country, and particularly all the rich countries in regulating prices on all essential raw materials; and this operation should be coordinated with the reform of the international monetary system. In actual fact, however, something entirely different is being undertaken.

That is not all. The Europeans seem to have accepted the idea that the international community will have to assist in the readjustment of the United States balance of trade to the tune of 9 billion dollars (which, in my opinion, is far too high a figure unless America is to be provided with the means of continuing her foreign investment policy; something I consider totally unjustifiable). It can only result in export problems for other countries and, by way of repercussion, deflationary pressures and risks of unemployment. Apparently, according to an O.E.C.D. report, 9 billion dollars would be a mere trifle; this figure is said to represent less than 1 percent of the gross product of the countries that trade with the United States. It is completely fallacious to reason and calculate in this fashion; indeed, were all the producers of all involved countries to undergo a 1 percent reduction in their markets, the damage would not be excessive. However, the contraction will be much more than that for certain countries and for certain industrial or agricultural products, while for others it will be less. Therefore, serious difficulties can be foreseen in the affected sectors; some companies will be forced to forego investment programs, to reduce their work hours, and to lay off workers. This process could spread to other sectors; something that always seems to occur with depressions. These prospects should be carefully considered by the European governments—and naturally also by the Japanese government.

Frankly, I remain skeptical about the chances of the United States to effect a rapid readjustment of their foreign accounts to the tune of 9 billion dollars. For one thing, capital will continue to flow out of the country. Furthermore, as the presidential elections approach Nixon will wish to keep his country's economy in high gear by relaxing taxes, prices, the budget, credit, and the like. Such a policy is incompatible with any true monetary readjustment. Nonetheless, countries which export abundantly to the United States, such as Germany and Japan, will be seeking replacement outlets and will try to penetrate more widely into third markets such as France (even though their recent revaluations may hinder them somewhat).

In this confused situation I greatly regret that all the Western European countries have not decided upon a collective economic and commercial policy. If the French had not systematically and for many years opposed the establishment of an efficient European organization, the latter might today have been in a position to face the dangers from abroad and to escape contamination from foreign problems. What is the actual situation? Each is going his own way. Italy now even seems to be refusing to apply to agricultural and food imports a revaluation of prices calculated in units of account. This leads France and the other Community countries to impose new discriminatory surcharges at their frontiers. Thus the Common Market is becoming less and less common. It is true that in 1969 the French government was the first to refuse to accept the consequences of the devaluation of the franc in the area of agriculture; that was a precedent for those who were to try to avoid the necessary discipline, first Germany, then Italy.

Moreover, if I am to believe a cable published by the Chinese Agency, Chancellor Brandt has recently promised Nixon to favor America's demands in the present negotiations. It is alarming to see what discord exists at present among the Europeans. One more opportunity lost, and a sizable one at that.

It is natural for the United States to wish to regulate its accounts and balance of payments. Nevertheless, the European countries—since their fate is at stake—should finally learn to work together.

I learn from another cable this morning that the high-energy reactor of the Grenoble Franco-German Institute has reached its maximum power and will be working under favorable conditions from now on. This message, which has reached me the other side of the globe from Grenoble, brings me great pleasure.

I shall be keeping close tabs on economic and financial questions because I now have an appointment with Mr. Chen Chieh, Foreign Trade Vice Minister, and Mr. Zung Zho-chang, Joint Director of the Foreign Trade Administration. Of course, the monetary tornado which has struck the western world does not inconvenience them; their country, exchange, and currency are somewhat isolated from the outside world. Yet this has not made the lengthy interpretations which they give me any the less interesting.

Mr. Chen Chieh prefaced his statement by describing at length the ground covered since the Chinese Revolution twenty-two years ago until the Fourth Plan, which began in 1971. Until then there was almost nothing: no steel production (more than 20 million tons are produced today), no mechanical industry, and no shipyards. Everything, such as grain and cotton, had to be imported. Unemployment, famine, inflation—all problems seemed to be insoluble. Now all of them, if not settled ("we are only at the beginning of our efforts and we still have many weaknesses"), are at least in the process of being so. "On the foreign plane, we have become independent: during the last few years, except for 1969, we have maintained a positive balance of trade. It is a basic principle that exports must always exceed imports; sales pay for purchases. China has neither national nor foreign debt. Her reputation for paying promptly is due to her policy of buying only according to her means. . . . Any surplus enables her to assist underdeveloped countries."

The Vice Minister of Foreign Trade attaches great importance to China's exchanges with the Third World; her aid comes in a variety of forms: open credits without interest or at a very low rate, development of light industry, and in some cases, delivery of complete factories; the Minister also mentioned the construction of the Tanzanian railroad. "Chinese experts and workers who go to Africa are at the service of the countries in which they work. They try to live like the Africans, and once their revolutionary duties and aid missions are accomplished, they return to China."

China's total exports and imports constitute around 1 percent of national production. Chairman Mao Tse-tung's principle is that the country should go forward on its own. I must point out that since China is a huge country with a great variety of resources, she accordingly is able to limit her foreign trade and to live in almost a complete state of self-sufficiency; a similar system, however, is not applicable to smaller nations. Switzerland cannot survive without a great deal of foreign trade because of her structure and in spite, or because of, her high degree of industrialization. She lacks many indispensable products and must seek them elsewhere. Thus she is forced to sell equally in return, so as to maintain the balance of her accounts. France, in an intermediate position, is less dependent on the outside world than Switzerland, yet more so than China. This is one of the reasons that justifies the attempts which have been made to broaden economic areas, the formation of a European Community, for example.

To return to China. She exports primary products (agricultural products, minerals, a little oil) and, to a lesser degree, a few manufactured goods such as textiles, machinery, and chemicals, especially to the underdeveloped countries. She imports machinery, materials for investment and transport, metals, fertilizers and also cotton, sugar and corn.

Her commerce with the socialist countries, which before 1960 amounted to two-thirds of her foreign trade, has been very much decreased since, while her trade in other directions has increased correspondingly. Japan has become her primary partner: Japan's purchases and sales form around 20 percent of China's total trade; to this must be added some of the transactions accounted for under Hong Kong, which in reality are with Japan. West Germany in second place comes far behind (her volume is about three times less than that of Japan), then Canada, Australia, Great Britain, France, and the Eastern European countries. China's trade with France, Germany and Japan is on about the same level and leads to much competition among them, which is likely to last a long time.

It is curious that France, which is on better terms with China, nonetheless trades less with her than does West Germany. In spite of this, Franco-Chinese trade is improving. China now customarily procures trucks, electric and diesel locomotives, and aluminum from us; occasionally she also purchases tractors, chemical and pharmaceutical products, and grains; she is interested in a variety of possibilities in very diverse fields such as aeronautics, telecommunications, electric power stations, and chemical plants. "Given equal prices and quality, priority will be given to France" was the Minister's remark regarding the Chinese purchasing missions in the textile, aeronautic, submarine cable, and petrochemical sectors, which have gone or are expected to go to France.

Nevertheless, in 1970 our trade did not exceed 850 million francs and this order of magnitude will not change in 1971, though there will be an improvement in the French trade balance, despite the strong Japanese and German export competition which I have already mentioned. We purchase a great variety of products from China but, because of their nature, in very small quantities: silk, cat-gut, hog's bristles, skins, furs, various oils, tea, pork, tin, and so forth. What else could we buy? This is a difficult question to answer and often comes up in conversation.

It is well known that the Chinese are rigorous businessmen who discuss at length such matters as price, delivery dates, and quality. The French businessmen are not used to this type of negotiation in which the Japanese, the English, and the Germans seem able to protect themselves more effectively and knowingly.

Although those who were speaking assured me that generally they do not systematically try to balance their trade with each individual country, and that they compensate for debts contracted in one by surpluses obtained elsewhere, they clearly wish to avoid prolonged and heavy deficits with their principal partners. It is not difficult for them to achieve that, because business transactions on their side have always been carried out by government organizations. The case, however, is very different for their western partners, who are often in search of something in return; China, for the time being, pays for part of her purchases from France in currencies obtained as surplus elsewhere, but this can only be temporary; it is acceptable for the time being because the business volume is so small. Nevertheless, she does not wish to prolong it. Finally the equilibrium is fairly easily maintained with the socialist countries, since bilateral agreements, with lists of products included, are drawn up each year.

It seems to me that the necessity to export must be a particular dilemma for states like China which have a planned economy. Their production programs each year are inevitably geared to give priority to the country's internal needs, which they are set on meeting as far as possible on their own. Thus, their plan is calculated mainly for domestic needs; it scarcely takes into account future exports, which are difficult to predict over long periods. When the time comes for such countries to purchase abroad, they have therefore no goods to exchange; this is the situation of the Soviet Union and even more so of China. I asked Mr. Chen Chieh about this question; according to him, in the future China will be signing contracts with her clients and suppliers which are to be fulfilled over several years. Chinese planning will be obliged to take this into account. The Foreign Trade Minister, with the cooperation of the State Planning Commission, will be able to establish import and export programs. Goods for export will thus be included in future production plans. This idea is interesting for it will call for a relatively new and daring approach to planning; Mr. Chen Chieh assures me that it is already in operation on a fairly large scale.

How does China bring her balance of trade into equilibrium? There was talk at one time of her having sold gold in order to be in a position to meet her obligations. Mr. Chen Chieh vehemently denies this; except in 1969, he says, their balance has remained positive, and China has been almost constantly buying gold. (In Tokyo I heard it said that China's assets in foreign exchange and gold amount to 600 million dollars.)

At this point I reminded them with a smile that Lenin had scorned the yellow metal which he felt was only worth using to cover the workers' toilets; and now China is gathering a treasure by accumulating gold: Mr. Chen Chieh protested that I had referred to a treasure; what they are setting aside is to assist poorer countries and also for China to be able to face a war which one day might be forced upon her. Meanwhile, therefore, the *ren min bi*—the currency used by the Chinese in foreign transactions—is very stable, as it is based "on large quantities of the substance." He obviously refers to gold. Besides, China has no choice but to buy gold with her surplus because "it is necessary to protect oneself against the dollar; and whereas Mr. Nixon's policies have repercussions in France, they certainly do not in China!"

"For we are and intend to continue to be independent of everyone." I believe this may be an allusion to the industrial dependence which characterized an epoch in Chinese-Soviet relations and the cessation of which has caused, over a period, serious trouble; China does not wish to repeat this experience.

"That is also why we do not borrow from abroad and do not pay on credit. Even if it sometimes causes delays, we only pay cash."

This naturally brought us to the subject of Japan's foreign trade for "she has lost all independence." I listened once again to the Chinese theory that the abnormal and unbalanced Japanese economy is propelling the country along the road to an imperialist economy which eventually will lead to political and military imperialism. Though I am fully aware of the difficulties the position of Japan is causing in the present state of international commerce, I do not believe Japanese military expansion to be really inevitable and I have not given up hope that events will move toward a less catastrophic future. Japan, however, will have to find new export possibilities other than the United States, and as a result will have to revise her production; Japanese industry can provide certain underdeveloped countries with the equipment or products they need, and it is therefore impossible to judge whether a peaceful solution can be found to the problems created by Japan's industrial and export capacity.

Mr. Hu Shu-tu, the Director of European and American Affairs at the Foreign Ministry, entered the conversation and spoke lengthily and in a very heated manner; he is, as I have remarked already, haunted by the prospect of renewed Japanese imperialism; the exaltation of the "Bushido spirit" in Japan angers him, as do Mr. Sato's visits to and meditations over military graves from which, according to tradition, the warlike spirit can be reborn. Mr. Chen Chieh expounded at length along the same lines. Were Japan to return to her former ways, she would come to a sad end. Militarism is exalted in many Japanese films similar to the one I was shown the day before yesterday. Were Japan, however, to choose a policy of "independence, peace, and neutrality," she would have a great future.

Mr. Hu Shu-tu added that for the time being there are 250,000 men in the Japanese army. Yet half this force of officers and noncommissioned officers would provide leadership sufficient for a far larger army. It is necessary at all costs "to stop Japanese militarism—denounce it and oppose it." At this point in the discussion an idea surfaced which I have noticed in several other conversations: Japan must have the right to "self-defense forces." Apparently this idea has not long been circulating in Peking; yet it implies a purely defensive, limited, and controlled rearmament for Japan which would be free from any foreign dependence or alliance. This will be a difficult matter for China and Japan to agree on when the time comes.

Mr. Chen Chieh says that they find it hard to expand commercial relations with a reactionary government like Mr. Sato's. Once the Japanese government changes, circumstances will change and the two countries will benefit mutually from increasing their trade: with only a short distance between them, Japanese can meet the needs of China while Chinese production can meet the needs of Japan. But before that the political obstacles must be overcome.

The reaction to the changes in the structure of Japanese exports that I suggested was: "That is their business; trade must satisfy mutual needs." In my opinion the matter does not concern Japan alone but it concerns everyone, because the entire world would benefit were the economic equilibrium in Asia to improve, were the dangers which trouble the Chinese to be reduced, and were the possibility of peace to be strengthened.

The New China News Agency in its English publication recently published a very interesting five-page article on Japan's situation. It criticizes the agreement recently signed between Tokyo and Washington concerning the restitution of Okinawa to Japan and the reconversion of its military base. In Tokyo the return of the island was greeted with joy and was considered to be a great achievement. Nevertheless, here it is regarded as a sort of technical adjustment intended solely to shift to Japan part of the military expenses which are for the time-being borne by the United States. Having commented favorably on the position the Japanese Socialist Party has adopted, *New China* attacks Sato's policy as being anti-Chinese, aggressive, and "at the service of American imperialism"; it suggests that the Japanese prime minister is trying to turn Japan into a United States military subsidiary; it adds that his policy can only end in utter disaster because it is generating growing protests from the Japanese people.

One of the most frequently stressed grievances arises from Japan's recent move at the last United Nations General Assembly where, with the United States, she signed the draft resolution to maintain Formosa's representation and, consequently, indirectly hindered Communist China's entry into the United Nations.

Finally *New China* gives a pessimistic description of Japan's situation: her exports are threatened, her production is decreasing, her factories are closing down, her entire economy is in recession; even the monopoly capitalists, particularly those in steel and iron, recognize defeat and losses sustained. This picture is however somewhat exaggerated and does not correspond to the possibilities which Mr. Chen Chieh seems to envisage—although these are for the future, of course.

There is an Iraqi delegation at present in Peking that I have encountered two or three times, of which I know neither its constitution nor its purpose.

I read that yesterday a banquet was arranged in honor of this delegation by Vice Prime Minister Li Hsien-nien. The speech made by the head of the Iraqi delegation naturally centered on the Middle East but he spoke also of the national revolts taking place in a great many countries in the world. He referred to the situation in Pakistan and to that in the Portuguese colonies. The Chinese Vice Prime Minister, after having forcefully stated his support of the Arab position and having condemned "Zionism and the Israeli aggression," went on to use a rather curious formulation which I believe has not been used before: "Their legitimate rights to return home and to their national identity must be restored to the Palestinian people and the Israeli Zionist aggressors must withdraw from the Arab territories they are occupying." Does this mean that the Chinese government envisages a solution which would insure peace for Israel on condition that the territories occupied (since 1967?) be evacuated and that she return to her former frontiers? This would correspond to the Security Council resolution of November 22, 1967 which China at the time condemned, while supporting the most uncompromising Palestinian demands.

Besides, I believe that when recently questioned about this November 22, 1967 resolution, a highly placed Chinese spokesman was very prudent and moderate in his answers. Perhaps China's entry into the United Nations may make her positions on a great many issues more political and better balanced than before.

Nevertheless China's policy in the Middle East, as everywhere else, is determined in direct relation to Soviet policy. She is obsessed by Russia. The systematic wariness, the continuous fear of the United States, which I heard expressed day after day when I was here thirteen years ago, today has been transferred to the Soviet Union. The ritual declarations against American imperialism naturally continue, but that deep fear which used to be so apparent no longer exists. Now the feeling here is that the United States is beating a retreat. On the other hand, the Chinese are obsessed by what they see as long-term threats from Japan (they expect her to be assuming to some extent the United States position in Southeast Asia and in the entire Pacific) and, immediately and before all, from the Soviet Union. Having often been overrun in the past, China lives in perpetual fear of new invasions.

Whenever this matter is brought up in conversation my answer is that the Russian leaders are realistic and level-headed people who know how to evaluate risks and who, in my opinion, would not risk starting a war in the century in which we exist. I cannot see what they might gain from one, but I can well see all they could lose from it—and not only from the point of view of their prestige and influence in the world. Although China's nuclear arms are not as powerful as Russia's, she could cause havoc by a retaliatory blow; moreover, a Sino-Soviet war would simply weaken both countries to the sole benefit of the "third bandit," that is to say the United States, which at some stage would most certainly intervene to reestablish order to her own best advantage. I cannot therefore believe that the Russians could be tempted to initiate a war. Nevertheless, my opinion is always greeted with violent protests. The Chinese are truly convinced that the Russians wish to attack them and they are deeply afraid of this.

Tchou, the young official of the Foreign Affairs Office who, on the day I arrived, was assigned to me as liaison with the various officials, has just said to me with slight embarrassment
that the North Korean Ambassador in Peking wishes to see

me. Looking surprised that I am willing to meet him, he has persisted a little heavily in underlining the fact that the Ambassador is from North Korea. For my part, I am surprised at his surprise because for some time now France and North Korea have been carrying on trade and relations. He must know that there is a French representative unofficially responsible for our interests in Pyongyang, while a so-called commercial North Korean delegation is stationed in Paris; furthermore other French officials more representative than I already have met this Ambassador in Peking. The appointment has, therefore, been arranged for tomorrow.

Peking is becoming a very active center for international contacts, for though few important members of the Chinese government go abroad, they do receive a great many visitors. There are Finnish and Yugoslav delegations here at the moment. Officials from all the countries in the world are constantly coming and going. In the hotel corridors I have come across Africans, Australians, and even some Americans (whom I have not yet been able to place exactly). It is understandable that these visitors are of great importance to the Chinese and that, for the time being, the latter prefer to "receive" rather than to travel themselves. That is why Chou En-lai, despite several very sincere French invitations, has left hanging the project of a journey to Paris, yet, on the other hand, insists that Schumann come to Peking.

Wednesday, 29th December

At nine o'clock in the morning they pick us up for a visit to an oil refinery forty miles away. Mr. Li Yao-wen, the young Vice Minister of Foreign Affairs, is in my car. He was at the airport to meet me the other evening and has since been present at nearly all the talks. He is charming, pleasant, intelligent, good-looking, and—I am told—has a bright future before him.

The asphalt road is good, wide, and has trees planted on each side. Near the road there are beautiful nurseries and the Vice Minister pointed out that millions of trees are planted each year. This has noticeably modified the climate in certain regions: for instance, there formerly were violent sandstorms in Peking; the nearby plantings reduce the wind and stop the sand; in fact there are now hardly two or three sandstorm days a year.

All around us the countryside is frozen. The ground is carefully cultivated. In this season the peasants are busy with somewhat marginal occupations: planting trees, carrying and removing stones, making ropes from rice stalks, and taking things to and from town. On the road, apart from heavy industrial trucks, there are numerous peasant carts pulled by horses, mules, and sometimes oxen.

The conversation with Li Yao-wen continued by fits and starts and we spoke again about the Middle East. I returned to the declaration by Li Hsien-nien that I read yesterday which refers to the Israeli withdrawal from the "occupied Arab territories" as some kind of preliminary. How should one interpret this phrase? Li Yao-wen insists that the Israelis must return what they have taken by force. I asked if this means that once they have evacuated the territories occupied in 1967, they will be able to remain safely in their own land, in short, if the State of Israel is a reality and will be permanently accepted as such (I avoided using the word "recognition"). It seems to me that is basically what the Vice Minister has in mind. But it is somewhat embarrassing for him to admit it and he would prefer not to take a definite stand. He deplores that after the First and Second World Wars the Jews, victims of persecution in Europe and elsewhere, should have collected in Palestine; it would, however, be difficult to go back on a *fait accompli,* he says. "There are delicate situations; an understanding will have to be reached." He once again insists on the evacuation of the occupied territories. Basically, without his actually saying so, he more or less accepts the United Nations resolution which, as he points out, was adopted at a time when China was not a member of the United Nations. There are two things in it, however, to which he objects: one is the fact that the "Israeli aggression" was not explicitly condemned; the other is that the existence of a Palestinian nation was ignored. I pointed out that, in a motion of this kind, where an attempt is being made to reestablish peace, it might not have been appropriate to condemn one of the parties involved, and that it was essential to find some basis for a compromise. He accepted this idea. As for his thesis concerning the reality of Palestinian national sentiment, (which indeed is something we should be aware of), one could point out that a national sentiment exists in Bangladesh, yet the Chinese government does not seem much disposed to acknowledge its legitimacy.

After an hour and a half on the road, we arrive in front of the refinery. We are the first French people allowed to visit this large complex which Chou En-lai mentioned the other evening. Both a series of refining systems (13 operations at present are functioning) and more complex petrochemical installations (for the time being, out of the 22 series of operations planned, only three are in service) have been combined here. The scene is vast and impressive. It has taken only three years to build and put into operation all we can see here.

How was the site chosen? Apparently for strategic reasons and also to avoid occupying agricultural land which would reduce food production. The oil is sent to be refined by rail from oil fields about 600 miles away, and similarly, tank cars ply between the refineries and consumption centers which are also far away. Moreover, to install the plant in this sector created certain difficulties. The nearby river could not supply the amount of water needed; a deep well had to be drilled. Since it was also necessary to recycle water, the appropriate equipment had to be devised; now, after processing, this water is used for irrigation. Nevertheless, this problem is still not completely solved. We were shown some vats filled with treated water, in which fish seem to live normally; a little further, we saw some ducks raised in this same water: they appear in excellent health.

The refinery yields 2,500,000 tons a year of a highly diversified range of products, from aviation and car gasoline to heavy oils, parafin, and asphalt, along with all the intermediate products such as fuel-oil and diesel-oil. The three petrochemical units which already are in operation produce synthetic rubber, acetone, and ethane. The other units still under construction will provide synthetic fibers, plastics, and the like, totaling about a hundred different products.

The workers come from everywhere. Some have not received professional training, while others already have worked in refineries and can contribute to the training of their fellow workers. Two primary, two secondary and one professional school have been built for their families. In short, a new community is developing in what used to be a practically deserted area. It will be interesting in ten years to see whether a truly humane town has been created or whether an artificial experiment necessarily ignores conditions vital for a normal life and has made it impossible.

The president of the Revolutionary Committee sees in these achievements, and in those to come, the expression of the "will for independence, autonomy, and self-confidence." For my part, I see in it another very interesting meaning. When in 1958 I came to China for the first time, there was much talk about the emphasis on metallurgy and on steel production; at that time I was shown plants or what were destined to be metallurgical plants. This time I am being shown a refinery and petrochemical plant. China has, therefore, in thirteen years moved from the beginning of the steel age to the beginning of the petrochemical age, which represents a highly significant developmental advance. It is true that large areas of under-productivity still exist and that labor resources (which indeed are practically unlimited) are sometimes badly utilized. Nevertheless, a considerable step has been taken and everything indicates that the forward march will continue.

China did not produce a single drop of oil thirteen years ago; she was totally dependent on other countries, the Soviet Union in particular. Now not only has oil been discovered on Chinese soil but it also is actively exploited, and enables China to meet her own needs and even to export a little. Actually her national consumption is low: there are very few cars, still very few trucks, and no fuel is used to produce electricity. The Chinese, however, are proud that they can meet their needs "by their own means."

There are 12,000 workers employed in the plants in operation and 10,000 in the construction of other buildings and plants here. When the entire project is completed, a force of 30,000 workers will be employed. Housing has been planned. Some already has been built and provides but the bare minimum; for the time being, priority is given to the production units.

Lunch was at the invitation of the Vice Minister of Foreign Affairs. We were given particularly well-cooked and tender fried duck. The conversation was friendly and relaxed, and for once hardly touched on political subjects.

As arranged, the North Korean Ambassador came to see me at half-past four at the hotel. He gave me a long description of his government's position; they are very pleased with the cautious yet real improvements in their contacts with France. Now there is a North Korean Commercial Delegation in Paris and a French Representative for Commercial Affairs in Pyongyang. But the Ambassador would like these relations to develop at a higher level and to become more openly political. He lays strong stress on the feeling the Korean people have against the division of their country into two artificially separated zones which was imposed on them. His government suggests the creation of reunified and common institutions through general elections in all of Korea; if this is not yet possible, a confederation of the North and the South could be formed; finally, if this second formula is not acceptable either, it suggests the maximum development of exchanges between the two territories: all sorts of communications, trade, economic cooperation, reestablishment of family ties, private and public contacts, and the like.

My answer was that we in France are particularly sensitive to the problems of divided states. One of them is our European partner and another is one of our former colonies. The German and Vietnamese situations naturally concern us more directly than that of Korea. There are, however, important evolutions underway. The nature of our relations with the German Democratic Republic is changing and one can assume that more official and even diplomatic contacts may soon develop (especially once both Germanys have entered the United Nations as is now almost certain). Furthermore, the solution which we hope may soon be found to the Vietnamese tragedy will, I would wish, include certain arrangements to improve the status of relations between France and North Vietnam. In my opinion, France should have more open and trusting relations with the Vietnamese Democratic Republic instead of courting the South Vietnamese regime which is unquestionably unrepresentative and reactionary. I view the situation in Korea in this same sense, though France has few material and moral interests there. For the general consolidation of peace it is good for us to be in closer contact. For I have been told of North Korea's very considerable economic progress, which is worthy of respect.

I had a friendly dinner at the embassy to end the day. Monsieur Étienne Manac'h invited Monsieur et Madame Quilichini who welcomed me in Peking in 1958 at a time when there were no diplomatic relations between France and Communist China. Monsieur Quilichini and his wife had stayed on to take care of various French properties and to manage a few buildings. They were very isolated here for many years and fulfilled a delicate task most skillfully. Above all, to the few French people who passed through here, they offered a haven which facilitated their stay and helped them to brave the concrete problems of everyday life in a country which was so totally "foreign." I had not forgotten their hospitality and this evening I enjoyed being able to have a quiet conversation with them.

Marie-Claire was not at the dinner as she has a very bad case of influenza. I never expected to be writing about Chinese medicine here, though already in Paris, then in Hong Kong, and here in Peking I had heard much about acupuncture. I have been told that a new doctrine has revived the old

Chinese technique and obtained extraordinary results with it. But how can the boundaries between western medicine and the new acupuncture method be marked off? That is quite simple. Once the patient has been examined, the traditional doctor and the acupuncture specialist decide together which technique to use. That is precisely what happened to Marie-Claire yesterday. She went to the hospital, where a doctor examined her as she would have been examined in France: the same questions, same gestures, even in the same sequence. Then he telephoned one of his acupuncture colleagues and the two seemed to have a detailed discussion; together they decided that this case did not require acupuncture. The doctor therefore prescribed medicines comparable to those we would have been given in France to fight the flu and bring down the fever: antibiotics, a pain-killer, and cocaine-based nose drops. He suggested exactly what would have been advised in Paris: rest and hot liquids.

Meanwhile, world affairs develop. Tonight there is just one subject of interest in diplomatic circles, and that is the arrival of an American delegation to make the technical preparations for Nixon's coming visit. Some say that the delegation is already in Peking, others that it will arrive on the third. The delegation will consist of people whose names are becoming known and who are responsible for solving the problems of communication, transmission, information (press, television, and so on) which will operate during the negotiations. Ziegler in particular has been mentioned; he is Nixon's usual spokesman in charge of relations with the press. With him will be representatives of the large American television channels and the technicians in charge of satellite telecommunications. Yet I feel sure that along with these activities to which the Americans attach great importance, there also must be certain more discreet political talks to prepare the ground on the controversial problems, so that when the meeting actually takes place, it can lead to positive results.

There is another point worth mentioning. On several occasions I have noticed that the government of the Chinese People's Republic and the Chinese Communist Party are much interested in the Persian Gulf and in Dhofar. I believe there must be a connection between certain underground fighting units in this region and China, which probably sends them instructors and arms. I also believe that China wishes to hinder Soviet influence in the Middle East and in the Indian Ocean. But there is another aspect of the problem, moreover, which should not be neglected: most of Japan's imported oil comes from the Persian Gulf. Japan is undoubtedly, as I have said before, trying to diversify her suppliers, which is what has led her to take a great interest in Indonesia, and, in spite of some hesitation, in Siberia. Nevertheless, were China to manage to control the Dhofar zone, this would be an obvious threat to the Japanese economy.

We are perhaps not generally well enough informed in France on the race for strategic position developing in the Indian Ocean, not only between the Soviet Union and the western powers (United States and Great Britain), but also and increasingly between the U.S.S.R. and China. From where did such strong feelings arise as those they each displayed over the Indo-Pakistani affair?

On this last point the Chinese press is making much of the unstable situation which appears to be continuing in Bangladesh; it seems that disorder and troubles are persisting there, but it is difficult to interpret them. One possibility is that, considering the cruelty of the Pakistani government's repression at one time, violent reactions are directed against any remains of the Pakistani presence and those one would call former "collaborators." If this is the case, India's presence could be useful in avoiding the aggravation of tensions and new massacres. The situation, however, is sometimes interpreted differently: divergent and hostile political movements seem already to be tearing the young state apart and it could be that the new authorities are directing the present repressions against a pro-Chinese Communist Party, a very active minority, in the hope of eliminating opposition from the extreme left. It is difficult to form an opinion from a distance.

There are complaints in Peking about the attitude of France toward Cambodia and the continuation of official relations between Lon Nol's government and Paris. It even has been hinted that France, or certain French circles in Cambodia, might have participated in Lon Nol's coup against Sihanouk, or that these circles had been at least informed of it. The Chinese suspect some complicity between the French (such as business and military men) and those who overthrew Sihanouk and took over from him.

I can in no way find out how closely these rumors correspond to reality. They appear to me likely, because I had already heard it said in Paris, that a lobby of planters, French colonists, and financial groups, still very influential in Cambodia, probably took a favorable stand toward General Lon Nol, at least after the coup, in the hope that he would better protect their private interests than Sihanouk's regime— suspected of being under Communist influence. That would explain why the French government has long kept a military mission in Cambodia and has continued diplomatic relations with the new team without recognizing Prince Sihanouk's exiled government.

Knowing the development of events in other countries and the positions often taken by business groups, I fear that the widespread interpretations here of French policy could be true. But what will happen when the Americans withdraw (which will finally be inevitable), when in turn Lon Nol's regime disappears, and when an independent government is established in Cambodia? The true interests of France will once more suffer the consequences. One decidedly never learns from past mistakes! It is true that the other day I heard Sihanouk speak very affectionately of France, and I know that many other Cambodians now in Peking do likewise. But these tend to be diplomatic attitudes, even if they do reflect some old sentimental loyalty. Political facts are much more realistic and harsh. We might feel their effects not only to the detriment of certain material interests in Cambodia, but also to the detriment of our cultural influence which is very strong there (there are more French in Cambodia today than there were at the time of the protectorate! Three or four thousand in all, including the *coopérants*). In a more general way, they might affect unfavorably our potential role in this part of the world.

This evening all the officials who have received me in Peking are coming to a dinner of thanks. There will be Vice Prime Minister Li Hsien-nien, Mr. Chang Hsi-jo whom I met in 1958, the Vice Minister of Foreign Affairs, the Vice Minister of Foreign Trade, several members of the Popular National Assembly, some members of Peking's Revolutionary Committee, and others.

Seated next to me is Li Hsien-nien and we survey several of the Southeast Asian countries. He gives me his opinion on Thailand: "It is a weak, divided state; once the Americans withdraw from Indochina, the situation there will change completely." On Burma: "We are on good terms with her and would like to reach an understanding with her in order to help her resist the more or less separatist movements which are under American influence and which control certain regions, especially near the Thai frontier." On India: "She has fallen under Soviet control, for Russia is pursuing imperialist aims in Southeast Asia."

An all-out attack on the U.S.S.R. followed this statement. She is planning aggression in the north and south; but in spite of her atomic bombs, she will not gain the upper hand, I too repeated myself: "When I visited you in 1958, I kept hearing that the United States was preparing to attack Communist China. I well knew that in some American circles such a temptation existed, but at that time, I told my Chinese friends that, in my opinion, in view of the nature of war in our day and the ultimate disapproval of world opinion, which everyone now has to take into account, the United States would not take such a risk. Now everyone is telling me that the Russians are preparing to invade China. Well, I feel the same way and even more so about this than I did thirteen years ago. I do not for an instant believe that the Soviet Union would take the initiative by attacking. Russia is governed by realistic people, capable of measuring all kinds of risks, not only military ones."

"You are an optimist," he answered.

After the toasts, he began talking about Stalin. Certainly, he said, Stalin did not at first trust the Chinese Revolution and allowed himself to be influenced too often by egotistic national views. Nevertheless, he was a vital force in the victorious battle against Nazism; and after China's "liberation" he generously assisted her.

What was the origin of the discord in its first stages between Stalin and the Chinese revolutionaries? According to the most rigorous Marxist principles, the Soviet Revolution relied on the working class, and therefore on the cities. Stalin and many Russians expected an identical blueprint for China. In the meantime it was necessary to take into account the weakness of the proletariat in a scarcely industrialized country, which is why Stalin suggested that the Chinese Communist Party form an alliance with "a certain republican and democratic bourgeoisie," in other words with Chiang Kai-shek. This tactic proved disastrous and in the end the Communists were crushed. Yet Mao Tse-tung had understood that the Chinese Revolution would have to be based on the masses, which in fact meant the peasants, for they make up more than 90 percent of the population. When he established the school that I visited two weeks ago in Canton, he was planning a new kind of Communist revolution which the Soviets found very hard to accept. But, my guests add, once Mao Tse-tung had been proved right, the Stalinist regime actively supported the young People's Republic, which makes the hostile policy of Stalin's successors toward China all the more inexcusable.

Friday, 31st December

This afternoon, making the most of the sunshine, I went for a long stroll through large commercial thoroughfares and small cross streets lined with low houses. Weekly rest days in

137

factories here are organized in rotation, so that teams work continuously day and night; therefore, with neither holidays nor slack hours, the streets are perpetually crowded with people going to or coming from the factory, or shopping on their weekly day off.

I noticed a large variety of goods in the stores, which appear to have ample supplies. The shops, grocery stores, large stores, and specialty shops (such as photographers and watch shops) are very crowded. It is possible that there are a limited number of retailers in proportion to the size of the population; that would explain why there are so many customers everywhere, and sometimes waiting lines.

I wandered into a pharmacy and then into a bookstore where books in foreign languages are sold (these turned out to be solely political works by Lenin, Stalin, Mao Tse-tung, Karl Marx, and others, translated into every possible language).

At the official exchange rate the goods appear to be inexpensive, although less so for manufactured goods than for food products. These prices should really be compared with wages, but this would be difficult for me to do since the information I have on the subject is very vague. However, it seems reasonable to suppose that wages are not high, as the standard of living is still fairly low. I believe that in any case the official exchange-rate favors those with foreign currencies; this does not greatly inconvenience the Chinese inasmuch as there is practically no tourism in China. Certainly not in the way we in Europe understand it. Imported goods, however, are expensive; in one shop I saw Japanese watches priced at 150 yuan, while Swiss watches of the best known makes were 550 yuan. Based on the wage-scale I was told about, who could possibly buy a watch at 550 yuan or even at 150 yuan? The "made in China" watches cost 30 to 50 yuan, which corresponds to the monthly wage of an average worker.

I went into a bank. It was actually a savings bank. Anyone can deposit money here and receive interest, the rate of which is a little higher for long-term deposits (one or two years) than for demand deposits. Apparently these are substantial, especially in the rural districts where the harvest has been good this year, but also to a certain extent in the cities.

I saw nothing worth buying, nothing tempting in the so-called antique shops. They sell mostly standard, somewhat common articles that one might find anywhere in Paris.

The street is bustling with activity; the people all seem hurried. Waves of cyclists pass by endlessly on new or nearly new bicycles (no rusty, grinding old crocks). There are some trucks, but very few cars. The passers-by appear good-humored and are neatly dressed and well covered for this cold season. The children look healthy, well fed, happy, and seem to enjoy themselves.

Recent buildings all around are not beautiful; they look like the low-income housing in our suburbs. Indeed, I do not have the impression that any real priority has been given to the construction of housing. It certainly is possible to see new apartment buildings, but all in all, there appear to be very few of them; the vast majority of the population still lives in ancient, dilapidated buildings.

Architecture does not seem to have been much considered: the important buildings are often imposing because of their size and a certain classical nobility, but they remain true to neo-Stalinist style, nothing of which evokes this country, its culture, or its spirit.

Each year on December 31st the French Ambassador is host to the diplomatic corps at a party which is much sought after. As though I were the keeper of great secrets, several ambassadors of Arab and African countries avidly questioned me on the talks I have been having during the last few days. Information is generally hard to come by here, so diplomats are always on the lookout for additional news. Unfortunately I have nothing to tell them. I am more interested in comparing their impressions with mine.

They all are speculating more or less about Nixon's visit. Their conclusions are fairly similar to my own.

Concerning Formosa, they believe China is convinced that,   139 in the long run, she will carry it off. She may be willing to proceed in stages in order to avoid overtraumatizing United States public opinion, but will in no case surrender her claim. Certainly, if Formosa's independence had been proclaimed twenty years ago, a different situation would have been created and consolidated, which it would be hard to correct. The Americans however preferred to play another game; they declared that Formosa was China. In fact, this was repeated both by Mao Tse-tung and by Chiang Kai-shek in turn, each for his own purpose. Therefore, while it is still possible to discuss or bargain over methods and delays, an eventual unification appears inevitable.

Where Vietnam is concerned the Chinese seem to expect the Americans to withdraw progressively but rapidly. In spite of unexpected turns of events and sometimes contradictions (for example, the recent resumption of violent bombing of North Vietnam), the Chinese are convinced that the departure of the occupying forces is inevitable, they simply wish to accelerate the movement. And they perceive a rough outline of a future solution, after the evacuation, in which South Vietnam would remain separated from the North for a certain time; later, however, a progressive evolution is likely to alter the entire structure of Indochina and, though this structure is hard to imagine precisely, China undoubtedly hopes to exert her influence over it.

The most delicate and most important problem which remained to be discussed was that of Japan's future. The Americans, who maintain a strong military presence in Japan, evidently are not preparing to leave. Nevertheless, the Chinese are aware that Japanese public opinion favors the evacuation of the bases and they are encouraging this attitude. They wish this presence which they consider threatening eventually to disappear. Furthermore, China is not about to forget the Japanese invasion and occupation, and since she fears a recurrence, she is seeking guarantees. This is the subject on which the Sino-American confrontation is later likely to become the most strained. Although she knows that it will take her a long time to reach it, China's objective is to obtain American agreement to relinquish American bases in Japan. As China has the impression that the Americans have decided to remain indefinitely in Japan (or even that Japan, remilitarized and allied with the United States, will take the military initiative), the acute antagonism will persist even if the problems of Vietnam and Taiwan are solved in the interim. Beginning in February, Japan's destiny will be the stake in a contest between Washington and Peking, a contest that will last many years. That is why China is not hurrying to start direct talks with Tokyo.

Everything that happens in Japan will be followed closely day by day. It is not a coincidence that yesterday the Foreign Ministry published a long statement on a few small neighboring islands whose exact legal status is unknown, and to which the Japanese are laying claim. China is angrily asserting rights of historical origin. (I, personally, never attach great value to these so-called historical rights of which the nations avail themselves; if the present were to be regulated on the basis of rights drawn from the past, Germany and France would have equally justifiable and absolutely irreconcilable claims to Alsace and Lorraine. And the historical arguments used in the same way by the Israelis and the Arabs could easily be repulsed by the "rights" that France acquired in Palestine at the time of the Frankish monarchy in Jerusalem; after all, did not the Crusaders maintain their position there for several generations? No, a valid claim to a territory cannot be based on the past.) In the case in point I do not know the exact situation in the contested islands in the China Sea and the wishes of the people who live there. Yesterday's statement, however, shows that Peking will miss no opportunity to voice its views whenever Japan lays claim to territories which depend (or depended) on China. When the time comes the discussions are likely to be tempestuous. This point has yet to be reached. China's immediate anxiety is not over Japan, but over the U.S.S.R. Although the Chinese fear Japanese militarism, they know that this danger lies well in the future. On the other hand, Russia is a constant preoccupation.

It is necessary to go over this again: China has often been

invaded in the past and has remained conditioned by her memories, which would explain her mistrust of the exterior world. This is concentrated on the closest and therefore most dangerous country, which stretches along her frontier for several thousand miles and whose industries and atomic bombs will, for a long time to come, surpass those of China. Added to this are ideological differences which always embitter relations and aggravate hostilities in such cases.

Viewed from here, the international scene on this New Year's Eve does not induce optimism. But for those to whom I have spoken and for me one large unknown remains: what will come of the American President's visit to Peking? It is unthinkable that this February meeting has been arranged by the President of the United States and the Chinese leaders without precautions having been taken to avoid a fiasco. It must be assumed that the protagonists probably already are well enough informed of each other's intentions (and the limits beyond which they cannot go) to be sure that there will be no setback, and that they already have agreed, to some extent, on the actions they are going to initiate.

Saturday, 1st January 1972

New Year's is a holiday here, as it is everywhere in the world. Everything is closed. I am taking this opportunity to write a few letters, bring these notes up-to-date, and read some French newspapers which arrived yesterday.

A different doctor came to see Marie-Claire, who is still in bed. The doctor, a young woman, gave her an intravenous injection. She was doing us a great favor, because here doctors do not generally make house calls. So long as the patient can move, he must go to the doctor's office or to the hospital; if he must stay in bed, he is hospitalized.

I watched the young girl at work. She was obviously skillful and intelligent. But what rudimentary instruments she used! Even at the worst times of the scarcities during the last war, we in France were never so badly equipped. In any case, she managed perfectly well taking the most meticulous antiseptic precautions, and greatly relieving her patient.

I am to visit a large printing establishment today in the west part of Peking on Hsiang Tong Street. This is possible only because Sunday is not a holiday here; the factories close without regard to day of the week.

There are 3,400 people working here and almost all of them live nearby. This is a local enterprise, like the medical instrument factory we saw the other day, with the same advantages and disadvantages. It is difficult to find out what the workers themselves think about it. Inasmuch as they probably are accustomed to this system, it must seem natural to them.

About 10 percent of them have been professionally trained, while the others are learning on the job. "Most of the young people come here after secondary school. They take their apprenticeships with experienced workers" and in the beginning, earn 33 yuan a month. The average general wage is from 40 to 50 yuan; senior workers receive 80 yuan and sometimes even more. There must, however, be very few of these, because the average age is low and I have not seen a single person over fifty.

The company provides lodging for almost all the workers, at a very low rent: 6 yuan a month for a "one-bedroom apartment," water, electricity, and heating included. There is also a canteen where inexpensive meals are served for those who prefer to eat on the premises.

The plant prints works by Marx, Engels, Stalin and Mao. It also publishes periodicals as well as color-magazines. The principal newsmagazine, *Znongguo Hua Bao,* has magnificent, absolutely perfect black and white or four-color photographs. It is a monthly *Paris-Match* with fewer pages and, of course, no advertising, and it includes "biased" material. They print 300,000 copies of the Chinese edition (sold for 1 yuan) and the same magazine with the same color pages is published in 16 different languages and sent by air in large bales to 120 countries.

The Vice-President of the Revolutionary Committee told us about the upheavals the Cultural Revolution caused in the factory. Before the Revolution, one workshop had only printed 1,260,000 copies of President Mao's works and very few of his portraits, because it was partly in the hands of reactionaries. The workers then seized power from the former management. Study of the Marxist classics inspired them, production was increased, and the 1971 work plan was completed forty-three days ahead of schedule.

I see a remarkable acrobatic performance in the evening in a packed hall with 2,700 seats. Once again I notice how young the audience is. In the last scene the actors wave the Little Red Book.

We return to the hotel after the performance, taking the long way around. The streets are dark, there are no lights in the shop windows, and naturally no shops are open. Oh, for the neon lights of Tokyo, Kyoto, and Hong Kong!

All the visible light comes from badly lit houses. The consumption of electricity, without officially being rationed, in effect is limited by the number, wattage, and price of bulbs for sale. Industry has priority on the use of electricity.

Monday, 3rd January

It is snowing; apparently this is quite unusual. The view of the city, which has become white, is not without beauty. But the cold weather, which lasts so long, must be miserable in the unheated or badly heated homes. I am spending most of the morning at the hotel putting my papers and things in order to prepare for our departure, which is supposed to be tomorrow. I intend to try to draw a few tentative conclusions from what I have seen and heard during what has been now nearly a month.

For some time we have been quite rightly told that we are moving away from the epoch in which "world politics could be summed up as a confrontation of two great blocs." During the last ten years an abatement or relaxation has taken effect in the group led by the United States, as well as in the Peoples' Democracies. But this is not the essential point. The essential point is that new power-centers have appeared on the scene, making the political game much more complex. Other powers—who well deserve that name—are now emerging in addition to the United States and Russia: Japan, an industrial force which will increasingly become a political (and perhaps military) force; China, now an unquestionable political reality, which in time will also become an economic power. One would like to add Europe to this list. So far, however, it has remained pulled and divided by different interests which are only minor if seen from afar, as I see them now; in the polycentrism which will appear, Europe also should learn to create its own personality and unity so as to be in a position to take its place on the international ladder.

Then there is the Third World, which is also far from forming any real unity. Nevertheless, about one hundred underdeveloped states are meeting and are beginning to work together. They have not yet acquired enough collective strength and it is impossible to foresee whether they all will later on focus their attention on the same issues. The development and problems of these states have probably been understood best by the U.S.S.R. and China, which would explain their rivalry in the Third World, where they are both exerting themselves to increase their influence. Strategic preoccupations sometimes are added and make the competition even stronger. China's bitterness, for example, at the Soviet Union's tightening of bonds with India and the new State of Bangladesh is understandable in this light. In fact, by paradoxically courting Pakistan for a dozen years or so, China, herself, was preparing the ground for Russia's policy. Yet this race goes on and gathers speed. China is now turning her attention to what is happening in the Persian Gulf, possibly in order to take the Soviet positions from the rear. There she may be able to settle behind the Russians' Suez and Middle Eastern positions. She also is establishing an active presence still further away in East Africa. One cannot help wondering when this game of leap-frog will end. It is not of a nature to encourage a climate of security and peace.

I discuss this as I take a walk with a journalist who has been posted in China for several years now. The snow has given Tien An-men Square and the Chinese roofs of the Forbidden City an unexpected aspect. Everywhere on the large avenues we can see teams of 50 to 100 men busy cleaning the streets with brooms, shovels, and all sorts of makeshift tools. The teams consist of civil servants, soldiers, and schoolchildren, since no workers are taken off production lines.

We are going to visit No. 31 Secondary School. It is an institution which strives to apply the new principles in education described to me at Tsing-hua University. However, the first thing to impress me here has been the traditional discipline they maintain. There is a physical training class in the courtyard where boys and girls separately run in tight rows shouting revolutionary slogans, while students in the classrooms are memorizing texts. Listening to an English class, I heard the same text (moreover revolutionary), repeated at least fifteen times. Apart from Chinese, English is the only language taught in this school. The teacher learned English at Peking University and speaks it well. He has no accent, so I asked him if he had at least for a while lived in an English-speaking country, but apparently he has never been out of China. I was less successful, however, when I attempted to converse with the students, for they did not understand my English at all; I must admit that I have a very bad accent. I noticed in one class—and only in one (why?)—that each student has the Little Red Book on his table.

Several teachers seem to me to teach their classes in the traditional authoritative manner. I was told at Tsing-hua that they wish to develop common research, open dialogue, and student initiative; it does not appear so here; I have not heard one child ask anything or speak unless asked a question by the teacher. Is this just because today there is a visitor?

The schoolchildren range from thirteen to seventeen years old. When they leave school they will spend at least two or three years in factories, communes, or military units. Already they all work one month a year in the workshops attached to the institution. Thus, allowing for one month for harvest and the holidays, they are left with eight months for academic work.

These workshops are in fact subcontracting units which make various parts or small implements ordered by outside factories. They are, as elsewhere, incongruously equipped with old reconditioned machines, homemade installations and various tools, as well as with some relatively modern machines.

The Revolutionary Committee consists of teachers, administrative staff, people from the neighborhood, and four Red Guards—students of the school who are from fifteen to seventeen years old. In conversation with the committee members I asked them if they wished to criticize anything. Three out of the four with much assurance recited the usual statements about the connection between school and factory, theory and practice, and so on. One girl, also a Red Guard, was more daring; remains of former customs, she said, persist; we must continue in our effort to correct matters, for we still have further to go. A teacher said that during the Cultural Revolution there was some exaggeration and that it had taken a great effort to reestablish order, but that things are running smoothly now.

I asked one of the boys what he did during the Cultural Revolution. He was eleven years old then and in primary school. He and his friends, led on by "a climate of anarchy," stopped going to school for a month. President Mao, however, said that everyone must return to school so he went back. He added that, generally speaking, in the primary and secondary schools there never was any great disturbance; in the universities, in contrast, some students did not comply, and the strikes lasted a very long time.

How are children admitted to secondary school? After the Cultural Revolution all primary school leavers were accepted without exception. But this had to be changed. Now the choice is made on the basis of "political consciousness" and previous school results. Does this method of selection (my choice of word) take into account the number of free places? Is there a limit to the number admitted? No—in Peking every child considered qualified to go to secondary school is accepted, even if this results in large classes (in the school I visited, there were often 50 in a class); however, there are not yet enough secondary schools outside the cities.

What about examinations? Wasn't it announced that these would be eliminated? The fact is that about twice a semester there are control tests which may be written, oral, or "open book."

Are diplomas awarded? Not since the Cultural Revolution. Nevertheless, when students leave school, they receive a "document" stating their achievements in "political consciousness" (always the most important factor), knowledge acquired, and physical health.

What are the relations between parents and school? In principle the parents are invited twice a year to talk with the teachers in order to keep in touch with the methods of administration and improvements in the course. About half the parents come to these meetings; the others do not "because they are often detained by their work in the factory. In that case the teachers go to see and talk with the parents at home."

I had the good fortune to be accompanied by our cultural attaché and a few French teachers, who talked freely with their Chinese colleagues, so we were able to exchange points of view on all we saw and heard. We all think that Chinese teaching still is in an experimental stage and that it is too early to make any definite judgments. There is undoubtedly a large gap between the words and the facts; but so far the words have changed much more than the facts.

On the whole, the new theory of education established five years ago maintains the characteristics of the old teaching theory, not only in its methods and practices, but also in the spirit which guides it: it still is based on national pride, patriotism, self-confidence, and even a feeling of superiority toward other nations whose cultures and civilizations are less ancient. Paradoxically, added to this is a wish to abolish whatever is connected with the past and not useful, and to substitute for it a refurbished, socialistic, and utilitarian education. Above all, today's needs have to be met, and all concrete and immediate tasks must be accomplished, which explains the importance given to applied and technological sciences. Of course, political education—the study of "the thoughts of Chairman Mao," foundation of all "useful" labor so long as it is constantly applied in practice—must never be forgotten. "Theory and practice must always go together" and practice, as was lengthily explained to me at Tsing-hua, is the most important factor; to give priority to abstract thought is a *petit bourgeois,* reactionary, hardened prejudice.

The schools are therefore attempting to give the children the feeling and understanding that manual labor is a noble activity and that intellectual life and those who devote themselves to it are not superior. All during their studies schoolchildren and students are in close contact with manual labor. At certain times they go to work on farms. Some schools have gardens where fruit and vegetables are grown for outside consumption. All of them have workshops similar to those I saw and these contribute also to the general economy. Thus the children are continually participating in production.

This is the underlying principle, yet I cannot help wondering if it may not be a little theoretical. Can the desired psychological effect be achieved in the student simply by a one-month interruption of the school year to do manual labor in place of studies? If this manual work were intermixed with everyday life, for example, were one or two days a week throughout the year spent with workers in a workshop, the mixture undoubtedly would be more effective; for I do not see how one out of twelve months of classes and lectures can be sufficient to ensure the desired integration. The sacrifice of one or two days of study could, of course, be detrimental to academic achievement and I can understand that they may hesitate to go that far. But then, isn't the present experiment purely symbolic? No solution has yet been found for this problem, admittedly a hard one, and no one so far has come up with the perfect answer.

Basically the objectives which have been established here

are of great interest. Their purpose is to keep schoolchildren from having the feeling as they leave secondary school that something essential has just changed in their lives as they begin their professional careers. They should pass smoothly from the years of school to the years of adult work. Besides a few years later they may apply to be sent to university for the completion of their education, provided they are chosen, subject to the usual criteria, by their commune or Revolutionary Committee. Chou En-lai himself told me that all of school, students and teachers alike, should spring from the workers, peasants, and soldiers—from the masses—and should never move away from them. The teachers should be recruited from among the masses and should be able to a great extent to understand workers and peasants, whose only education is experience. Nevertheless, at School No. 31 this was discussed with me with a certain caution. When I asked what the teachers' backgrounds were, the answer was that most of them have come either from universities or from teacher training colleges. Moreover, qualified people are sometimes called in to teach certain subjects at which the regular teachers would be less competent than people with practical experience; that is naturally the system adopted in the workshops.

The connection between school and production takes still other forms. Not only are the teaching establishments associated with workshops, factories, and farms, or are even integrated with them, but also the factories and communes themselves often have their own teaching centers. There is constant interaction at all levels between education and practical work. This is the only possible way to avoid returning to the teaching methods which formerly maintained or reproduced aristocratic structures and encouraged the mandarins. It is said here that such methods, which were those of the former Chinese Empire, are now returning in the Soviet society.

What can be fairly said about today's methods, as practiced or experimented with, is that they are providing the Chinese economy in its present stage of industrial and agricultural development with workers who have the wish to produce, who

are more sensitive to technological innovation, and have a great capacity to adapt to their future tasks, if only continually to seek progress and to achieve it "against all odds." This has been the source of workers' or retired workers' inventions (as they are called here); these are usually practical innovations, tricks of the trade, methods with which to increase productivity or to economize on time or supplies. The workers and peasants in China undoubtedly are receiving training which, at present, is superior to that of any in the past and which conforms to the level of the country's industrial development.

But that is not all. As Chou En-lai said himself the other evening, the length of studies has had to be diminished because of the country's urgent need for large numbers of productive workers as soon as possible. Besides, keeping students too long in a university can be harmful; in spite of all the precautions taken, there is always the risk that they may develop a separate mentality there. Studies are therefore being shortened by further reducing time spent on "useless subjects."

I would like to have questioned someone more deeply about their concept of discipline, since this very afternoon I again witnessed what had already impressed me the other day on my visit to the nursery school. It is, however, a difficult subject to broach. Yet it can scarcely be avoided when, each time I walk in the streets (even in the little villages I have been driven through), columns of schoolchildren of all ages pass by on long marches after school hours, with no freedom or gaiety. At the school I noticed the importance given to military physical training, rhythmics, dancing, group-singing, and physical exercise. This all must be to cultivate a strong feeling in each child that he is part of a system and that his intellectual education is less important than his training for life as a productive citizen, and for his future participation in the common cause. What is essential is for him to become a good peasant, worker, administrator, doctor, or civil servant. His health and physical resistance are important for the same reason; he must be fit to stand up to fatigue, danger, illness, and war.

Tuesday, 4 January

The founders, the men of the Long March, Mao Tse-tung's old companions, the first generation of the Revolution have indeed remained in power in spite of some disagreements between them and the disappearance of a few. It is the same generation and the same team which has governed China since the Revolution. The problem which is apparent today and will become so increasingly is that of their succession. I am thinking not only of Mao Tse-tung's personal successor—a matter never mentioned openly—but also of a broader problem which, in fact, arose in the Soviet Union near the end of the Stalinist era. Ever since the People's Republic of China was established, she has always been led by men who could refer back to past lives of fighting and resistance. Today's newcomers, however, have proven themselves during the Korean war or at various levels in the Party or in technical, cultural, or other activities. The process of renewing the political staff has to be undertaken gradually. Indeed we had a similar experience in France; for twenty years Resistance men governed the country whatever their successive political ideals. Today for the first time, at the head of the country's two main political forces we have Pompidou and Marchais, whose authority does not derive from their wartime activities. A similar evolution in the highest circles is inevitable in China. Nevertheless, after having been so generously welcomed everywhere and having heard so many explanations, I still feel very ignorant about this question, which will determine the policies of China during the coming years.

I have asked several times for news of Mr. Chen Yi, the Foreign Minister, whom I knew in the past and who is another veteran of the Long March. He is one of those sometimes called the "French Group," since when he was young he was a revolutionary militant in Paris like Chou En-lai, Chang Hsi-jo, and others. During the Cultural Revolution, Chen Yi's position was challenged and he came near to being unseated; Chou En-lai intervened and actually physically defended him during some violent incidents.

Unfortunately I cannot see him, as he has just undergone an operation and is very ill. He still has the title of Minister, but has not been able to carry out his duties for several months. That is why I have so frequently seen the young Vice Minister of Foreign Affairs.

Leaving for Shanghai, we found (at the airport) all the Chinese officials who had greeted us when we arrived and had then accompanied us on our visits, so I was able to thank them all warmly for their friendly hospitality. The French people from the embassy and, in particular, Monsieur and Madame Manac'h also were present.

We noticed the surprising presence of an American plane on the tarmac; it belongs to the mission sent here to organize the visit of the President of the United States. An American plane at Peking airport is an unexpected sight indeed and many an American or French magazine would pay much for the right to publish a photograph of the scene.

The journey, which took from 3:30 to 6:00 P.M., was uneventful. The view was snowy. We could see huge rivers winding their way across the country. It is easy to imagine them greatly overflowing their banks at certain seasons and devastating the surrounding area.

We arrived at Shanghai after dark and were given, as usual, a very friendly welcome by officials with whom I shall be spending some time in the course of the next few days: Mr. Tsi Wei-li, in charge of the Foreign Trade Bureau; Mr. Wei Min, in charge of Planning and Statistics; the Director of Urbanization and others. We have been given a luxurious room in the Hongshan Hotel.

The weather is mild here and much pleasanter than in Peking. This evening we were able to wander around town where there is quite some pedestrian and cycle traffic, though few shops are still open and it is dark.

I noticed in passing that *Le Grand Monde,* which I visited in 1958, is being razed. Is this due to the Cultural Revolution? It used to be an establishment where one could find entertainment and fun—-scarcely compatible with the present Puritan fashion—and it is probably too striking a reminder of Shanghai's colonial days.

Shanghai is not in the least like Peking. The capital is quite flat, composed, at least in the center, of houses of the same height in the middle of a limitless plain. This is best exemplified by the Forbidden City with its countless buildings of which almost all have only a single story. The most recent buildings, constructed since the beginning of the century under foreign influence, are the only ones of any height; these are often official buildings (such as ministries, and the post office) or apartment blocks, often on the outskirts, similar to our low-income housing. Shanghai, on the other hand, is a western-style city, with taller old and recent buildings everywhere. Space here is limited. Shanghai is a port situated between two rivers, which has always made available land hard to come by. This city resembles those of the West even more because the Europeans built a great deal here during the epoch of the regime of concessions, when they occupied and governed Shanghai. It is especially easy to pick out the many buildings by the quayside which must have been luxurious during *la belle époque:* banks, maritime companies, beautiful villas with balconies and colonnades and decorative details, all in the midst of gardens (where there are no more flowers to be found, for priorities have changed since then).

Wednesday, 5th January

On our way to visit the Shanghai metallurgy plant No. 1, we drive through endless industrial suburbs followed by abundantly irrigated marshland. Under a milder sky than Peking's, the peasants work in large numbers in the fields.

At the steel plant there are 15,000 workers, of whom 10 percent are women. Production reaches one and a half million tons of steel, of which a large proportion consists of special alloys. Chou En-lai had mentioned this factory to me, and said it has achieved great technical progress, but that its program is far from complete, and that it does not yet produce certain special alloys. The visit—very interesting, as usual—

nevertheless reveals nothing unexpected. The installations here are similar to those in many other countries.

I remember that the metallurgical industry here was just starting up in 1958; the construction in the villages of small high furnaces was being recommended. Today production exceeds 20 million tons (about the volume of French production). Though this still is very small in relation to the needs of a country of 700 to 800 million people, considerable progress has nevertheless been made.

The president of the Revolutionary Committee, who is about forty, congenial, open, and intelligent, explained that he himself was formerly a worker; he had had no professional training when he came to the plant. He appears to be managing it today with a zestful appreciation for work and efficiency.

In the afternoon we went to see Pong Pu city, a workers' quarter in the suburbs. In 3,300 of the 3,700 households there, both husband and wife work, and the population is 17,000. The average salary is 70 yuan. A family in which two members work makes 140 to 150 yuan. The monthly rent for a one-bedroom apartment with kitchen and bathroom is 6 yuan. To this, 4 yuan a month is added for water, electricity, and gas. There is no heating and they have no transportation expenses because almost everyone works close by.

We were given this information by the permanent representative of the Revolutionary Committee for the quarter, a jovial woman between forty and fifty years old. She came to live here with her husband in 1959 and by 1960 was "chosen by the masses" of the district to carry out this duty. She used to live in another district where she was responsible for the same work. She is in charge, among other things, of cultural activities: she teaches Marxism and the principles of Chairman Mao, takes care of the kindergarten and tries to make the women work who still remain at home.

Before the Cultural Revolution there were only 2,700 women working here, she told us. Thanks to the activity undertaken then, 600 more are working now, either in neighboring factories or in local workshops some of which were set up to fill orders from larger factories (thus we visited workshops where shoes, toys, and the like are being made), some of them to provide useful services for the district's inhabitants (such as mending and making clothes and sewing).

We visited a school for children between three and seven years old, who were animated and not in the least shy. There they sing and dance. There are also primary and secondary schools nearby.

A large antiaircraft shelter is being dug in the middle of the town, as indeed similar ones are being prepared in all the other districts of the city.

We saw two or three apartments; rooms, furniture and households utensils are minimal. Nevertheless, I suppose they are better than average or they would not have been chosen for us to visit. They probably represent what ideally would be offered to the entire population. But the rate of construction here, as in Peking, appears to be very much below the population's needs. Someone with us mentioned that since 1950 about a half million homes have been built in Shanghai; even supposing that during the last few years this rate has improved, it still represents a poor total effort in comparison to what is generally necessary in a city of 6 million inhabitants (10 million including the suburbs). Taking into account both the fact that some very dilapidated houses have become uninhabitable and that the city's population has increased, housing conditions today are, on the whole, no better than they were at the time of the Revolution.

I asked, in passing, a few questions about population development. Thirteen years ago the Shanghai authorities were complaining about a surplus of labor which could not be utilized. There was talk then of making workers and their families leave for other regions and I believe that is what actually happened on quite a large scale. But a systematic effort also was made to industrialize the area and more particularly the outer regions. This would explain why the steel industry was established relatively so far away from the regions which produce coal for coke and iron ore. Apparently the coal comes from quite a distance and part of the iron comes from Hainan which has high-grade ore deposits that can be brought here by water.

There is generally no more underemployment. The problem is no longer finding work for Shanghai's inhabitants, but improving their productivity in all the factories. The motto is: increase production without increasing the labor force. Industrialization must not, at least in its present stage, increase urbanization, for instance by drawing people from the countryside. For the time being, the population in the cities, and particularly in Shanghai, must not increase (apart from natural demographic growth—and an attempt is being made to limit this by a birth-control policy). This is probably one of the reasons why more effort is not put into the construction of new housing.

We stopped on our way back at Shanghai's "department store." As always, it was very crowded. There seemed to be a plentiful supply of very diversified goods of good quality.

This evening I am to see the film, *The Red Detachment of Women*. It has beautiful scenes and colors and magnificently produced ballets. Like all the productions I have seen, it has an essentially political theme, which exalts communist and revolutionary feelings. Basically, entertainment as we understand it in Europe has not existed here since the Cultural Revolution; films, plays, and concerts are used to arouse popular enthusiasm and to contribute to shaping the minds and the political point of view of the public.

During a conversation in the intermission I was told that Nixon has made very unyielding declarations on the subject of Taiwan; he is supposed to have said that there is no question of his modifying the American position and that he will never leave Taiwan undefended. But I cannot believe for an instant that he has any illusions about Taiwan's future. These declarations are perhaps based on the fact that the Chinese, without giving up their inflexible position with respect to Taiwan, are not calling for an immediate solution (Chou En-lai told me so the other evening) and Nixon evidently knows this. Thus he is able to cater to some of his supporters by maintaining his stand in principle, well knowing meanwhile that later he will have to be more flexible. By that time the elections will be over.

Nonetheless, Chinese-American diplomacy is very complicated to decipher. Would it not be preferable to allow a fresh breeze to enter in, to engage in more direct, frank diplomacy so that little by little the mistrust and bitterness of the past could be erased? China has just gone through a long period of segregation during which she was kept out of normal international life—an added humiliation which does not make it easy for her now to reestablish healthier relations with other countries, her neighbors in particular. Indeed, her accumulated economic and political satisfactions of the last year have raised her confidence and optimism, which could mitigate certain psychological consequences of the past. This is, therefore, a favorable moment for conversations finally to be opened; and no time has been lost. Timing probably is one of the considerations which led the President of the United States to propose the spectacular move he will make in the second half of February. But is this to be a short-term maneuver for him to extricate himself from an awkward position, or does he intend it to be a far-reaching political enterprise? If it is the latter, then I cannot see what good declarations like the one yesterday can do. For world politics will neither cease on February 21 in Peking nor in November, the time of the American elections, and there will still be many more years to come after 1972.

Thursday, 6th January

I have been asking ever since my arrival in Shanghai to see what we in France call a city-planning office, which is the organization where they work at planning future urban developments. It should be of particular interest in an area of this kind which is in the process of full change. The European concessions which formerly were administered like separate cities now are integrated into a single unit; the port was then the essential sector, and now industry is dominant. The city has spread widely in all directions. A large number of problems must have resulted and I would like to know what they are doing to solve them, how forecasts are being made, and how the future is being planned. But I am unable to make myself clear to those around me; for instance, if I say that I would like to have an idea of what the city will be like in 1980 according to their plans, they burst out laughing, as though my curiosity were both unexpected and amusing. Finally they have promised that a competent person will come to see me with whom I shall be able to "chat." When I insist that I would like to see plans and diagrams, they seem even more surprised. This is something which intrigues me and for which I can find no explanation.

This morning we are going to visit Hospital No. 6. There is no point in dwelling at length on the fact that buildings are in a dilapidated state, that there are large numbers of patients in each room, and that there is an extreme lack of comfort in the narrow operating rooms where two patients are operated on at one time amidst a shocking and disagreeable confusion of teams and equipment. All this is only too understandable; it is inherited from the past and nobody can blame it on the present administration.

It seems to me that it would on the contrary be more useful to note what has been accomplished and the experiments which are going on now. Mr. Liu Cheng, the vice-president of the Revolutionary Committee of the hospital described these to me. The latter plays an important part in local politics and quickly revealed himself to be an interesting and charming man of remarkable intelligence. I questioned him about the hospital's organization, the doctors' influence, and the role of political power; his answers were sometimes somewhat vague, which was certainly intentional.

There are two military officers among the members of the 159 hospital's Revolutionary Committee and one of these is the hospital's president. Several times I have noticed similar situations. The Army intervened a little bit everywhere at the time of the Cultural Revolution to insure at least a minimum of coherence and organization and thus assumed an importance and influence which later provoked adverse reactions. It is significant that in a hospital like this a military person should have been summoned to preside over the Revolutionary Committee and in some way still directs the hospital. The vice-president, however, was chosen from within the hospital; he was its deputy director before the Cultural Revolution. Later, here as elsewhere, the Communist Party was reconstructed and reorganized, which ought to bring it to dominance again. In some places this appears to have caused no difficulties with the Army; in others, to the contrary, there have been conflicts. Naturally nobody told me what the situation is in Hospital No. 6.

We were introduced to patients who were victims of work accidents and had to have a limb or part of one amputated, and have had fingers, part of a hand, even an entire hand grafted on.

People have said over and over that in the past under a capitalist regime workers and peasants could not obtain treatment; their sicknesses and suffering were neglected. Now the poor people, thanks to Chairman Mao and the Communist Party, can be treated, operated on, and cured. A young woman, showing us her fingers which were covered with scars, said: "I would no longer have this hand were it not for Chairman Mao; he gave it to me." If I were to tell these patients that in a capitalist state like France there exists Social Security which enables the working class to be treated under practically the same conditions as everyone else, they would not believe me; if I were to add that in our country women and children are protected, as well as the head of the family, they would believe me still less. In China even though the workers have 100 percent coverage, that of their wives and children is only 50 percent and for workers in typical communes the guarantee is neither absolute nor total. It is obvious that the validity of these comparisons is limited; one must never forget that China was living in the Middle Ages one generation ago and she can scarcely be expected to lift herself to the level of the most developed countries in a single attempt.

Then we were taken into rooms where operations were in progress. Acupuncture is used to anesthetize the patients. I was surprised and (why not say so?) uneasy that I, the three French people, and four Chinese with me should be permitted to enter the operating theater during an operation and that the surgeons and their assistants should let themselves be disturbed, where there are sometimes two operations taking place simultaneously—using matching teams— . . . not to mention the patients! The latter, who are perfectly awake and conscious, chat with the nurses and through the interpreter, at times, also did so with us.

I can, of course, give no competent opinion on what I saw there. But I certainly feel great respect for the spirit of research which urges on these Chinese doctors and for the results they have obtained (which are very positive according to certain of their French colleagues with whom I discussed the matter).

We asked the directors if foreign doctors have already visited their hospital and in particular the part where the experiments are taking place. The answer was positive. Can foreign doctors come here for a training course to learn and study those new techniques and use them? The answer was more hesitant. We do know that requests of this kind have been made and that up until now they have not been welcomed. Indeed, since 1966 the cultural gap between China and the outside world has widened; Chinese students working in France at that time were called back and none have returned since then; in the other direction, French researchers, students, and teachers have found it very difficult to go to China to work (apart from a few very rare exceptions).

Hospital No. 6 does not merely treat patients in-hospital. It receives 3,000 out-patients a day, who come for consultations or treatment. It administers a "hospital at home" service whereby patients or convalescents in town receive treatment and visits at home from either a doctor or nurse, according to their needs. This saves on the available hospital beds, which are scarce, and permits those who participate to benefit from family surroundings. In fact this system is being developed in a certain number of French towns.

The hospital also trains teams for work in the country and in factories. These are generally composed of individuals who are called "barefoot doctors"; they are young, even very young, people of both sexes, often former workers or peasants who are given an accelerated professional preparation before being sent to give advice and treatment particularly in the communes and villages. Their number has considerably increased during the last few years. Their main duty is to improve sanitation in rural areas. They are expected to watch for contagious diseases and to report them without delay to the proper authorities, to give preventive vaccinations, to set up individual health records for the population, to give the required advice in cases of mild illness, to establish contact as quickly as possible between patients and qualified doctors when necessary, and to send patients to hospitals. The "barefoot doctors" are also responsible for hygiene and cleanliness. (Mao has always insisted a great deal on the need for maximum respect for the rules of cleanliness.) Finally, they deal with family planning and the birth-control policy. The regime is attempting to encourage late marriages (while also trying to reduce premarital sexual relations to a minimum); it recommends two children to a family (apparently without much success, and in many cases, authorizes and facilitates abortions). This systematic activity is largely in the hands of the "barefoot doctors," in spite of the fact that many of them are so young.

It must also be noted that, in order to keep in contact with the working population, the "barefoot doctors" continue, within the limits of their time, to work at their former occupations, especially, for instance, during the harvest season or at times of intense and urgent work.

This afternoon, we have indeed been invited to visit a commune some miles from Shanghai. The Malou commune has

25,000 inhabitants, 17,000 of whom are regularly employed; the "nonworkers," children and old people, are, however, called upon for extra help at times of great seasonal activity.

I am certain the village was "scrubbed" for our visit, yet some unmistakable details (the condition of its buildings, new construction, and the appearance of the equipment and furniture there) reveal its prosperity.

In the past 6,000 small farmers worked singly on this land. Now they have formed a collective farm to which some social services have been added (such as a hospital, a school, and road works), some agricultural professional activities (such as workshops to make agricultural tools and to treat products and by-products), all of which provide work for the quiet season and increase individual incomes. To use a paradoxical comparison, this is somewhat similar to what one might see in an Israeli kibbutz.

There is always intense activity here, even in winter. Groups work on seasonal tasks in the fields. At the moment they are pulling up weeds and parasitic plants by hand. Elsewhere some are planting trees, some are building houses, some are collecting the mud at the bottom of the river to use as fertilizer, and others are repairing tools and the like. The countryside is strewn with water reservoirs. The region is abundantly irrigated by rivers and canals; junks and barges, often pulled by boatmen, provide water transport. There are apparently a few motor boats but I saw only boats with sails or maneuvered by sculls or oars.

The commune produces mainly cotton and grain. The grain yield per *mou* (about one-sixth of an acre) has almost quadrupled in twenty years; the cotton yield has increased almost tenfold.

Each year the state establishes a plan of production which the commune discusses. At that time they must take into account the needs of both the state and the locality. The commune is owned collectively. It pays for fertilizers, costs of upkeep, agricultural taxes, administrative expenses, and the wages of the peasants.

How are wages calculated? On the principle that "to each according to his labor," that is to say, based on three criteria: attitude to work, technical level, intensity of work; based on these criteria each person has "points" credited to him and this is how wages are calculated.

The members of the commune work an average of three hundred days a year. Certain activities such as livestock-rearing entail more days of work and consequently pay more. The working day lasts about six hours in winter, whereas in summer, particularly at the rice-transplanting season, it sometimes exceeds ten hours. When it rains everyone rests, but there is no pay.

The accounts are settled once a year, at which time wages are distributed. Meanwhile the peasants can ask for advances, but they rarely need them because they can feed themselves from what they produce on their personal plots of land and usually they buy durable goods only after they have received their annual pay.

I have the impression that there is a general excess of labor in relation to the work to be done, although it is hard to form a precise and definite judgment on this question in winter; the seasonal underemployment certainly does not continue into spring and summer. But China's present demographic policy must also be considered, for it tries to avoid crowding of the population in the cities and attempts to keep any possible excess in rural areas. At China's present stage of development, this policy seems reasonable to me.

Malou's 1970 total gross receipts were distributed in the following manner: wages, 50 percent; exterior purchases, 35.4 percent; running and upkeep, 0.5 percent; state tax 4.2 percent; and equipment and collective investments, 9.7 percent.

The members of the commune themselves decide on investments to be made on roads, schools, tractors, and so forth, and, in a more general way, on the distribution of returns. There is a tendency sometimes at these debates for requests to be made for immediate distribution as wages of all disposable sums. But long-term advantages must never be forgotten, as I was told by the vice-president of the Revolutionary Committee, a dynamic, intelligent man of forty-two. He prefers to invest rather than to distribute wages. He is obviously competent, yet he assured us that he had received no more than a primary education. He has always lived here, knew the former divided land plots, and went through the progressive regrouping of the land and the commune's entire history. On the other hand, the president came to Malou after the Cultural Revolution and does not hide the fact that he was sent to supervise the "management of the commune." President and vice-president seem to form a good team. I was struck by their competence, as I was yesterday by that of the woman who received us at the workers' village, and by that of the other organizers we have met on most of our visits.

I asked—it is becoming a habit with me—what the relations are between the Communist Party and the Revolutionary Committee of the commune. The answer was decisive: the Party commands, the Revolutionary Committee deals with the practical execution. Here again, the Party has the upper hand.

The Cultural Revolution started with the uprising of some leaders against the "bureaucracy," that is to say the Party as it was then constituted with its officeholders and profiteers. Indeed the revolutionaries affirmed that they were protesting against certain leaders whom they accused of monopolizing the responsible positions and advantages and of losing touch with the masses. The revolt which Mao initiated against this organization of public life stimulated particularly the young people and the Army. The floodgates were opened, allowing all initiatives, all protests, to develop freely. This is what made it possible for the Party to be overrun. Then Revolutionary Committees were installed everywhere to represent the winning forces. Nevertheless, once this had been completed it was necessary to start up the machine again and to reestablish some discipline. It had been good to revolt against the former bureaucracy's rigidity and to appeal to the spontaneity of the people. At the same time it became necessary to establish a new organization. 165

That often was put into the hands of military men, since they were accustomed to commanding and obeying. They controlled many hospitals, factories, government offices, communes, and even branches of the Party. Six months ago 60 percent of the Party's regional secretarial posts were still occupied by them. But now a definite system which would conform to that of all Communist countries must be instituted. The Party must hold the authority, not the Revolutionary Committees, the Army, or the groups formed in the heat of the Revolution. This new change is not being accomplished without incident. I have heard dissatisfied people speak of a Thermidorian reaction! It is understandable that the Revolutionary Committees have not always been willing to be subjected to the new controls after their relative autonomy. The Army also has resisted at times (which, in fact, is one of the causes of the great Lin Piao affair). At present therefore, this is a period of reconstruction for the Party, which will be concluded at the time of the meeting of the Fourth National Assembly, which has been delayed several times and now is announced for the spring.[3] It is indeed expected to consecrate the reestablishment of order in the entire Chinese political system.

At the same time that one considers this evolution, the growing influence of Chou En-lai, which everyone repeatedly confirmed, must be taken into account. A few years ago he was not a leading figure in the Party. Although he was at the head of the Chinese government, he was not a leader within the Party itself. His power has done nothing but increase, especially since Lin Piao was dismissed. There is no doubt that his policy prevails in matters of foreign affairs.

Returning to Shanghai, along the road we passed groups of youths carrying knapsacks or blankets on their backs. I am told that they are sent on long marches to train for war. Sometimes they go very far and are away for several weeks.

I have observed all over town that old notices, inscriptions, and slogans are being replaced by new ones; portraits of Mao are being freshly painted, and numerous houses, shops, or stores fixed up. This great cleanup is part of the preparation for Nixon's visit.

Whenever possible, I inquire about prices and make comparisons. At the official exchange rate merchandise, and particularly food products, are relatively inexpensive here also. The State must sell food at a loss, or in any case at no profit, while on the other hand it must take a healthy share on industrial, manufactured products. If prices, like wages, seem low to me when converted at the official rate, it means, for one thing, that the yuan is undervalued which invalidates all comparisons.

I had a conversation with Mr. Tsi Wei-li who is responsible for the foreign trade of Shanghai. He is mainly in charge of the exports and imports which pass through the port (which I am to visit tomorrow). Shanghai, formerly an important port which surpassed even Hong Kong, for the last twenty years has had great difficulties which seem on the way to a solution. Mr. Tsi Wei-li tells me that the flags of about sixty countries are seen here more or less regularly: Japan, which ranks first, England, some Pacific countries, and also some African and European countries. Unfortunately there are few French ships among them; last year was an exception when the corn we sold to China was delivered.

Out of Shanghai China exports many food products, pork, for example. Mr. Tsi Wei-li complained that France at one time refused to import Chinese pork for sanitary reasons; the necessary precautions had not been taken, the meat did not have the required guarantees, and the like. The matter was cleared up eventually and the quality of the Chinese shipments finally was recognized.

Many Japanese ships come to Shanghai. What are relations like between the Japanese sailors and the workers in the port, and with the population in general? Once again I heard the same old story: the two nations are made to understand each other; the past is the responsibility solely of a certain Japanese military clique; there is no hostility and they can have sincere, friendly relations; the two countries must come closer to each 167 other and work together; unfortunately, however, this is not possible with the reactionary group which governs Japan today.

I asked Mr. Tsi Wei-li about all the excavations in the roads I have seen here and in Peking. He tells me they are underground shelters which will make it possible for the city to face up to a war of aggression: "We are threatened and must take precautions. We will definitely not attack anyone. But if we are attacked, we shall furiously defend ourselves till the end and the assailant will be overcome." When I asked if this attack they feared was expected from the north rather than from the east or south, he answered cautiously, but spoke for a rather long time about American imperialism and the possibility of aggression coming from that direction.

Friday, 7th January

In the morning we visited an important machine-tool factory. First we drove through an endless industrial suburb. Factories were everywhere, with their products stored all along the road, perhaps for lack of warehousing. Once we had left this zone and had gone through a bustling village, we abruptly found ourselves in front of the largest machine-tool factory in all China. It is clearly a remarkable production unit, with the kind of modern equipment one would find, for instance, in the Western European countries. Those machines which are American, English, or Swiss have probably been there for a considerable time, but the majority appear to have been made here in China. Qualified labor is obviously employed here and the work they do requires attention and genuine professional skill. The workers, of which there are about 6,000, often have the diploma of the second level of secondary education, and the others have been trained in the firm itself. They even have within the factory a technical university where the workers' professional, political, and general training is completed. The course, which is very specialized in certain aspects, lasts two years. Some evening courses are less difficult, and lead to lower levels of qualification (over 600 workers are registered for these). Thanks to this system of promotion, the factory has trained 350 technicians on the premises since 1953.

The entire plant is managed by the Revolutionary Committee, of which the President is a military officer. The Vice-President, a former worker, received us. When I once again asked how matters are decided between the Party and the committee, I received the usual precise answer: the Party controls everything. I also asked if there is a workers' union in the factory. During the Cultural Revolution, I was told, the unions were strongly criticized because they laid special stress on production and the welfare of the workers, rather than on proletarian politics; they made no attempt to improve the political consciousness of the workers. Now there is a popular organization under the Party's direction, a "Congress of Workers' Representatives," which forms a living bond between the working class and the Party.

In the afternoon we visited some quays at the port. By coincidence they are the very same ones I was taken to visit in 1958. Once again I found myself looking at the large ships (which weigh up to 15,000 tons) continuously loading and unloading. One is Cypriot, another Dutch, another Japanese, and several are merely Chinese. While I passed in front of the Japanese ship, I again asked about the relations between the port workers and the Japanese sailors. "They are excellent. The Japanese sailors can wander around town. No hostility exists between our two nations now, as it did after the war when nobody here could forget the suffering they had endured at the time of the occupation. Chairman Mao has since explained to us that our resentment should be turned not against the Japanese people, but against their former bad advisors. We have all understood, and today we feel nothing but friendship toward the Japanese sailors, who, indeed, also get on well with the Chinese people. Our two countries must come to an understanding, but for that there will have to be a change in government in Japan. The present government does not inspire confidence and does not really want a reconciliation."

169

On the evening I arrived in Shanghai I was struck by the fact that the city was so dark and the streets so relatively calm. In the daytime it is quite the contrary: traffic is intense and there are unbelievable crowds and great activity everywhere, no matter what the hour. The stores are bursting with goods and customers. At the end of the afternoon, however, everything stops, the lights are turned out, and everyone goes home. Even shows, cinemas, and ballets begin and end early. At that moment the crowd is very dense and appears good-humored. Indeed, the passers-by, astonished and intrigued by the presence of Europeans, stare at us in surprise.

At the end of the day, I am finally to meet the representatives of the services for Planning and Development of Shanghai—directed by Mr. Wei Min, who is in charge of Planning and Statistics. The discussion will unfortunately be difficult because several of Mr. Wei Min's colleagues speak only Shanghai dialect which my interpreter does not understand. We must therefore pass through two translators, which complicates the conversation. But above all, I believe that none of those to whom I speak quite understand what it is I want to find out from them. They give me endless accounts of the city of Shanghai's achievements "since the liberation" and especially since the Cultural Revolution, but practically no precise information on the general plan for Shanghai and on perspectives for the future. I can just make out a few very general points from their reports.

The Revolutionary Committee of Shanghai, under the control and direction of the Communist Party, directs the administration of the city. Mr. Tchang Chun-chia, former secretary to the Party for Shanghai, now is the president. At the same time, he is a member of the Party's Central Committee Political Bureau. The vice-president, who also first campaigned within the Party, is a member of the Political Bureau as well. Since both of them often are detained in Peking because of their high offices, the city is managed in their absence by thirteen other vice-presidents who parcel out the work more or less in the same way as do the deputy-mayors in large French cities. The committee consists of 150 members, 20 of whom are revolutionary staff elected by people in industry, agriculture, and financial services; 20 others have been "chosen by the army after discussions with the masses"; and the remaining members, who represent the workers, peasants, and intellectuals, are chosen "as a result of widespread consultations and discussions." In all, half the members are workers or former workers. The committee was formed during the Cultural Revolution; a third of its members are under thirty years old and half are between thirty and forty-five years old; the average age is therefore young. Nobody knows when and how the committee will be reelected.

The cities and regions have relatively few sources of revenue of their own: some taxes (on bicycles, cinemas, theaters, and electricity) and part of public utility profits (such as on water distribution, electricity, gas and transport) which must be and always are in the black. These services are state-owned, yet return part of the profits to the local community.

Otherwise, cities depend on state grants to finance investments decided upon by the plan's central administration, or to pay for running expenses. Thus the cities and regions appear to have very limited autonomy. Most of their work is planned by the state, which provides them with the necessary financial support.

On housing policy, those to whom I spoke gave me chiefly separate examples of what has been done in this quarter or that suburb. They more or less avoided answering my questions on the total extent of their achievements in this field. The total result seems to me somewhat meager. From a series of calculations which we made together, it is possible to deduce that during the last twenty years about 450,000 homes have been built in Shanghai, while the population has increased by one million inhabitants, which is 250,000 households. Taking deterioration into account the net total is scarcely satisfactory. Those to whom I was speaking admitted that even fewer homes were built in 1970 and 1971 than dur-

ing the preceding years. Effort has been concentrated on building in districts outside the city, like the one I visited the other
day.

On the plan for education the development has been far
more spectacular, but mostly in primary schools. There were
300,000 schoolchildren in 1949; today, there are ten times as
many. The number of students in secondary schools is said to
have risen from 850,000 to only 900,000; I believe there must
be a mistake, because the last figure seems low to me.

In twenty-two years, I was told, "Shanghai has become a
real industrial center, whereas before it was simply a consumer
city." Total production in 1970 was twelve times that of 1949.

In spite of that avalanche of figures, I still do not have the
information I have been seeking on the problems of urban
planning which must, nevertheless, be fascinating in a city like
this, where a profound transformation of the basic structure is
being undertaken. First, does a local plan exist? If so, by whom is
it spelled out and to what extent is it subject to controls from
higher authorities? How is such a plan put into action? Those
to whom I spoke could give me no indication. Neither the
mayor of Grenoble nor his deputy in charge of town planning
would find the equivalent of their town-planning agency here.
I would like to have seen the offices where these problems are
handled, but my hosts do not seem to have caught on to this
idea very well. Coming to see me at the hotel to give me the
preceding information, they brought no documents, with the
exception of a few photograph albums (with pictures of com-
pounds similar to our low-income housing, of improved streets,
and so forth). Nonetheless, I find it hard to believe that there
exists no overall policy in a city where such large problems
must constantly be arising.

Thirteen years ago I heard there were too many people for
the number of jobs in Shanghai. Plans were drawn up which
not only prevented immigrants from settling here, but also
sent some inhabitants to other regions. Apparently, factories
were displaced inland and the appropriate workers had to
move each time this occurred. Any increase in local population

is the result of natural growth and of a fairly high birthrate, in spite of the dissuasion regarding this matter. The authorities needed and brought about a certain amount of emigration toward other regions and that perhaps is why there is little concern about the construction of much new housing.

Although I have been unable to obtain much information on local planning, it is clear that state planning exists. A central office sends the orders and the credits for them to be carried out locally. However, in its regional and local formulation, I can see nothing of what we would call city or regional participation. Local institutions such as the Revolutionary Committee have the responsibility of applying the plan rather than formulating choices and decisions.

Besides, on what basis are credits distributed by the staff of the state planning office? Which regions, what kind of production, or which social groups will benefit? The people to whom I was speaking never mentioned this to me and, curiously, did not even seem to envisage the necessity of criteria or priorities. They must certainly exist, because it would be impossible to satisfy all demands indiscriminately. I was told several times, "We send in requests, state our purposes, and if the State approves of them, it gives us the necessary credits." But on what are the decisions of the authorities based? After three days I have been able to grasp only a few vague allusions according to which the president and vice-president of Shanghai's Revolutionary Committee, very powerful individuals, and members of the permanent Central Committee, effectively protect the interests of Shanghai in Peking. We are familiar with this in our own countries, too, but we don't call that planning!

A large dinner has been organized in our honor by Mr. Wang Chao-yong, a vice-president of the city's Revolutionary Committee. There I meet the local authorities and those who are responsible for the most important public services. We received an affectionate, somewhat southern welcome: I enquired about the geographic origins of the guests; very few of them were born in Shanghai; they came from everywhere, most of them in order to carry out their duties. Are there any workers or former workers among them? Yes, several, but no peasants.

Incidentally, I tried to return to city-planning problems with my neighbor at dinner, Wang Chao-yong, but obtained no more details than I had this afternoon. I shall have to remain curious.

The conversation, once again, turned to international problems and the coming visit of Nixon, who is expected to pass through Shanghai. The people near me at the table are cautious. Perhaps they do not yet know much of what will be expected of them during the visit. At least they assure me that, no matter what, Nixon will be "politely" received, though they cannot force the population to cheer him. They condemn the United States for its imperialist, aggressive policy, and especially for the savage bombing of Vietnam which, Wang Chao-yong indignantly tells me, is inconsistent with its alleged intention to achieve peace. He doubts the sincerity of these intentions. We did not bring up the subject of China's disagreements with the Soviet Union. There is a slight difference, which I have definitely perceived, between what I heard in Peking and what is being said here. Might there be a fundamental divergence between Communists in Shanghai and Communists in Peking? Shanghai has always belonged to the uncompromising wing of the Party.

Saturday, 8th January

In the morning we visited two factories: jade, ivory, and semi-precious stones are carved in one of them and the other is a carpet factory. The work is handicraft, but it is done by groups, which reduces costs and facilitates the training of apprentices. There are about 600 workers in the jades and 700 in carpets. At least three-quarters of their production is exported, mostly via Hong Kong. Schools or public institutions buy a small part (objects that are particularly artistic and very valuable). What happens to the rest? There must be very few customers at home for this kind of inevitably expensive luxury merchandise.

We lunch in a large restaurant in the center of town. The people around us look very surprised; astonished to see four Europeans among them, calmly having lunch around a table. Later, we found it very difficult to wander around town. Our car attracted attention and as soon as we left it, a huge crowd of people, especially children, surrounded us. They were not in the least disagreeable, but it was awkward and embarrassing. We finally gave up, after passing a procession of about twenty-five identical cars, which probably belong to the American delegation, here to arrange for Nixon's trip next month.

Taking the train to Hangchow in the late afternoon, we found both the station and the train very crowded.

Many women on the platform were crying. It is not a mobilization, as it might appear; the system by which labor is organized results in family separations which, although temporary, often last a long time. The train was packed with young people on their way to the country, distant factories, or frontier areas.

We arrived in Hangchow three hours later. The station there is very large and modern. The town of 700,000 inhabitants is developing rapidly, which probably explains why it has such a large, new station.

We were put up in a magnificent building, a sort of "V.I.P. residence," where the service is cheerful, pleasant, and competent.

Sunday, 9th January

Hangchow is made up of two completely distinct parts. The one, the tourist district with many hotels, good roads, bright lights, and very beautiful gardens—everything expensively maintained—is intended for visitors and convalescents who come here in the high season; then there is the industrial area—less beautiful, but more active.

We travel about 15 miles out of town this morning to see a commune famous for the tea it grows. Considered a model commune, it is visited by many important people and tourists. The woman in charge of the Revolutionary Committee receives us in a beautiful old house, formerly a rich landowner's home which belongs now to the workers of the commune. We listen first to an intensely felt description of all that has been achieved here; since the liberation, and especially since the Cultural Revolution, everything has been constantly improving; we are given a list of the many improvements in production and productivity. I am constantly at odds with our hostess since she pointedly avoids answering some of my questions. She is so concerned with showing how things have continued to progress that she reaches the point of denying variations which are the unavoidable consequences of meteorological conditions—bad weather and so forth. Since this commune is devoted almost entirely to the growing of tea, I would have been interested to understand what methods are used here to allow for a regular guarantee of investments and workers' pay when money resources are not absolutely stable or continuously growing. I find it impossible to have this point clarified.

As we walk along, the representative of the Revolutionary Committee explains to me that the commune's members "chose" not to depend on other communes or regions for supplies for themselves, and therefore "decided" to grow wheat and rice, although up until then they had produced only tea. Their attempt has encountered some serious difficulties, such as bad weather and other problems. Yet, they have persevered and are determined to be self-sufficient against all odds. Mao's constantly repeated theory that each man, enterprise, commune, and province must be self-sufficient and must never count on others is being applied here. In this particular case I have the impression that the absence of division of labor is having uneconomical consequences. All in all, this visit gave me the opportunity to see a beautiful region and a very well maintained commune, but taught me nothing from the standpoint of economics. All I can say is that the village is well kept, very clean, and even charming. Its houses are in good condition and new ones are under construction here and there. It has modern equipment for processing the tea, and everything breathes of prosperity.

We went out on the lakes in the afternoon, passing pretty islands and very beautiful gardens. There were many strollers on the islands. On the banks of the lakes are large hotels. One of the best is reserved for Chinese who come here on vacation from abroad. This is a sign of the new relationships which have developed during the last few years between Communist China and the Chinese scattered all over the world, especially those in Southeast Asia. Formerly, expatriate Chinese were considered deserters, cowards; the breach widened after Peking became communist and the groups of Chinese abroad remained loyal to Chiang Kai-shek. All this has changed considerably. Along with the regime's continually growing prestige, emigrants' hearts have felt twinges of patriotism toward their country. The government has successfully regained some of its scattered subjects—now considered a vanguard—a factor in the country's spreading international influence. There is even a network of banks which returns to China the savings of workers abroad, including the possibility of freely taking them out again despite exchange controls; this is a very substantial source of foreign exchange.

At the end of the day we were invited to a dinner given by the president of the Hangchow Revolutionary Committee. He is also a vice-president of the regional committee, which consists mostly of people from the town (workers, students, intellectuals, and so forth) even though out of the 31 million inhabitants of the province, the town has only 700,000. Our host is himself also a military man.

A simple evening meal during which, however, there was one small unpleasantness: I wished to visit, tomorrow, an important metallurgy plant or a plastics factory, one or the other, which have been built recently; instead, I am to visit a silk factory. It is impossible for me to go to the others since "the road is being repaired"; the workers can reach them, but we cannot! I made no attempt to hide my doubts and annoyance, but, so as to avoid the incident becoming serious, I agreed to go to the traditional silk and brocade factories tomorrow morning.

Monday, 10th January

The silk factory is half-mechanized and employs 1,700 workers, half of whom are women. Almost their entire production, which is very beautiful, is exported, and there is not enough to meet the demand.

We went afterward to visit some strange and fascinating Buddhist temples. It is obvious that they have been restored at great cost and at a recent date. Nobody worships there now, but it is a very popular tourist site.

The visits to temples, lakes, and beautiful gardens have given my stay in Hangchow a tourist-like quality. But I could have seen some very interesting things, since I would have liked to find out more about the rapid and important industrial expansion which is taking place here. In fact, I have learned nothing about the enterprises which have been established here (metallurgy, chemical products, plastics, and the processing of the region's agricultural products).

We drove around town after lunch. There are large straight avenues, several of which have been built quite recently; old houses and even entire districts often must be destroyed to allow new streets to be built.

There are a great many bicycles here as everywhere else, and I have noticed once again that most of them are new or nearly new. This is an unmistakable sign that living conditions are improving. A large part of savings certainly is spent buying a comfortable means of transport which helps to save time and gives a sense of independence—like a car in our country. This evolution must have been encouraged by the Plan, which must have provided for massive bicycle production.

We are becoming accustomed to the scene on the streets here: the dense crowds dressed in monotonous and somewhat depressing clothes which, however, never look dirty or neglected; the construction of underground shelters; and the numerous trucks.

At 3:30 P.M. we returned by train. During the trip we again passed very well-kept countryside with the countless carefully cultivated small rectangles, where no space is wasted. This region is particularly fortunate because there is water everywhere.

In Shanghai, there is interesting news. The Japanese-American negotiations seem to have come up against serious obstacles on every subject: economic, commercial, military, and political. Whatever conclusions the present conference between Sato and Nixon may reach, the problem of United States–Japanese relations will be constantly present for the next few years, and these relations in all likelihood will take a new form. Anyone who can say what their relations will be in several years is very shrewd. While Europe is experiencing a calm period, "moments of truth" will be multiplying in Asia.

The growing importance of naval forces—Soviet and American—in the Indian Ocean also gives rise to a number of questions. Points of contact and confrontation are imperceptibly increasing between the world's two greatest military powers—precisely there where Japan and China will progressively be confirming their presence which, although less dangerous immediately, will, nevertheless, be important in the future. It is strange how American-Soviet relations sometimes give the impression of parallel development or even of some cooperation while, at other times, they appear as preparations for confrontations which could become increasingly harsh.

There is still no way of knowing what is happening in Bangladesh or what kind of difficulties they are continuing to face there. It is not surprising that, after the events of the last few months, calm and order have not been restored from one day to the next. Nevertheless, one would like to discover the nature and intensity of the tensions which persist there.

Tuesday, 11th January

This morning, the death of the Foreign Minister, Marshal Chen Yi, was announced; he had been suffering from cancer for some time. While I was in Peking I wanted to see him, but his illness prevented him from receiving visitors. In the past I had long talks with this striking character, one of the elders of the great team of founders. Chen Yi remembered our language and understood it well; at times he could even talk about day-to-day matters in French, which made our contacts better and more direct. He was a good-natured, solid man, sure of his cause and a true fighter, but he was also happy because he had in full faith participated in a glorious adventure and in its risks, and because this had brought him great satisfactions. I am sorry I was unable to see him again and to hear his evaluation of this new China, to the building of which he gave so much.

China has just completed a new nuclear test. I heard the news by chance, since none of the Chinese to whom I have been speaking mentioned it. Yet this must be an important event for them, judging by the prominence it has been given in *The People's Daily News,* in large type, where it appears on the front page. Although I can appreciate the size of the type, I cannot unfortunately read the article. In it, I am told, the Chinese government repeats—as usual in similar circumstances—that it will never be the first to use the atomic bomb in an international conflict. It demands that a world conference be called to discuss the complete prohibition and total destruction of nuclear weapons. Whenever this statement of principle was repeated to me in Peking, I asked what controls are thought of here to enforce such decisions once they have been reached. Although I totally agree with the principle, it seems to me that such decisions would necessarily have to include a very strict control system. The great powers, however, do not seem to agree. I have never gotten a clear answer.

I also have discovered the translation of another article which appeared in *The People's Daily News* a few days ago and which is evidently intended to influence public opinion into accepting a more relaxed policy toward the United States. Of course, it has been said for some time now that no real conflict exists between the Chinese and American people, and that all of the disagreement has come from the actions of the imperialist government in Washington. But now this idea is developed with an unexpected complacence and abundance of details in the article, which describes the presence in New York of Communist China's delegation to the United Nations General Assembly. The title in heavy type is significant: "Deep Friendship Between the Chinese and American People." It is followed by the statement: "The successive reactionary United States governments . . . have not succeeded in destroying the feelings of friendship which exist between the two peoples." That is why the Chinese delegation received a "warm welcome from the great American people," who expressed their feelings "everywhere, particularly in the streets." The article cited countless examples of individuals who spontaneously and enthusiastically greeted the Chinese. A lawyer and his wife stopped them in the street to say: "Welcome"; a taxi driver stopped his car and greeted them warmly; a woman from Miami sent the delegation a photograph of her nine-year-old son; also, two young people on bicycles called out, "Long live Chairman Mao!" when they met the Chinese on Park Avenue. Officials at the United Nations say that there never have been as many visitors as since the arrival of the representatives of the People's Republic; the meeting halls are packed whenever they make speeches, which are widely covered by newspapers and television; besides, the head of the delegation has received thousands of letters from Americans who have heard his speeches on television. (I wonder what the average reader here thinks of this, since it is very rare for him to hear political declarations of foreign statesmen on the radio or on television, if he has one.) The article also gives the names of people who sent expressions of admiration and encouragement and who asked for autographed photographs; a seventy-year-old lady wrote that she had lived in China when she was young and she is "very moved and very happy" to have heard about the changes and progress there. A secondary-school child expressed his admiration "for the great Chinese leaders"; others hailed "Chairman Mao's enlightened leadership" and asked for the Little Red Book; a letter is quoted, according to which "the days of the two superpowers are numbered; . . . nothing will ever again succeed in obstructing the understanding between our two peoples." The Chinese delegation arranged for the showing of *The Red Detachment of Women* in New York; not only was the film a success, but also in the audience some cried and sang "The Internationale." In a secondary school the students organized a conference on China, and so forth.

The publication of such a long, detailed article in the official newspaper of the People's Republic is an attempt to create the proper climate for President Nixon's welcome to China next month. Not that enthusiastic displays should be expected (this is the very thing I have been told during these days in Shanghai). However, there is a wish to spread the belief that there is no reason for hostility between China and the United States, but only a past of misunderstanding at the government level. From the moment the President of the United States, representing American popular feeling, asked to be received in Peking, it was essential for his presence to be understood and approved of since it could promote the peace which both nations desire. Naturally that does not mean that Peking is prepared to make important concessions in controversial matters; but it ought to justify the latest decisions of its leaders in the eyes of a population which for many years has heard of the United States as an imperialist, aggressive nation. Indeed, the facts about America have been depicted, on the whole, extremely unfavorably, even though the Vietnam antiwar demonstrations or the black freedom movement were being mentioned here. An attempt is being made now to make acceptable a new political psychology in response to the surprise and even resistance which must have been expressed by the public, the Party, and in ruling circles. Apparently the conflict between the present governing team and the Lin Piao group arose partly from a deep disagreement on matters of foreign policy. Lin Piao was said to oppose the visit of Nixon to Peking; even if the conflict extended to other issues as well, the turn taken by Chinese diplomacy must have provoked many discussions.

My new friends in Shanghai gave me a particularly delicious farewell dinner because they had found out, though I do not know how, that today is my birthday. It was a pleasant, relaxed meal; we exchanged toasts and my hosts drank a great deal. I neither tried to follow their example nor did I take up their challenge to do so.

There were the customary speeches; I warmly thanked those who have taken so much trouble to acquaint me with their city where, perhaps better than in Peking, I have been able to appreciate the improvements which have taken place in industry and employment.

Then we left for the airport. We said a somewhat ceremonious farewell and soon the Air France plane took off.

All at once I am back in French surroundings. The stewardess gives me a complete collection of French newspapers dating back to the tenth. I have not enjoyed myself so much for a long time.

But I read first a short cable from the Hsinhua Agency which warmly approves of the conclusions of an article signed by Michel Debré which was published in the *Revue de la Défense Nationale* and in *La Nation*. I cannot get an exact picture of Debré's ideas and point of view from this summary alone; he is essentially dealing with military and, above all, atomic power. The Chinese dispatch reprints only a few very general sentences on the French wish for independence, security, and defense. Communist China's official press agency has commented favorably on these truisms.

So now we have reached the end of a far too short sojourn amidst the immensity of the problems of China. I must sort out my impressions which have sometimes seemed confused, sometimes even contradictory, during the last few weeks. Although I have just seen some strange and occasionally, from a human point of view, even painful aspects of the regime at work, I cannot help feeling true admiration for this nation 183 which has embarked on an experience of such magnitude. It is an intelligent, refined, clever nation, proud of its ancient culture, yet also humiliated and hurt by past trials. This gigantic country, which has practically no frontiers, has throughout its history continually suffered invasion and infiltration from the north and south, not to mention landings on its coasts. It is not surprising that the Chinese are constantly tormented by the thought of new invasions and attacks.

It is not difficult to imagine what the Chinese must have experienced as they watched the European colonialists taking advantage of their strength and settling on Chinese territory. I can well see what the Chinese reaction must have been to the insolent spectacle of "legations" established in the very center of their capital, right next to the Forbidden City, with heavy, imposing buildings, parks closed in by walls, offices, barracks, and the like. Although all this has disappeared and no more material traces remain, no one has forgotten.

I saw no reminders of the former French concession in Shanghai. Nevertheless I could easily recognize vestiges of the former English settlements in a section near the port with its large colonnaded buildings where banks, transport agents, insurance, and navigation companies proclaimed their opulence and power, and, further on, rich villas surrounded by gardens which were once full of flowers and where the foreign masters led a sheltered life. How could a starving, suspicious population have been expected to accept all that without anger?

At the moment we are flying over the Yunnan, where France at one time dreamt of extending her Indochinese colonization and where she had indeed sent a vanguard of banks, trade agencies, missionaries, and a railway line (the very one used today by the Chinese to supply Vietnam with arms, food, and the like).

Yes, China was carved into pieces, each country taking a share. It is not surprising that China still suffers from a complex and often—sometimes excessively—blames the old colonization for her present underdevelopment.

184   Because the Chinese feel that they were ill-treated, scorned,

and exploited in the past, they still today tend to believe that they are surrounded by hostility from foreign countries, not only countries of the capitalist world, but also—and this feeling exasperates them—from the Soviet Union, which is historically the first communist country and claims the leadership of the world socialist movement. Now that China has regained her independence and is building her future, everything has conspired to make her seek a course which is neither that of capitalist imperialism nor that of Soviet socialism. Many Third World countries, especially those once colonized, tend to imitate their former masters in their countries. The popular democracies, however, generally have adopted the Soviet model. China, on the other hand, intends to keep her authenticity and personality, to remain herself, to overcome competition, and to prove herself in the future both in a quantitative and a qualitative manner by developing her own unique formula.

This mentality sometimes leads to questionable choices, mistakes which could weigh heavily on her production plans. But it is imparting a specific character to the Chinese experience, an originality which throughout the world is not failing to attract nations who are also seeking their directions. In spite of errors, weaknesses, and imperfections, China without doubt has made substantial progress in the economic sphere; but whether or not she has found a new form of socialism is as yet unproven. It will take time, experimentation, successive approximations, and even reversals before this question can be answered. Then it will be necessary to question the cost of the experience. Would another course have been faster and more efficient, would it have yielded more? It would be presumptuous even to attempt to answer this now.

Very far to my left and to the south is Vietnam, which I cannot leave unmentioned as the plane follows a route parallel to her frontier. How many times during the last few years have I pondered again and again on the drama which has lasted for two generations with only the briefest hopeful interruption in 1954! How I respect these men's tenacity, the dignity, courage, and determination with which they have faced so much suffering in their fight for independence, and of which few such examples can be found in history!

In 1954 I thought that the Vietnamese would finally know peace and quiet, would be able to build up their nation and, having freed themselves from colonial domination without submitting themselves to their great allies, would choose the institutions and social order best suited to their national genius. Today I still believe that this was possible and, contrary to what is often stated, that China would not have obstructed it by trying to impose her dictatorship on Vietnam. We could have been of assistance. Our policy should have been to maintain contact at first with both the governments of South Vietnam and the Democratic North by offering totally disinterested economic aid to each one. In the South we would have had to promote and facilitate an experiment both national and democratic, which a large majority of Vietnamese desired. Some thoroughgoing reforms (such as agrarian reforms, suppression of usury, development of cooperatives, elimination of exploitation by business groups left over from the large landed proprietors of the colonial period, and an effective rural democracy) could have commanded widespread popular support. Thus South Vietnam and the D.R.V. would have furnished two kinds of progressive evolutions and their rivalry would have been a favorable factor. Later, the people would have chosen or enforced a compromise and that could have been done in peace.

It is not a wild dream. But of course such a policy could never have been adopted by the Ngo Dinh Diem team, a symbol of the reactionary forces which were most hostile to change and to democratic progress. The Americans did not see that they were making a grave mistake in vehemently supporting him. Gradually many of the liberal administrative staff and also the Buddhists, so influential in the region, were driven into the opposition and took their support to the popular resistance. The country was irrevocably cut in two and the bloody confrontation brought on the war which is still continuing.

I remember the animated and disagreeable discussions that I had on this subject with Foster Dulles, particularly in November 1954, in Washington. He did not believe an authentic experiment of freedom and autonomous development in this region was possible. I was not aware then that certain decisions had been made in Washington which were revealed only recently by the publication of the *Pentagon Papers*. I felt we should play the game loyally in Vietnam and respect the wish of men who had won their freedom by paying for it with their blood. But very soon the French military forces (traumatized by a defeat due more to the politicians than to them) and then successive French governments stopped contributing to the success of an enterprise which, if it had succeeded, would have set an invaluable precedent. After we had continued obstinately for eight years with a war which was contrary to all our traditional principles and also to all realism, they then lost interest in Indochina and some of them were only too pleased to hand it over to the United States.

This bitter story, this wasted bloodshed, provided the arguments for those who had criticized the Geneva Agreements from the start. I continue to believe, with no hesitation whatsoever, that it was the only resolution—and I might add the best investment—that France could have made then to win back the hearts and friendship of the nations she had disappointed. All I have heard these last few days in Japan, Hong Kong, and China, where people have often spoken to me about Geneva, is proof to me and confirms it for me. Above all I am thinking of the thousands and tens of thousands of human lives which were saved. Today, in France and in Vietnam, there are men alive who would have been massacred had the war continued. (Of course, tragedy has since returned to the Vietnamese; but the war was stopped then and it should never have begun again.) Thanks to Geneva, men's lives were saved, young and old, yellow and white, and I shall never regret having done everything in my power to stop the massacre of innocent people.

I really admire the coolness of those who regard as diplomatic blunders the "Geneva wager," as they call it, and the one-month ultimatum to make peace. Have they forgotten that every day that passed meant more bloodshed, more deaths? Moreover, my feelings are the same about the Carthage policy which avoided other tragedies and victims in Tunisia and would have had perfectly satisfactory results for Tunisia and for France if the entire issue had not been reawakened by the horrifying Algerian war. I shall never forgive myself for having been unable to attempt the same thing in Algeria, for having been unable to persuade the Assemblies and the deluded public opinion right from the start that only an emancipatory and generous policy could hope to avoid the tragedy which cut short so many young lives and plunged us into a national crisis, the effects of which still are apparent.

Wilfred Burchett, an Australian journalist who has often been to China and is particularly well informed about what is happening there, is traveling on the same plane. We have been talking though we are frequently interrupted. What does he expect will come from the Nixon–Chou En-lai meeting? Nixon, in his opinion, will not wish to go far enough or fast enough. Even if he is aware of the true situation in Vietnam, he will not dare admit to failure and to plan a complete retreat. So Burchett does not anticipate a concrete result from the Peking talks. Personally I also think that we cannot expect an agreement, that is, a solution, to result from the coming meeting (principally because the Vietnamese have every intention of arranging their own affairs and of not finding themselves faced with a solution imposed by others). Nevertheless, it seems impossible that the Peking talks will not end up with some consultation and negotiation procedure, or by affirming principles on which later discussions will follow. No basic decisions will be made, but the result of the meeting will be the start of something new; that, at least, is what I hope for.

In the meantime, while the conflict continues, the fighting areas are spreading. I have often said and written that if the Vietnamese affair were not settled rapidly, it inevitably would extend toward the west. That is what has happened: Laos,

Cambodia, and now Thailand have in turn become involved and this may not be all. Yesterday the North Vietnamese carried off great victories in Laos, and the Vientiane government's position is becoming increasingly endangered; the other side had to call for massive Thai reinforcements. The latter, well armed and well organized by the Americans, may be capable of controlling the Pathet Lao offensive, but in the end it will be to the detriment of their own country's unity. When will the Americans understand that there is nothing to be gained from broadening the battlefield and that it is in their interest to finish with all this by a direct and full dialogue with the Vietnamese?

Solutions for the postwar period remain to be envisaged. It is clear that China does not wish any power in which the North Vietnamese are preponderant or dominant to spread over the whole of Indochina; they speak of the independence of each political unit, not only of Laos and Cambodia but that of South Vietnam as well. There is a slight difference, to say the least, between the attitudes of the North Vietnamese leaders and Peking's views, not to mention those of Prince Sihanouk, the Laotians and even the South Vietnamese, were they communist.

Finally, Burchett is convinced, as I am, that the most difficult issue in the end will be that of the status of Japan. Her economic, political, and military future is as important to China as it is to the United States. How will the problem be approached by the two who are about to talk in Peking— and by a hundred million Japanese, conscious of their new power?

What gigantic and impressive issues there are all over this continent!

But now other considerations are awaiting me. Japan, Hong Kong, China . . . up until now, I have not seen the true Asian underdevelopment. I have not yet seen countries where poverty is endemic and is sometimes even increasing. Japan, on the contrary, is the essence of accelerated development; China is organization, the attempt to master fundamental problems,   189 and the vista of an economic and industrial modernization after the basic problem of famine has been eliminated. As for Hong Kong, I would prefer not to mention it. . . . From now on I shall be seeing countries situated on the other side, Burma and India, which, together with other similar countries, represent almost half the world. Once again I am about to face this great problem of underdevelopment which I already have observed in Africa, in Latin America and, once before, in India. This is a problem which has so often troubled me and which has not sufficiently attracted the attention of French public opinion (including that of all the leftists). Although I shall be passing through too rapidly, I know in advance that I shall once more come up against these seemingly unsolvable contradictions, these apparently insurmountable obstacles, which will have to be resolved and overcome if we are not to accept another failure of our times. I have a feeling of anguish each time I approach the underdeveloped countries where these immense problems exist.

Underdeveloped countries? Officially they are called, rather, developing countries. That term is, in itself, a hypocrisy. The countries which have really been developing over the last twenty years have been the secure, industrialized countries, in the east and in the west alike. Not only have the others lagged behind, but the distance which initially separated them has only increased. Shortly before I left Paris I studied the progress achieved during the 1960s, which the United Nations valiantly called the "decade of development." I found out that those countries with the lowest per capita income, less than 150 dollars a year (in fact, two-thirds of the Third World's total population), achieved an annual per capita growth of 1 percent; the per capita growth rate in the other underdeveloped countries came close to a 3 percent average; while the improvement was far above 5 percent in our secure countries of Eastern and Western Europe and North America. No comment.

Burma

Two representatives from the Foreign Ministry, the French Ambassador, and the Chinese Ambassador welcomed us at Rangoon Airport. I was informed that General Ne Win, President of the Revolutionary Council of the Federation of Burma, and Prime Minister, wished me to be his guest and to stay in a government residence. We are therefore settled in one of the gracious, comfortable "guesthouses" which were built by the British throughout Egypt and Malaysia for their high officials and military commanders. Its style is classical colonial; there are green lawns and tennis courts.

Wednesday, 12th January

The windows open onto a beautiful, calm garden with bright flowers and a large silent lake beyond. The morning sun is very hot. What a change!

To start the day I read the local newspapers. There is talk of the opening of schools where journalists will be obliged to attend courses in order to learn to remain loyal to the true interests of the country and to the ideology of the Revolutionary Council.

We visited Rangoon, a beautiful city designed by the British. It is vast, with wide avenues, official buildings, and numerous pagodas one of which, the famous Golden Pagoda, dominates the entire landscape. The city has two million inhabitants while the population of the country is about 30 million. In the streets we saw large and small markets, children running about, and handicraftsmen working on the pavements or in vacant lots. But except for the center, which consists of a few streets near the port, Rangoon is made up of wide colorful spaces, with large trees and houses, almost smothered in bougainvillea and other flowers. After having lived for weeks among crowds of people dressed in blue or khaki uniforms, which are quite depressing, here we are mingled with a motley population, dressed in loincloths, sarongs, and dresses in every color of the rainbow.

The brilliant orange saris of the many shaven-headed Buddhist priests stand out. Among them there are often young boys, similarly dressed, between ten and fifteen years old, who are preparing to become priests themselves or who are experiencing some phase of religious practice.

There are apparently about three hundred thousand Buddhist priests throughout the country; they dedicate their lives to prayer, preaching, and education; I have heard that their teaching is not very good. They can own nothing and exist through public generosity. In the morning they leave their monasteries with a bowl and, going from door to door, collect a small quantity of rice which is the contribution of the faithful to their needs.

The population near the port seems very poor. Thousands of Indians and Chinese who work on the docks or in nearby enterprises are crowded into large tall buildings. Here, there are two huge markets, one for day and the other for night, where quantities of all kinds of goods are sold, food products, clothes, materials, and household goods. It all somewhat resembles Dakar.

After shivering in Peking and Shanghai, we have been plunged into a furnace. It has not taken us long to miss the northern frost.

This afternoon we went on the river and then visited a state-run bottle factory which is equipped with West German machinery.

Later we visited a refinery which uses mostly British equipment. The entire petroleum industry (extraction, refinery, distribution, and export) is also nationalized, with the exception of exploration (several inland sites are in the hands of Schlumberger, while the Americans are searching "offshore"). Among the underdeveloped countries those with petroleum are the fortunate ones. Nevertheless, this advantage has not yet been greatly exploited here. The local industries extract the products and by-products (such as asphalt and plastics) which are necessary for local needs. Because their production units are so small, however, their costs are high and exports remain low. Yet there is hope for the future.

We were very graciously received for dinner at the Embassy by Monsieur and Madame Pérès. Since only French people were present, I was able to question them freely.

One must remember that Burma, because of her precious resources, principally rice, oil, teak, and jute, was perhaps one of the richest British colonies. Today the average standard of living of her relatively small population, with a moderate birthrate, is still higher than that of most of the neighboring countries. Her principal export is rice, which is sold to India, Pakistan, Japan, Ceylon, Indonesia, and the Soviet Union. China also purchases some (she exports some to others and by selling it to Ceylon forms a triangular operation; this is convenient to everyone concerned because it reinforces China's political position both with Ceylon and Burma and enables the latter to pay for part of her purchases in China). The Burmese also export cotton, rubber, vegetable oils, and, of course, teak.

The present regime, which came into power after a coup in 1962, is organized according to a military method, a system called the S.A.C. (Security and Administrative Committees). Under the leadership of General Ne Win, a centralized secretariat consisting largely of officers is in charge of all political and economic activity. This body chooses the heads of the various services, which explains the presence of many military men in regional and local administration and in industry. (This afternoon, when we visited the bottle factory, we were received by a high officer who manages it.) There are groups on the local community level in charge of disseminating and implementing the central administration's orders.

Every now and again there are discussions about limiting

the military style of the system by transforming the Revolutionary Council into a government . . . composed of the same men who would have left the Army.

Whatever comes of this, they are actually facing serious difficulties, primarily about the plan for national unity. Groups of underground fighters have formed in the border regions near China, Thailand, and Bangladesh. The newspapers carry accounts of the incidents which occur here and there, particularly on the Thai frontier where the Army at the same time claimed to have definitely put down the rebelling minorities. Economic problems are linked to the troubles which continue in the frontier zones.

The troubles in the north, however, are of a particular nature as China is close by and the underground fighters are known to have been supplied with outside aid and sometimes even with actual military support, at least that is the rumor. After General Ne Win's visit to Peking there was very definite improvement and even a lull in the revolts in the north. But recently the troubles seem to have broken out again, without any visible reasons or any certainty as to what extent China has encouraged the troubles.

These rebellions near the borders are among the principal factors which have curbed and limited the export of teak, wood, oil, precious stones, and minerals, because the zones where these resources are found often are unsafe. Moreover, because of the instability within the country, a third of public expenditure is committed to military expenses. The situation is further complicated by the propaganda of the two communist parties, the White Flag, which is linked to Peking, and the Red Flag, which claims connections with Moscow.

Finally, there is the resistance of right-wing circles, the former industrialists and the property owners who disapprove of the present socialist policy. The government actually has nationalized a great deal. The entire banking sector, a large factory which makes jute sacks (which are needed for rice), a pharmaceutical-products company, a steel factory, sugar refineries, some distilleries, and the entire petroleum industry, as I already have mentioned, have come under public control. The dispossessed but still quite powerful proprietors support U Nu, the former head of government who has found refuge in Thailand but who, apparently, sometimes crosses the badly controlled frontier and comes to stir up the separatist movements.

The noticeable decrease in export prices, particularly of rice, in the course of the last few years has made it harder for Burma to solve her economic problems. Because receipts from foreign trade have fallen, the authorities have been forced to tighten exchange controls and to limit imports of manufactured products, with the immediate result that a black market has developed.

Various countries provide Burma with a certain amount of foreign aid. Japan heads the list and in a different way China is one of them. France is scarcely represented; apart from providing electric locomotives, our industry is not visible here.

Although I have had a busy day and it is late, before I go to bed I cannot resist looking through a collection of English and American newspapers that were left in my room. In them are long accounts of the United States—Japanese talks and of Nixon's meeting with Sato. As could have been foreseen, the discussions seem strained. It is true that the Japanese-American cooperation and security treaty has been confirmed. It is true that Washington has made a few concessions by agreeing, for example, to hasten the restitution of Okinawa by several weeks and, what is more significant, to withdraw progressively its nuclear forces from that island. But discord persists between them on the one hand over China, and on the other over commercial affairs. For purposes of their new Chinese policy, the Americans need to have their hands free, and they reserve the right to make concessions in Peking next month, or possibly later, which could cramp the Japanese. But the latter no longer wish to be faced with accomplished facts. They find it hard to accept that the Americans should make all the important decisions unilaterally. An uneasiness begins to be felt and the debates between these two countries, which have been closely associated for a generation, increasingly will be charged with mistrust. Japan will seek a new course, probably after Sato leaves; she will have great difficulties because "no one will make her any presents." But inevitably all the problems will have to be reviewed, and it is significant that Foreign Minister Fukuda (whom I unfortunately missed in Tokyo, because he left for the United States just as I arrived), should already have found a very subtle way of demonstrating that Japan's obligations to Taiwan are of a different nature and far less constraining than America's. This is significant, for if Fukuda is to succeed Sato this year,[4] as many people are confident he will, certain initiatives can be expected on his part which will be intended to free him to some extent from the American hold. This is particularly so because of the vulnerability of the United States on account of its grave anxieties over the dollar.

Concerning this question, the latest French papers mention a revival of monetary problems. I am not in the least surprised by this. At the time of Pompidou's and Nixon's meeting in the Azores and later when the Ten conferred, I had the impression, as I have already stated, that the real problems had not been dealt with. Had the hasty decisions that were taken included a certain dollar convertibility in some form or another, they might have been able to last for a while. But it was not possible. Under those conditions, the dollar devaluation was not a solution: the price of gold went from 35 to 38 dollars an ounce, but what did that mean and what did it change when it was impossible to convert dollars into gold? The public instinctively sensed that nothing had been settled and that the entire monetary system remained as fragile as ever. Thus a justified anxiety concerning all currencies in turn brought about movements of all kinds: on the stock exchanges, in gold prices, and so forth. In the absence of fixed rules of the game, clear and comprehensible (like the gold standard in the past, although I am quite convinced that the gold standard is no longer viable), any arrangements must remain precarious.

The newspapers announce that during the last few months

European and Japanese central banks have once again accumulated considerable amounts of dollars. What will eventually become of these dollars? How will they be used? This is something that Japan's Foreign Minister declares he is wondering about himself, for he has not the slightest idea what he will do with the dollars his central bank is reluctantly continuing to amass. His European colleagues must be facing the same dilemma.

Thursday, 13th January

This morning we went to Pagan, one of the historic capitals of Burma. We visited countless temples, pagodas, and ruins. There are, they say, six thousand pagodas and, though it is impossible to count them, it is easy to see that they are everywhere, dilapidated or glorious, small or vast. But most of them have been abandoned for a long time.

The town has only five thousand inhabitants in all. The splendor and size of the ancient structures show that formerly there was a much larger and more flourishing population there.

Each time I come across a similar situation (in the country of the Mayans or in the ruins of Palmyra), I try to imagine what events, what tragedies must have led to such vast deterioration. The political explanations often given for this do not suffice. The deep causes, which generally are economic, should be found. All they say here is: the kings changed capitals. But precisely why did they change capitals? It is perhaps a consequence rather than a cause and, in any case, that cannot account for the poverty which followed former wealth.

To visit Pagan is impressive and one should devote more time to it. But even our hosts did not urge us to stay because of the lack of accommodations. They have only just built a "guesthouse" which will be able to provide for a few tourists. The government has not made much effort up until now to promote and increase tourism, though a contribution from tourism to the balance of payments would be very useful. However, in this country which is closed in on itself, they do not much like the presence of foreigners; they mistrust them and wish to preserve the purity of the national lifestyle and perhaps also to keep the controversial influences of the outside world at a distance. This mistrust is understandable. The only foreigners Burma has known in the past have been hostile, pillaging, dominating invaders. The Burmese still retain disagreeable memories of them. Nevertheless, they possess so much scenic wealth that visitors in search of new places are sure to invade their isolation a little, in the future.

Friday, 14th January

We visited Mandalay, where there is at least one clean, pleasant hotel ready to receive tourists (since there are already a few here). Mandalay became a royal capital only in the nineteenth century, just before Burma's independence came to an end and before the British colonization. This is another matter of curiosity: how did Mandalay collapse and how did it lose the resources which had enabled it in the past to construct such powerful fortifications, palaces, and temples? The arrival of the English is not a sufficient explanation.

Because of successive waves of destruction, especially those of World War II, today only a few traces remain of former splendor. Mandalay is on the famous so-called Burma Road, which played a large part in the military history of the region and in supplying the Chinese who were fighting against the Japanese. The city was bombed first by the Japanese and then by the British. Nothing is left of the famous royal palaces.

With 50,000 inhabitants it is nevertheless the second largest in the country, but it is more typically Burmese than the capital, which has become somewhat cosmopolitan due to British colonization and to the presence of large Indian and Chinese minorities.

Daw Tinhla, the curator of historical monuments and the person in charge of the town's cultural affairs, took us on the traditional visit to the pagodas and handicraft workshops. She is a curious, interesting person, a descendent of an aristocratic family which played an important part during the epoch of the kings of Burma; she evokes historic events, of which Mandalay carries so many scars, with a sort of nostalgia and moving tremor in her voice. At the risk of disappointing her, I must admit that, in spite of Mandalay's historic fascination, I find the Pagan site more interesting, stranger, and finally, of more character, perhaps because of its greater age.

On our return we made a detour to visit a museum, or rather a collection of ancient, mostly religious objects which have been collected by archeologists and some Buddhist priests and amassed in a jumble in huge showcases. The whole thing is guarded by an impressive priest, with shaven head and draped in an orange robe, who took great care to ensure that we go barefooted into this place, which is so full of images of Buddha. As we were leaving he offered me as a gift two ancient statuettes, which were actually a little damaged, but were not without attraction. I could see that I was offending him by offering to buy them and we had a long discussion, for I was embarrassed by his gift and he would not hear of any payment. Finally I accepted his present and into a kind of moneybox I put a small contribution for the upkeep of the museum and the exhibits. He pretended not to see.

When we arrived at the hotel last night, a group of Japanese were having dinner; they are tourists. Today we noticed a large table of Chinese; they are experts come to help with the construction of a paper-paste factory. This is a comparison worth noting. The Japanese are becoming wealthy and they are beginning to spend it on travel, and the wealthiest among them at least already travel all over the world, especially in Southeast Asia. This does not mean that they are not working here; on the contrary, they play an important role in Burma's foreign trade. The Japanese are, for instance, the principal buyers of rice, providing manufactured products and technical equipment in return. Chinese activity is just as great, even though it does not include tourism. The Burmese are trying to maintain an equal balance, giving neither country the impression that it is at a disadvantage compared to the other in the commercial (and inevitably political) competition which is developing on their soil.

Marie-Claire asked a Burmese, "Which of the large countries in the region do you fear the most?" The answer was, "Look at the map. It is obvious."

The alliance between Pakistan and China which has developed during the last few years is the source of great pressure on Burma, which she feels strongly. In this situation she has found relief in the advent of a Bangladesh independent of China, and in the partition of Pakistan, for this gives her the impression that the balance of forces in the region has been somewhat reestablished. This is why she already has recognized the new government of Bangladesh.

Nevertheless there is an overriding desire in Burma to remain neutral in the conflicts which are everywhere threatening the peace. This is both because the structure of the Burmese state is insecure and conflict would encourage the centrifugal movements and lead to its disintegration, and because the standard of living is generally higher here than in India, Pakistan, China, or Thailand; everyone is aware of this and wants to preserve it. Moreover, in the past the Burmese, like the Chinese, were constantly invaded. Contrary to what might be expected, their mistrust of foreigners does not apply so much to Europeans (since there no longer exists a European threat) but to the neighboring overpopulated and poor countries. There are also large Indian and Chinese minorities in Burma that the government is trying, without much success, to send back to their native countries. All this explains the xenophobia and also the fear in Burma of the neighboring nations.

Saturday, 15th January

This morning we are to visit the Shwedagon Pagoda, which is the largest, most magnificent, and most frequented in Rangoon. It is a kind of city within the city, with an imposing number of buildings, courtyards, and temples. Lodged on a hill, its gold shining brightly, it is visible from everywhere in the capital. The dome's outer layer is continually maintained in perfect condition with sheets of pure gold.

Unlike most of the pagodas we have visited during the last few days, there is constant activity there and it is filled with an immense crowd. We were ceremoniously received by a council of "trustees" who are responsible for the complex and its upkeep and who showed us around the inside of the enclosure. There we found a profusion of pictures, statues of Buddha, and symbols of all kinds, as well as offices, workshops, restaurants, and countless "temple merchants" who sell groceries, toys and objects of worship. Nearby, there are places for prayer and relaxation set aside for the priests and there are sacred relics and so forth.

I cannot help pondering the enormous sums contributed by the faithful and, to a certain extent, the taxpayers for the upkeep or reconstruction, and sometimes even the construction of all these places for prayer and pilgrimages. Would it be sacrilegious to point out what a large part of its meager resources this country, whose population still lives so poorly, gives to this? That it uses imported gold by the pound to cover statues of Buddha or temple domes, while it cruelly lacks foreign exchange? Naturally, every nation has a right to choose its own ethic and to worship its god in its own manner, bearing the sacrifices it has chosen. But I find it hard to accept in this case.

For beneath the folklore I am seeking reality and its hardships. For reasons of her own and more general reasons shared by most of the poor countries, Burma has notoriously serious difficulties in bringing her external balance into equilibrium. Receipts have fallen as a result of lower prices for primary products on the world market; during the last few years the terms of trade for underdeveloped countries have continued to deteriorate because the prices of their exports have been decreasing, while those of manufactures from the industrialized countries have continued to increase. Malaya, for instance, had to export twice as much rubber in 1970 as in 1960 to pay for the same quantity of imported goods, and Ceylon had to export one and one-half times more tea to pay for the same manufactured goods she purchases from abroad. This is a general phenomenon of which Burma, which exports raw materials and agricultural products, has suffered the full consequences. 203

And that is not all. Like other underdeveloped countries, she has been obliged to ask for loans from abroad in order to meet her urgent needs. A large proportion of her currency reserves goes to pay interest and to repay debts, thus reducing by that amount the sums available for new purchases. This is the fate of almost all Asian and Latin American countries; which explains their aversion to contracting new debts and further encumbering their future balance of payments.

This situation benefits the industrialized countries wishing to go into Burma. They make very alluring financial propositions to the government in exchange for commercial or industrial advantages . . . which enables them to recoup themselves. In such a race France is at a great disadvantage; she offers the standard conditions for financing, which are obviously costly. Meanwhile the Germans, the Japanese, and others, on the contrary, apparently allow generous credits. I have been told of a transaction which the Germans suggested of a loan, payable over fifty years, beginning only after ten years, at 2.5 percent interest. The prices of the goods supplied at the same time certainly include as an invisible rebate the financial loss accepted on the loan. (Considering world interest rates, no private enterprise nor any bank today can provide a loan that the supposedly beneficiary countries could afford—without some sort of hidden counterpart. These loans should be made solely by disinterested international institutions subsidized for this purpose by the rich countries, since it is the only way to avoid this racket which continues to work to the detriment of the least favored.) Meanwhile the Germans, who systematically make use of this type of operation, increase their already active position in the Burmese market. The same applies to the Japanese who are very dynamic and show much ingenuity. For example, an American company proposed to undertake oil explorations in certain probably propitious areas; there was, however, a financing problem, since the firm in question did not have the necessary means. The Japanese, who were interested in the affair, could not, however, take over from the Americans as they did not have the proper equipment. Finally, the Japanese financed the American exploration on the understanding that if oil were discovered Japan would have priority on the purchase of the output. Triangular operations of this kind well illustrate Japan's skill and versatility in her projects here.

I had an appointment at 11:30 A.M. with General Ne Win who received me at his residence with Colonel Hla An of the Medical Corps, the Minister of Foreign Affairs, the Minister of National Education and Public Health, another military minister, and General Koko, General Secretary to the government, who has the reputation of being very influential in the regime. The head of the government was dressed in civilian clothes and the others were in uniform. The others hardly joined in the conversation. Their behavior and discipline is totally military. There is, however, a rumor that the government is gradually going to become civilian and, to prove it, the ministers will soon be leaving the army.

We first spoke about Burma's industrial development. The General is categorical: with a few rare exceptions, he opposes the creation of foreign enterprises in Burma, even when these would be viable and contribute to the country's expansion and growth, for in the long run foreign intrusion always entails unacceptable political consequences. The necessary investments will be made as they gradually become possible, but by the Burmese themselves. It is unfortunate if her economic development is restrained by this; one must have the courage to make such a choice. However, General Ne Win does not on principle refuse financial aid from abroad if it is to be used by the Burmese themselves. The Chinese delegation I met yesterday in Mandalay is, he says, a good example of this. For some time now Chou En-lai has had a 20 million dollar credit open to Burma, which has the right to use it as she thinks best and under the conditions she alone will choose. Even if Chinese experts have come to study the installation of a factory in the Mandalay region, even if several Chinese technicians later participate in the enterprise, it will remain a national undertaking and he will firmly see to it himself.

This being so, for the plan—even on a reduced scale—

to be realized, Burma would still need to import equipment, machines, and manufactured products. Other than the very limited financial aid the country receives from international institutions, most of the bill for these purchases will have to be paid for by Burmese exports, which consist exclusively of unprocessed products or raw materials: rice, jute, teak, wolfram, and a few other minerals. I asked if they have any plans for processing their products locally, at least in part, in order to increase their value added so as to obtain a better price abroad. The General replied that this is exactly his objective, but it is difficult at present. He neither gave anymore details on the subject nor did he appear very optimistic about the possibilities that may exist. I have the impression that the structure of Burma's foreign trade will not change much for a long time.

As a matter of fact, the western countries know what they can sell to Burma. France, for example, provides her with locomotives, trucks, industrialized products, and such things. What, however, can she purchase in exchange which would "carry the load?" This is the important question here, as it is—though on a different scale—in China. It is a fundamental problem which remains unsolved in the relations of the industrialized world with what used to be called the new nations. A solution can only be political and must include the notion of asymmetry and imbalance. In exactly the same way as taxes function within national communities, the solution must or should entail a transfer from the rich to the poor.

However, up until now these ideas, which at times have been timidly suggested, have made no impression on those responsible, either among the leaders of the West or among those of the socialist countries.

General Ne Win did not linger on economic questions, preferring to talk about international affairs. He first affirmed his intention of remaining loyal to his policy of neutrality, although it is not always easy to have it respected by his neighbors. Indeed, it has successively provoked difficulties with the Indians, Pakistanis, Chinese, and Thais. Nevertheless, considering Burma's military forces and geographic position, neutrality is the only possible policy for her to adopt.

Naturally the head of state is interested in Nixon's visit to Peking. He does not believe anything concrete can come of it at once, yet he is just as convinced that the meeting cannot end in failure. In fact, since the decision to confer with the President of the United States was not unanimously agreed to by the Chinese leaders, even provoking very active opposition, Chou En-lai's group must now prove that it was right to wish to negotiate. As for Nixon, with the American elections approaching, he cannot afford to return to Washington without proof that his policy will open the way to some solutions. The Peking summit meeting could therefore end with "beginnings" from which it will be possible to approach the settlement of the problems themselves. Then I asked the Prime Minister if he did not agree that the most difficult discussions would not be over Vietnam and Formosa, but rather over the future of Japan; will that not, from now on, be the main conflict between China and the United States? Undoubtedly, he answered, yet he has thought of possible solutions. The Americans could evacuate the bases they occupy in Japan, starting with the withdrawal of their nuclear installations, and could still make a military agreement with Japan which would guarantee her security in the event of an aggression. Japanese public opinion would be able to approve of American withdrawal if it were done in this way. Would the Chinese accept this formula? General Ne Win skeptically repeated the question several times. He believes they will be very demanding.

In any case, it will not be possible for a Japanese-American dialogue to settle all the unresolved difficulties. Countless elements will interfere. Moscow will attempt to make it difficult if not impossible for China and the United States to cooperate. The Asian nations do not wish to have their conduct dictated to them in an authoritarian way. The Vietnamese, Cambodians, and Thais will not accept without protest any arrangements or compromises reached by their powerful allies without their participation. They have taken their stand, are passionately involved, and have shed their blood. Their wishes cannot be ignored and to do so will result in more than one complicated situation. For instance, how will the Cambodian tragedy be settled? It is probably the most ticklish of all those in this region.

Ne Win spoke for a while about Thailand. Incidents have continually occurred between his country and Thailand, especially since he has been in power. Part of the Burmese opposition is in exile in Bangkok, where it has found aid and protection, and there are constant hostile infiltrations over the border. Ne Win does not wish to give in to a resentment which would, however, he says, be quite justified. I nevertheless encouraged him to talk by mentioning that, although Thailand's intervention in the Indochinese war for a long time remained limited or at least cautious, during the last few weeks she has provided the Americans with strong and even visible military aid. What will happen once the latter have withdrawn from the Indochinese peninsula? The present regime, groups, and classes in power risk finding themselves completely isolated and unable to maintain the government. General Ne Win, without committing himself, assured me that there are alternative groups of capable men who could take over. He added that certain rebel forces hold several regions of Thailand particularly in the north and northeast. Does he support them discreetly in the same way as the people of Bangkok help his rebels in the eastern part of his country?

Ne Win has also been following the evolution of the Indo-Pakistani conflict very attentively. On principle, he does not believe that one country should be allowed to dismember a neighboring country by military means; and, without expressing it openly, he let it be understood that he did not approve of India's intervention in East Pakistan. (He probably is thinking that several of Burma's peripheral regions, to an even greater extent than before, could also receive foreign military support which would endanger the unity of the Burmese Federation.) Nevertheless, yesterday he recognized Bangladesh. As neighbors the two countries cannot ignore one another. Besides Burma is already providing the new state with food supplies. "We have been asked to provide a million tons of rice;

due to our other commitments, we do not have that much in stock. But we will do our utmost." Burma expects to increase her trade with Bangladesh in the future, particularly by buying her bad quality jute which will liberate large quantities of better quality Burmese jute, which sells well on the international market. General Ne Win protested against my insinuation that Burma cannot have been displeased to see Pakistan —so closely bound to China—removed from her frontiers. Although in the past there were some incidents between China and Burma, all their disputes have been settled. The Chinese know that Burma does not have a hostile policy toward them. Ne Win seems quite confident about this and consequently affirms that the alliance between China and Pakistan causes him no anxiety.

However prudent and tactful he may be about international affairs, when dealing with internal problems he becomes authoritarian and conservative; he is like a different person. He constantly mentions authority and discipline as necessary for dealing with young people and students. He firmly insists that order must be imposed in the universities, that the students must be selected not only on academic merit but also on the basis of the political guarantees they can offer, that the religious schools must no longer be too modern and liberal, and that communist influence must be eliminated everywhere. The Foreign Minister intervened vigorously several times, expressing similar principles, and I soon understood why. He is also Minister of National Education.

What a strange character is General Ne Win! A corpulent man of sixty-five, who has retained a military style and temperament, has nationalized industry, and declares himself a socialist; he suppresses communist propaganda yet seeks to cooperate with China; he would like to modernize his country yet fears any contact with the outside world; and he wishes to have a liberal reputation yet is harsh with journalists, students, and Catholic or Protestant missionaries. He is deliberate, strong, and obstinate. He is also distrustful—of foreigners in particular. Nothing could have been more significant than his reaction when I said, after mentioning the Pagan and Mandalay treasures, that with a little encouragement countless visitors would come here. He quickly answered that he does not like to have too many tourists in his country. They spread ideas and customs incompatible with those of Burma. There is some good in the western world, but it also sows bad seeds. Ne Win wishes least of all to have hippies arrive; at times some have infiltrated, but they were expelled. Once foreigners are encouraged to come, how can they be selected? And so on. Yet, as soon as we left his anxieties over internal affairs behind, the General regained his composure, particularly over international politics. I left him, intrigued and curious to know what his country's position and future will be under his guardianship.

After lunch we bought a few last-minute gifts in the shops in the center of the city. We again had the impression of a densely populated tropical city in the quarter around the port in contrast to the vast geen areas and spacious properties on the periphery. The market is alive with countless small shops, local craftsmen, and also a few more modern shops or enterprises (such as garages, people selling bicycles and tools, and so forth).

Is there a birth-control plan here? No. The authorities do not believe in it, for they consider that the country can easily feed 50 million inhabitants and that it is unnecessary to reduce the birthrate, which is indeed moderate. Burma prefers to increase her population density since she is surrounded by nations where demographic pressure is far higher (Bangladesh, Thailand, China), and were she to remain a low-density zone, it would simply encourage her less fortunate neighbors to infiltrate and eventually overrun the country.

After dinner with M. and Mme. Pérès we left Rangoon for New Delhi. At the airport we found the Burmese officials who have so kindly taken care of us during our very short visit, as well as the French Ambassador and his colleagues who welcomed us so cordially and amicably. Unfortunately, because of a technical matter, the departure of the BOAC plane was delayed. One of the small lights on the control panel was not working. Because of security regulations, the crew could not take off under these conditions. They had to cable London for permission to leave. The answer took four hours to arrive, so we spent most of the night in the uncomfortable humidity of the airport.

India

We slept late this morning as we well deserved.

Then, quickly, a rather cosmopolitan lunch: an eminent member of the Indian Supreme Court of Justice, Mr. Grover, a well known and respected jurist; an old acquaintance, Mr. Younes Nekrouf, Moroccan Ambassador to New Delhi; Monsieur de Lagarde, the French Ambassador, who was once chief advisor to my friend R. de Moustrier; Monsieur Doré, the French Cultural Advisor; and many Indian officials.

It did not surprise me that they asked me many questions about my visit to China. Here, everyone is concerned and constantly anxious about China. Although I did not refuse to answer their questions, I nevertheless tried mostly to make them talk. They all told me what a great relief it is for India to have freed herself from what was felt to be a constant threat; Pakistan's presence on both the east and the west. Now this has been reduced to a single territory on only one of the borders of the Indian Federation.

Nevertheless they are deeply disappointed at the American attitude. The United States always was considered an ally, by reason of the substantial material aid which it provided to India as well as the indirect protection it assured her against Chinese pressure. Now at this crucial moment the United States has taken a stand against India. Nobody can understand it. The Indians, however, are very pleased about the British stand, for in spite of all the past troubles they have had there is still a family feeling here toward England. Their solidarity, therefore, has not come as a surprise. Can she take America's place? Sentimentally, yes—but economically? No, the British certainly cannot take over financially. Nor could the French; especially since there has been some ambiguity concerning their position. It was clear that France sympathized with Pakistan and was delivering arms to her at the beginning of the conflict. France also had a more or less privileged status dating from the De Gaulle period. However, it became plain that Pompidou effected a change as discreet as it was real; for, without turning totally to India's support, the French stand appeared more balanced, possibly neutral; this was manifested by France's abstention from several United Nations' votes at the time when China and the United States were strongly campaigning against India. The press has immediately hailed France as a "friendly power," the Indians are pleased to see that she has at last adopted a moderate, understanding attitude, and the press is publicizing the coming arrival of a French ship bringing powdered milk and pharmaceutical products . . . with no mention that it is a good ten months late and that thousands and thousands of Bengali children, meanwhile, have died of hunger.

Nevertheless, the Indians will not easily forget that the outside world remained silent and indifferent while tens of millions of refugees fleeing East Pakistan piled into Indian camps throughout 1971. The refugees poured into the Calcutta region, which was already underfed, and the tragic problem of supplying them with food was made all the more difficult through the necessity of facing it practically without international aid. It is generally agreed that the Indian resolution of the serious problems which arose then was a true test of strength. What was extraordinary was that all the refugees were vaccinated, and, contrary to all expectations, not one case of cholera broke out, even in full summer. Public clamor was greatest when the passivity of the governments and international institutions, acting as support for Pakistan, became known. Finally, while a gigantic genocide took place on their frontier, while millions of people were being massacred and millions of others were stagnating in camps, the Indians felt themselves so totally cut off from the rest of the world that they found it all the easier to decide to intervene in Bangladesh.

Today, they are bitter and bewildered. The United States, to complete the picture, has abruptly stopped its very substantial financial aid to India, and that at a time when she is bearing exceptional burdens (the refugees, her military contribution, relief to Bangladesh). It is true that Britain, West Germany, and Japan (and perhaps also France) have announced that they will somewhat increase their economic support, but this probably will not amount to much. Will India's difficulties become insurmountable? A lot depends on the coming harvest which appears to be progressing fairly well.

There is nothing in all I have heard over lunch to encourage optimism.

Leaving there I went for a quick walk to rediscover the city I had not seen for so long. I always enjoy the beauty of the forms and colors of these relics of a noble past; old temples, tombs, fortresses from the Mongolian period, which have been treated with respect and very well exhibited.

I am having dinner with several administrative officials, in particular Mr. P. N. Haksar, who is apparently Mrs. Gandhi's chief advisor. There must be several shades of opinion among the high officials at table, yet they don't express them. This is perhaps because Mr. Haksar, who obviously intimidates them, is present. Because of recent events, this former diplomat, who is conscious of his influence and importance, has developed a deep mistrust of the United States and China, and also has acquired great assurance as a result of the outcome of the conflict. Each time I tried to make him talk about the problems still to be settled—how to ease the situation with Pakistan, how to overcome India's and Bangladesh's economic difficulties—I found myself up against a wall of optimism. India can provide her own food supplies; there already was much improvement in the last harvests and the next one will be very good. Bangladesh is a wealthy country, with resources which were not tapped by the Pakistani government; they will, however, now be developed to such an extent that she will even export food products to India. She will have no difficulty in keeping a positive balance of payments. She will have no difficulty finding qualified men to fill the necessary important positions because there will be those who formerly were needed in West Pakistan but who will now return to their own country. Others in East Pakistan whom the former authorities kept, but in inferior positions, now are available. As to Pakistan, she now must radically change her policy, putting an end to her past aggressiveness. India bears her no grudge and has no intention of doing anything violent. Nevertheless, it is up to Pakistan to take the initiative to improve their relations.

Speaking of China, Mr. Haksar believes that even if her leaders continue to increase their anti-Delhi statements, they are too realistic to believe seriously that India is hostile to them. They are pretending to be threatened simply for propaganda purposes; they are well aware that India has no intention of attacking China and will not even allow herself to be dragged into an anti-Chinese coalition. The Chinese have been clearly told that they have no reason to fear any danger from the south or from an India-Bangladesh-Soviet Union alliance.

I must admit that I am somewhat amazed by such excessive confidence. If that is the attitude of the Indian government in its entirety, it must favor the continuance of the existing misunderstandings and tensions. I foresee no progress in India's economic recovery for I believe it would require a more solid estimate of reality than I can sense.

Mr. Haksar's tendency to relate every subject under debate to matters of principle, morals, or insights into historical philosophy made it all the more difficult to converse with him. His theories may be valid about more than one point. I am not among those who criticize India's past policies. Nevertheless, there are some major and urgent problems among those yet to be solved, such as the consolidation of peace, and the economic situation. These could cause renewed outbursts which would be dangerous to the already precarious state of affairs. There is the risk that with excessive optimism this may be forgotten.

Most of the Indians I saw yesterday are members of the Congress Party, the great historic creation which resulted from the struggle for independence.

The party is more of an organization for the administration of the masses than a political party. It has always expressed any currents of thought, which may have developed among the Indian people, adapting them to its general policy and to the limitations which go with the exercise of power. The other parties are much less important, acting as pressure groups upon it. But the opposition and the disagreements of substance give rise to debates and finally to arbitration within the party rather than between it and the others.

India has tried, under its guidance, to follow a peaceful international policy and to maintain a neutral position. She slowly has been drawn into an alliance with the Soviet Union, rather through circumstances than by the will of her leaders. Some of them regret that the days are over when Nehru and Chou En-lai lived in friendly, peaceful coexistence.

The great achievement of the Congress Party in internal affairs has been the attempt to unify this extremely diversified, even heterogeneous state. It is a difficult task to turn a gigantic country, with five hundred million inhabitants who speak four or five hundred different languages and dialects, into a true nation. At the same time the party has been turning toward the strengthening of the socialist and reform aspects of its policy, such as planning, control of the main centers of production, nationalization of banks and insurance companies, and reduction of the old princely privileges. It is true that such decisions were made gradually and always implemented fairly prudently and there has been no true agrarian reform. Even so, the spirit which generally has prevailed is definitely progressive, and the large companies continually complain about it. This on my last journey here.

Since independence India, in spite of the difficulties she must have had to face, has exemplified a country whose leaders and administration have attempted to maintain and reinforce freedom and democratic structures. I shall always remember how Pandit Nehru at the end of his life, in spite of failing health, was bent on having discussions with his parliament and the opposition, and gave a daily account of his actions to the voters to accustom them to the most open democratic discussions. The Indian regime has put its trust in the British parliamentary system in the hope that economic development will go hand in hand with the practice of the greatest possible freedom, a concept which is very rare in the underdeveloped world. Even though rivalries and disagreements have shaken it, one must acknowledge the decisive role of the Congress Party in this experience.

The party recently split into two antagonistic organizations. Mrs. Indira Gandhi's group has won the Congress Party's force and traditional means of securing its power. Elections are planned for next month; there is no doubt in anybody's mind that Mrs. Gandhi and her party will win a widespread victory even in the States, where up until now they have never held the majority.

Mrs. Gandhi's prestige is enormous. Young people and the more progressive party members have always supported her. The spirit she has shown in the most difficult moments and her tenacity, each time she has had to fight to reach objectives for which she has needed to mobilize public opinion, have helped her to win and hold the majority in the party. That is how she also won the reputation of being a radical leader, fighting against reactionary and conservative forces. But her popularity has increased considerably since her recent victory, for, in the middle of a tragic political deadlock, she managed to give the entire country the impression that it was at last to be free of the Pakistani threat.

When I last saw her many years ago, she was working with her father. I would never then have foreseen that she would one day succeed him as Prime Minister, or that she would show statesmanship such that it indeed surprises her friends and adversaries equally. I find she has changed little, looks scarcely older, though perhaps somewhat thinner because of the effort and tenacity needed to fight the tumultuous battles within her party, for her country, and on an international scale. Her frail and very young appearance, in spite of her gray hair, only adds to the impressiveness of the determination and will that one can sense in this woman.

She received me in a bare office, nearly empty. There is, naturally, a portrait of Nehru on the wall; there is a large bare table devoid of papers. This is a place of total sobriety and great silence, where matters of state are deposited, become the object of neat and firm decisions, and depart again, without leaving that impression of clutter and nervousness which reigns in the French ministerial bureaus. No one interrupted her, no one called her on the telephone during our ninety-minute conversation.

Mentioning our previous meeting, I expressed my admiration for the spirit she has shown for so many years in mastering all sorts of political trials, and said that I wished to ask her about her country's situation and its future. But she said that, since I have just visited Tokyo and Peking, it is she who would be interested in hearing my impressions. She proceeded to draw from me a detailed survey of all I saw there and of the feelings about her country I had heard expressed in Japan and China. I made a point of answering as objectively as possible. I did not hide the fact that in China there is much anxiety over India's behavior and that there her attitude over Bangladesh is condemned. Mrs. Gandhi strongly protested against the malevolent intentions attributed to her and affirmed that she feels no hostility toward China. It is not true, she says, that India has submitted to anyone and that, besides, the Soviet Union is not harboring the aggressive plans Peking attributes to her. I answered that I do not believe in these intentions either, but that the Chinese anxieties are a reality and as such must be taken into account. Every attempt must be made to strengthen the chances of peace and to minimize mistrust wherever it arises, even if it appears to be unjustified.

When I thought our conversation was over Mrs. Gandhi

said to me, smiling, that she had not forgotten that I also had some questions I wanted to ask her. I therefore returned to the Bangladesh-Pakistan affair and to New Delhi's relations with Rawalpindi; whatever happens they are neighbors and cannot live indefinitely in a state of cold war interrupted by episodes of heated warfare. Mrs. Gandhi says that it is up to the Pakistanis to become conscious of the new situation; it is the result of their mistakes, of the provocative policy which they have carried out. Now they must take the consequences. We have no intention of starting a war with them, she continued, and they have no reason to doubt that. They should therefore change their behavior toward us. Moreover, the last word always belongs to the realists; the Pakistanis will eventually have to take that into account.

I am not entirely convinced by this line of reasoning. Surely it is up to the victorious state to make honorable propositions to the vanquished. The Pakistanis today are embittered by their defeat. In such a case, the worst passions, hatred, and feelings of revenge will inevitably develop. In the long run this could make the situation more difficult in the future than it has been in the past. Time does not always work in favor of peace; it can imprison nations in irrational, chauvinistic positions, while their leaders become paralyzed by nationalist exaggerations. I expressed the hope that therefore India would actively seek constructive solutions and that she would do so quickly, while nothing is yet irrevocably set. I ventured to make a comparison: "After the Six Day War, I thought that the Israelis should have taken the initiative of making a generous proposition. At that moment it would have been possible to achieve anything. Such a gesture would have seized the imagination of the Arabs who were abashed and crushed by the suddenness of their defeat. Many Israelis, however, believed that the hour for such a move had not yet come, that time could only act in their favor, and that the Arabs would eventually face reality, at which time a solution would be possible. I have always been convinced that it was a serious mistake, for I believed that the value of the Israeli trump cards such as the occupied territories would gradually diminish and would not facilitate future negotiations. Indeed, although I have no thorough knowledge of the Indian subcontinent's problems, I feel that my reasoning is equally valid here today."

I had the impression that Mrs. Gandhi did not much appreciate this comparison, but that she was nevertheless struck by my words. She somewhat nervously took down some notes in a small notebook, which surprised me since a secretary sitting in a corner of the room was taking down the conversation in shorthand.

"Do you have a concrete proposal to make to me?" she asked me finally, as if she believed I had come with an unofficial message. I by no means wanted her to think that, just as I was not claiming to bring a solution to a conflict, the facts of which she knows far better than I. Nevertheless I continued: "I am talking as a friend of your country. You must act while there is still time. Today everything is fluid. In six months or a year both sides will have taken fixed stands, will have sworn oaths from which neither you nor your former adversaries will be able to free yourselves. That is what happened in the Middle East and that is what now makes a settlement so difficult."

I felt that she was not indifferent to my arguments. I wonder, however, what will endure of this when, in the work of the day, she again faces the problems one by one, the difficulties one by one; when without surcease she must deal with what is most urgent, and in the course of this, let time—not always a gallant gentleman—flow by. She is at the moment involved in a tough electoral campaign: no political leader is ever interested in taking a moderate stand at a time like this.

She is basically still very bitter about the way she was totally abandoned in the dark hours of the crisis and the Pakistani genocide, while at the same time in India the anger of the army, the nation's rancor and resentment, and centrifugal forces of all kinds threatened to plunge the country into despair and chaos. So she returns to the past—possibly in order to escape from the present for an instant. Throughout

1971 her cries for help and her appeals were left unanswered. She visited the heads of state in the West. She was politely received everywhere, but nobody seemed to hear her, nobody wanted to know about the atrocities being committed in East Pakistan, nobody cared about the millions of humiliated miserable refugees. The United Nations should have intervened, to force Pakistan to adopt a more humane policy. Nothing was done; all great principles were forgotten. Today everyone feels free to reproach her for having intervened in favor of people who were being massacred and were calling for help; and the United Nations has dared to condemn India. She is very upset about it. If the great powers and the United Nations had done their duty, millions of human lives would have been saved. For three million civilians died in Bangladesh. All these memories are still fresh and obviously do not encourage the Prime Minister to make the effort I had hoped for to ease the situation.

She has been disturbed more by the American attitude than by international indifference and nonchalance. She said: "I said the same things to Richard Nixon as I did to Georges Pompidou and Edward Heath. I explained the same things to all of them. Pompidou and Heath understood me even if they did not entirely approve of what I was doing and did not give me aid. Nixon, however, did not really understand a thing. He did not want to consider what we are going through here, the suffering of the population. Why this harshness toward us?"

She continued: "Today, the United States says that it will provide us with no more financial aid. Well, we do not need it and, in any case, we will never allow anyone to threaten our independence by such pressure. We will manage on our own, we will maintain our independence. It is true that we are grateful to the Russians for their support, but we do not depend on them; we have paid for the arms they provided us down to the last cent."

The audience was over. The Prime Minister very graciously said that she was very pleased to have had this conversation and invited me to return to India from time to time to see her. These words did not seem to me to have been said purely out of courtesy.

Afterward I had a second meeting with Mr. Haksar. I arrived at his office late, as the conversation with Mrs. Gandhi had lasted longer than expected. He would not let me apologize, finding it quite natural that I should have lingered with the Prime Minister.

I was immediately struck by the contrast between the beautiful, austere, noble office of the head of the government and this one which was ugly and smothered in a snowstorm of folders. One senses that all official business passes through here to be studied and sifted by some outstanding aide responsible for centralizing, sorting, and studying it closely before it reaches the Prime Minister's table. From there, the decisions having been made, it must return to Mr. Haksar to be implemented by him.

Both the atmosphere and style of this office also are different. The telephone rang several times and Mr. Haksar did, in fact, have his secretary answer that he was busy. But I once again encountered this man's philosophical or sociological temperament. He referred at times to Rousseau and to Clausewitz to demonstrate India's rights and her indisputable eventual success. His manner of approaching problems is evidently conditioned by a set of convictions and unshakable certainties. Listening to the impressive profusion of knowledge and erudition in his discussions, I cannot help comparing him to the very influential advisor of another head of state. Mr. Haksar resembles Mr. Kissinger psychologically and, to some extent, physically. The former is bigger and conveys a certain power which Kissinger does not, but they are ponderous in the same way. Both of them are obviously indefatigable, meticulous workers who for a long time have thought about and developed certain opinions and doctrines and, as a result, fight tirelessly to shape their countries' policies.

I am certain that Mr. Haksar is sincere when he declares that this country nurtures no aggressive or even hostile feelings toward China. He does not, however, seem to take into account the fact that the Chinese have the opposite conviction and that, in spite of difficulties, it is necessary to try to assuage their anxieties and mistrust.

Mr. Haksar returned with perhaps more precision to what Mrs. Gandhi just had been telling me: "We will make the necessary effort to manage without foreign aid. Half of what America lent us annually was spent on interest or debt repayment, while the other half was "conditional aid." That is to say, we were obliged to use it to purchase goods in America for which we paid 15 percent more than their real value. A splendid deal, as you can see. We will modify our habits in order to do without foreign support. In any case, we will never accept its becoming a threat to our independence."

Mr. Haksar, in any case, is now waiting for Pakistan, China, and the United States to modify their positions "to coincide with reality." They will end up, he says, seeing things as they are. Will this spirit assist the normalization of relations in Asia? In my opinion, it is clear that India's neighbors will seek any possible means of preventing the consolidation of the present situation. Did not Chou En-lai speak to me at length about the centrifugal forces which one day could break up Indian unity: Sikh, Tamouls, and other minorities—not to mention the small but ardent Maoist groups? I chose not to repeat this to Mr. Haksar.

In the fifties Peking and New Delhi had excellent relations; when did the first misunderstandings arise between them? Mr. T. W. Kaul, whom I met next, the most important official in the Foreign Ministry, knows very well this story in which he played an important part, particularly at the time when the agreements were signed by Chou En-lai and by Nehru. He assures me that even now he wonders what reasons caused China to end this accord which was advantageous to both, by sparking off one fine morning those grave incidents concerning the resolution of their common frontier. Mr. Kaul does not understand what happened.

We spoke about Vietnam and he recalled the part I played in 1954 in words which pleased me greatly. The attitude of the French government of the time, he says, remains in the memories of the Asian peoples, and especially in India's, because of the settlement that was reached at that time in a democratic way on the Pondicherry problem. Although theoretically India was not a member, she nevertheless played a big part in the Geneva Conference through the skill of Krishna Menon; because of this she was chosen, along with Canada and Poland, to join the commission for the supervision of the agreements. Mr. Kaul wonders if what remains of the conference—for instance, the combined Anglo-Soviet presidency—could be of use in establishing a solution for the future. I personally believe in the principles we set up in Geneva; but the situation has evolved so much since then that it is unlikely that a solution could be reached based on a seventeen-year-old framework. China since then has achieved international status which is clearly more assured and more ambitious. In another quarter India, whether she wanted it or not, appears to have openly taken sides in the Moscow-Peking conflict. It seems to me for all these reasons that it would be difficult to revive the Geneva Conference. Furthermore, changes have occurred in Cambodia, Laos, and Thailand. What kind of balance will prevail among these countries? Since North Vietnam will certainly emerge strengthened from the ordeal, will she dominate the situation? If the total unification of Vietnam is to take place, it will do so progressively; the delays and way-stations will depend entirely on the North and South Vietnamese who will at first be separately constituted nations. Elsewhere, Cambodia has demonstrated during the last few years a desire for independence which cannot be ignored. Neither the "Sihanoukists" nor the Cambodian Communists will allow themselves to be dominated. This is also the opinion of Mr. Kaul, but all this is hard to predict.

We returned for a moment to the subject of Sino-Soviet rivalry in Southeast Asia. Mr. Kaul made one precise statement in which he categorically denied that India has granted the Soviet fleet any facilities whatsoever in their Indian Ocean ports, particularly in the Andaman Islands.

I was entertained at lunch by the ambassadors of the Common Market countries . . . including Great Britain. I had an interesting conversation with these men who obviously are very close. The policies followed by their governments may not always be in harmony, but, in the face of Southeast Asian events, that harmony is realized among them here at least. I was struck by the uniformity of their judgments, both concerning the crisis of the last few months, and the outlook for the future.

With a few small differences, these diplomats all warned their governments about what was happening during the critical months of 1971: that the profusion of refugees pouring in was an unbearable burden for India, that India could not avoid being implicated in the East Bengal situation and could not usefully support the rebels without intervening, and that she undoubtedly would do so if no exterior pressure were placed on Pakistan. For a few weeks some thought that discreet nonmilitary Indian aid could solve the problem and that the Bangladesh revolt could come through on its own; but the Pakistani army, which firmly held the towns, the airports, and so forth, was opposed only by unorganized peasants. It spread dreadful panic which increased the exodus of refugees and the indignation of the Indians. Public opinion became more and more heated here as the entire world remained passive. Finally it became impossible to avoid the conflict.

Those to whom I was speaking considered that from that moment hence there could be no further doubt about the result. It seems, however, that opinions differed. In the same way the reports differed, on the one hand, between the United States official representatives in India (who foresaw an Indian victory and considered it best not to take sides) and, on the other hand, the military men and special services, who favored Pakistan and believed the latter could win. They believed the Indian army incapable of fighting, whereas the well trained and well led Pakistanis were inspired by a warlike spirit. The debate in Washington appears to have been lively and has been the subject of some lively revelations in the American press which show that Dr. Kissinger, principal instigator of the United States–Chinese negotiations, supported Pakistan, which had indeed played an effective role at the start of these negotiations. He also wished to avoid displeasing Peking. His policy was adopted. This would explain the United States attitude before the outburst during and since the hostilities. It is at present maintaining its negative attitude which settles nothing, mainly by announcing the cessation of economic aid; this will merely cause India to change her economic policy and adopt ways of doing business about which the Americans will be the first to complain.

We went on to other subjects. The West German Ambassador, who participated in the 1954–1955 Franco-German talks as an advisor to Adenauer and Hallstein, remembered the forthright discussions we had and the reactions of the old Chancellor, who was not too fond of me. The Englishman made an ironic remark to which the German replied sharply. Then I said, "Now that we are all in the Common Market, the real difficulties are about to start."

I would have liked to hear the Italian Ambassador a little, since he is one of the most reliable experts on the Arab problems in the Middle East. I unfortunately did not have time as, before going to visit Sirdar Swaran Singh, the Foreign Minister, I had to fit in a visit to Mr. S. K. Banerji, General Secretary to the Ministry of Foreign Affairs.

He also started by going back to 1954, Geneva, Pondicherry, and the effort to achieve peace and understanding on all sides. After briefly discussing what India could do to normalize her relations with her powerful and mistrustful northern neighbor, he took me to Sirdar S. Singh. He is a great old man of noble bearing, a Sikh with the traditional round beard and magnificent white turban. He is well acquainted with most of the world's foreign ministers as he customarily attends international meetings. He, in his turn, mentioned the 1954 Indochinese agreement and asked me what, in my opinion, could be the solution to the renewed conflict in Vietnam. The Americans, I said, must be aware that they will have to withdraw and I believe the earlier the better. The Chinese, for their part, declare that they are prepared to act as intermediaries, but that it is up to the Americans and Vietnamese alone to conclude the real business. Isn't there, the Minister asked me, an inclination in Hanoi to absorb the entire peninsula? I do not believe that the South Vietnamese, Cambodians, and Thais would let themselves be dominated, pure and simple. As for the Chinese, it appears they do not wish a too important political entity to form on their southern border; they would prefer, if I am not mistaken, several separate national units, provided these are genuinely independent and could not be of service to a venture of a third state, which might be directed against China.

Sirdar Singh then gave me his opinion. Peking's leaders have just scored a great victory by entering the United Nations. He is pleased that right from the start India fought for the recognition of China's rights in the United Nations. France, he says, undertook the same thing, but we were a long way ahead. After the 1954 breakthrough in Geneva the French governments once again started ignoring China until De Gaulle established diplomatic relations with her. But "by a curious change of attitude, now that they are in the United Nations, the Chinese use this forum, which at last is open to them, to attack and insult us. We have had the presence of mind not to respond and we do not regret having worked for them to be admitted to the organization. It was just and reasonable. After all, during the Indo-Pakistani crisis it was better for them to be able to voice their feelings in this body than to be tempted to take up arms in support of their Pakistani friends. Now that they are participating in the life of the international institution, they can no longer gratify themselves by taking verbal and demagogic positions of principle and by taking initiatives which are more or less dangerous to peace. They will be obliged to accept responsibilities, participate in votes, have their points of view confronted by those of other countries, take into account the opinions of others, and exercise their right of veto. In the last analysis, the United Nations will be for them a good school in international politics. All told, even if they use it against us, it will be a positive factor for peace."

We discussed the subject of Japan and her future. Sirdar Singh is aware both of the opposition which is emerging there over foreign policy and the negotiations which ought to open between the Japanese and Americans on the one hand, and the Japanese and Chinese on the other. But here everything depends on the Chinese. What are they thinking? Are they ready for talks or will they delay them?

The Minister firmly repeated that in any case India would do nothing that could poison situations anywhere. She has informed Peking that she, for her part, is ready for talks and improved relations. Contrary to reports in certain newspapers, India has not given the Russians any military bases or any special port facilities anywhere. India will not be dependent on another state or submit to another's foreign policy whoever it might be (and here, once again, was the affirmation that she has totally paid for the arms she received from the U.S.S.R. in 1971 and 1972).

We continued our conversation later, as I again met Sirdar Swaran Singh, along with other officials, at a dinner given in his honor by the French Ambassador. Present were Mr. T. N. Kaul, Mr. S. K. Banerji, several members of Parliament, and Mr. Patel, General Secretary to the Ministry of Finance, whom I know, having met him several times in Paris when he was at the head of a large economic mission. (In addition, I am seeing him again tomorrow.)

The discussions this evening were mostly about Pakistan and Bangladesh. I asked what might happen if the Indian government were to propose forming a confederation, a common market, or any other kind of collective organization with them to enable them to settle together those matters which none of the three countries could resolve separately. India would thus prove her willingness to work with her neighbors on an equal footing and to embark at last on economic projects which are in the genuine interests of the people of all of them; for these nations should undertake positive programs rather than clinging passionately to old hatreds. India, Pakistan, and Bangladesh, which supply 80 percent of the jute produced in the world (if Burma were to be included, this figure would be even higher), combat one another in world markets and end up by impoverishing one another. If they were to unite, they could restore prices, reduce the exploitation imposed on them by middlemen, use their primary products and manufacture goods themselves, transporting their exports in their own ships—in short, improve their terms of exchange. Together they could build large dams to control the rivers which cross their frontiers and finally make use of the water, instead of wasting it (when they were not being devastated by it) as they have up until now, because anger and political resentment made it impossible for these countries to collaborate. West Bengal has a good deal of coal which it could supply to Pakistan and Bangladesh who until now have bought it thousands of miles away. There are many other possible examples.

I am clearly telling Sirdar Singh nothing that he does not already know. But "it would not be prudent for us," he says, "to take such an initiative at this moment. Coming from India, the most powerful member of this uncertain three-sided organization, the suggestion would be misunderstood and wrongly interpreted as demonstrating a wish to dominate the group. We will later, however, be able to consider these ideas."

I am not very pleased with this procrastinating reply. If there is a danger that a proposition might be misunderstood, one can and must take certain precautions. Nevertheless, I am still convinced that it is up to the victor in this kind of situation to show political intelligence, skill, imagination, and even audacity. India must not adopt a passive wait-and-see attitude, must not allow positions to harden, mistrust and anxieties to increase. This would be to risk unexpected flareups in a situation which is far from being stable.

Although I did not say so, I have the Naxalist Party in mind; a small left-wing group, it has much ardor and fighting spirit and is known to be under Communist China's influence (to the extent that it proposes to construct socialism on a rural basis, which relates it directly to the Mao school of thought and not in the least to that of the Soviets). This particularly restless party could at any time stir up popular movements especially in surroundings where there are difficulties about food or social problems.

Marie-Claire returned full of enthusiasm about her day at Agra and Fatipur-Sikrit, of which I have marvelous memories. Unfortunately, because of lack of time, I wasn't able to go back there.

Tuesday, 18th January

I have been invited to speak this morning at the School of International Studies, a branch of Nehru University, which has many foreign students. I have warned them that I will not be giving a lecture since I really have not had time to prepare one, but have said I am willing to answer questions from professors and students. The dean told me that most of the questions are likely to be on China. In fact, right from the start there were all kinds of questions on China's foreign policy and on "her territorial ambitions." I therefore found myself responding at length to questions I believe to be important.

I do not in the least think that China has any territorial ambitions, as we understand this expression in my country, be they imperialist or annexationist, nor that she has any wish to enlarge at the expense of her neighbors or to absorb them. There are, however, three exceptions to this:

—The first is Formosa, which is clearly a very special case, as both Mao Tse-tung and Chiang Kai-shek have always considered Formosa a Chinese province, especially since the Cairo Conference at the end of the last war.

—The second concerns Hong Kong and Macao which Peking declares to be Chinese territories; their populations are Chinese and they will at a given time have to be returned to their motherland. The Chinese government has, of course, shown no impatience over this matter, but in the longer run there is here something resembling a territorial aspiration.

—Finally, since Communist China has continually protested against what she calls unequal treaties which, in the nineteenth century and at the beginning of the twentieth century, deprived her of Siberian territories, there can be no uncertainty as to her intentions in the northeast. Her leaders have indeed never explicitly said that they claim part of Siberia; but they have proclaimed their refusal to recognize the validity of the past treaties signed by the tsars and Chinese emperors.

Apart from these three exceptions—and they are important ones—I do not believe China to have territorial ambitions. Quite frankly, I cannot guarantee that she may not develop such ambitions later, but I have heard nothing to make me think this is the case. What we know of China's history seems to prove that China has never tried to conquer and to annex, but, as the victim of many invasions, she has always been interested in what is taking place in the neighboring territories, for fear that hostile governments might settle there. For instance, the American presence in Vietnam long appeared to her to reflect their wish to use it as a springboard to attack and invade China. Thus she wishes to be surrounded by friendly, neutral, or sympathetic regimes which should not be powerful enough to pose a threat. This is, in my opinion, the interpretation of China's political psychology regarding the states around her.

This, in fact, explains her anger over the events in Bangladesh. As Peking sees it, the danger lies in the fact that India and Bangladesh are supported by the Soviet Union and could become satellites to be used by the latter in its anti-Chinese undertakings. In the course of the talks I had with the Chinese, I tried at times to get them to accept a more optimistic and peaceful view of the future. I came up against a mistrust and anxiety which are facts which cannot be ignored. Even if one considers that the Chinese are wrong in their view that aggressive plans are directed against them almost everywhere, their view must nevertheless be taken into account. The Indian government must, by its attitude, do everything it can to calm these suspicions and reestablish contact. It has tried to do so according to what I have been told; it must persist in that endeavor.

I was asked what I thought about Nixon's visit to Peking, which is in the minds of many Indians, coming as it does at a time when China and the United States, having recently taken a position against India, are about to strengthen their bonds. Naturally, I knew no more about the coming talks than those to whom I was speaking. I simply explained to them my belief that the pending problems will not be settled in one session, that Chou En-lai and Nixon both need, if only for internal political reasons, the meeting to open the way to future developments and long negotiations which will be complex and extremely lively. The two partners will probably outline general principles within which talks will then be able to continue. Perhaps this preparatory work is already quietly under way, even before the trip of the American President.

At 11.30 A.M. I have an appointment with Mr. Patel, a charming, open, liberal person who obviously enjoys discussions. I had hoped to talk to him about financial questions but it was impossible and we could not escape the present political problems. Knowing his influence, I once again repeated my hopes that the Indian government would take the next initiative to unblock the situation and to begin true negotiations with Pakistan. It is time for India to overcome the irritation caused in the past by the attitude of her neighbor, to put aside her resentment over the refugees she has taken in and who are still in her country, and to give up uselessly judging the former Pakistani government; solutions must now be reached. I believe more and more, after listening to the Indians to whom I have spoken, that there are countless technical, commercial, economic, and human problems that Pakistan, India and Bangladesh should deal with together. This is an opportunity for India to call upon so many men and women who are suffering and show them that they can unite against poverty and famine. Mr. Patel is skeptical. We may perhaps be able to reach that stage later, he says, but the moment is not yet ripe. I am disappointed to see that an expert of his competence should allow himself to be dominated by a paralyzing political situation.

I then met another expert, Mr. Ashok Mitra, and this time I was determined to limit our conversation to economic matters. Mr. Mitra is a high official, known for the independent, courageous stands he takes. Without breaking away from the official point of view, which continues to be very optimistic, he added some interesting and, in my opinion, realistic nuances to it.

At my request, he started by describing the Bangladesh economic situation to me. Fortunately the war has not been as heavily destructive as was feared. Certainly, peasants returning home often do find that their cattle have disappeared or that their tools have been scattered about, which will mean that agriculture will be slow in starting up again and that the 1972 harvest will be less than in previous years. But this is all temporary; the country will be able to develop fairly rapidly and to improve its balance of payments soon; the intermediary period will be difficult. The new state will have to build up an administrative corps and eventually an army, which will take both time and money to accomplish.

Jute is the principal export of Bangladesh and her new government has nationalized the jute industry. India, which also produces a large amount of jute, has always competed with East Bengal in world markets; this will no longer be true. From now on the two countries will work together. They will not, however, be able to make use of their position to impose excessive prices arbitrarily; competition from synthetic fibers as well as other producers, Pakistan and Burma, will prevent this.

Up until now Bangladesh imported some of her food supplies from West Pakistan. This is now out of the question, at least for the time being, so she will try to increase her domestic production. This poses a delicate problem: should they increase the area devoted to the production of jute or rather that planted in rice and in grain? In the first instance, the new state will export more jute and will be able to obtain some of her food supplies from abroad. In the second instance, by purchasing less grain, she will compensate for the loss in export revenue. She will have to choose one or the other of these alternatives. One must bear in mind that Bangladesh is, in any case, short of food (though indeed by very little); one can hope that an effort to stimulate and increase production by 10 to 15 percent could solve the problem; but that cannot be done from one day to the next. There is always this race against time and this terrible interim period during which it will not be possible to avoid difficulties and tensions of all sorts, marked by inflation and leading to mass reactions.

Even so, the country still has enormous potential resources which might eventually even include petroleum. It has a prosperous future before it but until then it will be a heavy burden for India. Will this be partly assumed by the U.S.S.R.? Nobody can say yet.

The Dacca government is preparing to face all these unanswered questions. It has nationalized not only the local branches of the large West Pakistani firms and the jute industry, but also the export trade in tea, cotton and cotton cloth, raw and manufactured jute, and the like. It intends also to nationalize banks, insurance companies, certain sugar and textile factories, and part of the import trade, not for doctrinal reasons but because these are sectors which were formerly in the hands of Pakistani business groups and at present there are no private groups capable of taking them over.

India and her new situation remained to be discussed. Her own problems are serious, in spite of the apparent optimism, even euphoria, I have found here. The last few years have not been bad, chiefly because of an improvement in agricultural production within the framework of what has been called the "green revolution." It must be noted, however, that this improvement does not apply to rice but chiefly to wheat, which is less widely consumed on the Indian subcontinent. Having been possible on only the large agricultural acreages, this improvement has thus aggravated the social disequilibrium between the large and medium-sized landed proprietors and the mass of small peasants. Even if food problems on the whole are less serious than they were several years ago, they remain preeminent because productivity in agriculture has not progressed as much as it should. According to Mr. Mitra, the intervention of fairly energetic, stimulating measures could bring about improvements, but the resistance of the large landowner class must be reckoned with for they always have created obstacles to changes such as agrarian reforms, a more aggressive fiscal policy, and the development of cooperatives. They are all the more powerful because the separate states are responsible for most of the measures to be taken (India is a federal state and the central administration has only limited powers) and the influence of the proprietors and principal producers is still important in most of the states. For this reason, the coming elections are of exceptional importance; if the results favor the new outlook which Mrs. Gandhi and her party represent, there could at last be certain changes.

Mr. Ashok Mitra, as everyone, foresees a substantial reduction in foreign aid. He is not over anxious about this, as long as the Indian authorities are clear about the important points on which they must revise their policy and about the new policies they must adopt. More discipline will be necessary not only in agriculture but in many other spheres. The economy will have to be more strictly managed, to keep to a more commanding plan and to better control foreign trade and industry, and so forth. It will be necessary to restrain imports of products which are not absolutely indispensable and, in certain cases, to give preference to local products even if they cost more. He favors at the least a protectionist policy (if not autarchic), relying mainly on domestic resources even though it might entail inconvenience, constraints, and even deprivation at times. In fact, these privations would affect primarily and particularly the more favored categories: the large landowners, merchants, exporters and importers, bankers, and businessmen, but they are powerful people.

Mr. Ashok Mitra's ideas are based on an intelligent doctrine. But in the last few days I have heard similar comments which, however, have more often been based on nationalist or chauvinist feelings than on objective analysis. I have also heard theories being developed, which a year ago were not in the least in favor here, according to which foreign aid is a delusion which does not really meet the country's needs, which indeed only a national effort can do. What also is stressed is the amount of expenditure for luxury, semiluxury and amenities which inevitably accompanies this aid and its allotment, as well as a certain amount of corruption in some circles, all of which does not encourage the growth of national saving. There is much truth in these propositions. No one, however, can deny that considerable support from outside contributed powerfully to the expansion of Japan and Israel, for example (but in each of these cases it was thanks to a native discipline which the countries importing the capital were able to count on). Those here are nevertheless right to stress the fact that the foreign aid they were receiving was increasingly "conditional," for its net value was less than its face value. All in all, these explanations help them to face their present misfortune.

It is clear that the compelling pressure of events has led to a new policy of developing basic industries such as steel, machinery and equipment, and energy production by imposing privations in the economy regarding consumption. They assert that Indian industry is already diversified enough to provide almost all the goods needed although possibly at high prices and subject to some delivery delays which should indeed be tolerable if priority is granted to essentials. Official speeches on economic problems already are appealing to national pride and the wish to dispense with assistance and become independent. Just before leaving Paris I had read very rapidly the proofs of several pages of a book by Mr. Tibor Mende on "the temptation of voluntary quarantine" which I believe would apply to what they are getting ready for here. I wish the author would return to this country for he could witness the psychological development he has described so well.

The most serious among the experts are naturally well aware and do not hide the fact that India will in all likelihood continue to depend on the outside world for certain raw materials, spare parts, special equipment, and the like, but they believe that exports will finance these purchases. They will have to be certain of a given volume of sales abroad in order to obtain the exchange, even if in order to do this they are obliged to export goods (sometimes at a loss) which would be of use within the country. This will guarantee the most vital supplies.

This vision of the future can be realized only if the people understand and support the objectives of improvement and independence. The political mobilization of the country is a decisive factor. This mobilization should not inflame the always latent nationalist or chauvinist tendencies, especially at this time when it is necessary, for the very success of the new policy, to seek cooperation with the countries in the region, particularly the immediate neighbors.

I have often considered these problems, written articles, and participated in conferences about them. A more satisfactory utilization of natural and human resources requires a kind of collective planning whose principles often have been advocated by the Economic Commission for Asia and the Far East, a special organization of the United Nations. If those countries who up until now have been rivals were to reach agreements, it would enable them to put an end to their present anarchical competition and to improve their sales of raw materials and manufactured goods to the industrialized nations (the Common Market, the United States, and Japan). They ought to go still further and build up manufacturing industries among the Asian countries, at least basic manufacturing, which would work for their common needs. However, these countries would have to accept collaboration in order for such collectively organized projects to succeed. They would have to harmonize their production, new industries, foreign sales, and planning; in other words, they all need to have a true wish to cooperate. This will become possible only once they reach some military and political understanding. I am surprised that the leaders, whose qualities, strength, and courage I have certainly seen, have not yet sufficiently understood this necessity.

In the afternoon the same ideas came up at a meeting which I was invited to attend of some of the China scholars whom Monsieur Vincent, the New Delhi A.F.P. representative, had gathered together. There I found mostly Indian men and women, but also a few French teachers, journalists, and officials who are deeply interested in, and sometimes even fascinated by, what is happening in China today. But they all are very much disturbed by the misunderstandings which have arisen between the two countries. They would like something to be done to bridge the gap and reestablish better relations between these two most populated nations in Asia. So, after discussing economic matters, we broached the political and psychological problems. I gave as objective an account as possible of what I learned in Peking and once again insisted on the need for India to prove that she has none of the evil intentions attributed to her there. There are no shortcuts that will assure the rapid success of this kind of plan for easing the situation. Only a long-term policy undertaken with much patience and prudence can accomplish it. I still believe that positive initiatives concerning Pakistan would be a good investment even if the other side does not immediately understand them.

One of the people present returned to the subject of the economic policy which has become necessary here and spoke discerningly about certain of its aspects. Its inevitable effect will be to shut in the country's economy, reduce imports, and the like. The burden of foreign financial obligations will continue, even more than before, to appear in her foreign balance of payments. India has received, like many underdeveloped countries, short, medium and long-term loans. She must therefore repay the principal and interest on these loans, the burden of which has increased. If the volume of her foreign trade decreases, the burden will become relatively heavier. Already during the last few years she has been obliged to ask her creditors for certain adjustments, consolidations, conversions, or reductions. That is, among other things, what brought Mr. Patel to Paris. India is going to be driven by necessity to ask for new easy terms in the course of inevitably disagreeable negotiations, since she will be obliged to discuss and bargain especially with governments that are not very favorably disposed toward her, like that of the United States. A country's financial credit is not improved by such a situation. I have always noticed how the Soviet Union and China understood, right from the start of their revolutions, that it was indispensable to them under all circumstances to be scrupulous debtors and to meet their obligations meticulously. This has assured them indisputable international credit, in spite of the fact that their political regimes very much displease their creditors. Meanwhile in order to balance their accounts, the U.S.S.R. and Communist China condemned themselves to importing less, and producing for themselves—sometimes at the expense of quality and cost—what they would otherwise have had to purchase abroad. The final results of this are positive.

To ask for more time when payments are due is to arouse fears among potential lenders, especially if they are private firms. Private investors who have been investing in India during the last few years will accordingly become fewer and more exacting. I do not believe India can avoid the kind of economic and financial policy toward which she is heading. If I have been emphasizing its consequences it is not because I believe another policy would be better, but because the Indian leaders may not yet be fully aware of the obstacles and difficulties which they will probably have to face for a long time to come.

I tried to obtain more information on these problems by questioning a very able international expert who is in New Delhi for a short visit. He has reached the same conclusions as I, that, quite apart from India's difficulties outside the country, at home she is embarking on projects which are likely to meet with obstacles and resistance, such as imposing more stringent controls on costs, prices, and profit margins, which have been fairly slack up until now, and making a new effort to develop education (unquestionably progress has been made in this field but it is far from sufficient). All this marks a route strewn with pitfalls and resistance—even if one ignores external difficulties. But his main interest is in the agricultural sector. He spoke to me at length about the "green revolution," the massive introduction in part of India of new high-yield grains. Why have they had satisfactory results with wheat and practically none with rice (when similar attempts in the rice-growing regions of Africa have been successful)? It is indeed unfortunate that they have not been able to consult here with Chinese experts (who have been of great assistance in other countries). Nevertheless, their future prospects are not necessarily grim, so long as they initiate resolute agrarian reforms after the elections. These would have an important technical and, what is more, a psychological and sociological impact. While the "green revolution" has noticeably increased the production of wheat up until now, it has benefited mainly a privileged minority (sometimes urban, capitalist, and commercial) because it owns a large portion of the land and because it can speculate on millions of indigent small peasants. If agriculture becomes mechanized, it will simply accentuate social differences even more (at the present stage, it would be inadvisable to discourage the use of animals for pulling plows and so on everywhere, since this method can still yield results; the "sacred cow" is not necessarily unproductive). In sum, the "green revolution" should be made available to the multitude of small and medium-sized producers through a redistribution of land and an appropriate system of cooperatives, which have become more urgent now than ever.

The subject of agriculture did not come up in my next conversation which was with Mr. Nanda, an important Indian manufacturer. Listening to him merely strengthened my conviction that there will be much disapproval of the government's new economic policy. This gentleman is not in the least satisfied with the orientation of the leadership and has come out against bureaucracy, administration, and controls very strongly. Yet, he says, I am not hostile to the government; after having opposed Mrs. Gandhi for a long time, I have now rallied to her support because I unreservedly approve of her patriotic behavior during the past few months. Moreover, she enjoys an immense, well deserved popularity such as no one up to now has known, neither her father, nor Mahatma Gandhi.

I brought the conversation back to economic questions. He immediately renewed his criticism without ever aiming at Mrs. 243

Gandhi herself; she and her immediate advisors are the only efficient people in the government and administrative circles; they are the only ones from whom one can obtain a decision without having to wait through endless delays.

Mr. Nanda is convinced that matters would flow more smoothly and the economic expansion would be greater and more rapid, if the state were to stop trying to meddle in and regulate everything, as much within the country as for foreign trade. He quoted occasions when the administration has hindered or delayed advantageous transactions and prevented the follow-up of profitable initiatives by Indian or foreign manufacturers.

I compared his opinion with what I have been hearing the last two or three days which has led me to believe that there is likely to be an accentuation of the prevailing point of view and an increase in administrative controls. Mr. Nanda does not appear to be prepared for this. Here is a man who is certainly intelligent and experienced, who has on his own organized large companies which play an essential part in his country's development and expansion, yet who does not at all seem to be conscious of its serious problems. How will he react when he learns soon about certain decisions which have been made in preparation for a tightening of controls and doing what is most necessary to achieve the plan's objectives?

Here he is demanding freedom in foreign trade. Businessmen would buy more and sell more and the balance of payments would benefit. He does not seem to realize that India lacks foreign exchange and that the shortage will become worse in the future and that, in any case, certain imports must have top priority. How can one expect private businessmen to understand this?

Frankly, what he said to me did not surprise me much for I have very often heard the same talk in France. I know that competent and efficient industrial magnates have often declared that they were discouraged by the regulations, for they could see in them only the aspects which hindered or irritated them, and did not attempt to understand the need for them. Meanwhile others purely and simply used "every possible means" at their disposal to oppose and obstruct the successful implementation of the government's policy. (It is true, moreover, that officials and politicians, on their side, are sometimes unaware of economic and human realities and do not take them sufficiently into account in making decisions and, even more, in their behavior.)

I met more businessmen, officials, and diplomats at a cocktail party given by Mr. Chandhuri, who is on the economic staff of the government. I put in only a quick appearance as it was getting very late. Many of the guests were complaining about the fact that New Delhi has been almost in a state of siege all day; the government district, in particular, has been completely isolated and blocked off by the preparations for the huge military parade which celebrates the national holiday every year but which will be particularly large this year in honor of the still very recent victory and of the military units which distinguished themselves in the fighting. The entire city is preparing for it. I must admit that I do not much like this atmosphere of military pride, which always encourages nationalist inclinations, especially when the international situation calls rather for flexibility.

Finally, very late, we are having dinner on our last evening with the ambassador of Morocco. His wife has prepared a remarkable Moroccan meal for us of couscous, stuffed quail, and the like. Mr. Younes Nekrouf talked about his memories of Paris and the sudden turn of fortune of North African policy fifteen years ago. A relaxed and charming dinner.

As we were having coffee, a young German journalist arrived. For a year she has been following the Indo-Pakistani conflict in the field. She described atrocious scenes she has witnessed. There are, she says, between the Pakistanis and Bengalis, memories that will not easily be forgotten. The Pakistani genocide was even more frightful than that of Hitler: more than three million people were massacred. It is as if, in France, two million murders had been committed within a few months.

She was authorized to see a Pakistani general who is at pres- 245 ent in prison in Dacca. Her interview with him very much disturbed her. She asked him about the killing that took place, particularly in December and January, under his orders. On the very eve of the cease-fire, he had called a meeting of several hundred Bengali intellectuals, doctors, professors, and writers; all those that went were simply shot. She asked the general: "Is this story true? Is a thing like that possible?"

"Are you not a German journalist?"

"Yes."

"In that case, after what happened in your country not so long ago I am surprised that you should be so indignant"

She is still upset about it.

I asked her if the violence and the reprisals are directed against the Pakistanis or the Bihari minority that is being collectively accused of "collaborating." Yes, passions are still intense; there were violent reactions right after the end of the war. Now things are settling down but anger and bitterness have remained deep in the population. That is, she says, why the Indian army is staying there, at least in certain parts, for several more weeks, because wherever it is there are no reprisals; it has a calming effect.

I would have liked to continue this fascinating conversation and to enjoy further Mr. Younes Nekrouf's hospitality. But it is late and tonight we have reached the end of our journey.

The
Return

Wednesday, 19th January

Our plane took off at 1 o'clock in the morning, local time. We have started what will be a very long night, since we are moving towards the west and constantly keeping the sun behind us.

We are flying over Afghanistan, Iran, Turkey, Greece—countries where there is much injustice, insecurity, poverty, and oppression. The men and women there, constantly anxious about the next day, live under the threat of civil, religious, racial, or international war. That is why, in spite of their poverty, willingly or unwillingly, they devote such a large part of their resources to armaments, encouraged by the suppliers who most often are from rich, industrialized nations.

Far to the south, there is an area where the peace between Israel and her neighbors is in danger of being broken every day. When will peace all around the world become the primary objective of the responsible leaders? Unfortunately, it always seems to be easier for them to start or continue wars than to make or maintain peace! Our colonial wars in the fifties taught me that it is so easy for people who obstinately want to remain at war and broaden it to find a warm reception! While those whose purpose is peace and who value it as the necessary condition for all progress have so much difficulty being heard! How many young lives have we thus sacrificed in Indochina, Algeria, and elsewhere? A similar drama here is prolonging fanaticism and demagogy.

Truly it is easy to preach wisdom, moderation, and a spirit of compromise! That is more or less what I have been doing since the beginning of this journey. I suggested to the Chinese that they not allow themselves to be carried away by their recent political success; to the Indians that they should rise above their victory; similarly, I wish the Israelis to understand the necessity of restoring their adversaries' dignity despite the threats and provocations with which the latter have drenched them for so long. Yes, it is easy to be generous with advice. But it is difficult for statesmen, when leading their people, who are prey to passions, resentment, and ancient hatreds, to take the risks—which clearly exist— of a policy of psychological demobilization, of calm, and of respect for the opponent. For internal reasons and as a result also of accumulated mistrust and resentment, they have a natural tendency to allow themselves a while to catch a breath, to wait to see what will happen to their opponents, and to give themselves time for reflection. But that time can cost them a great deal.

After a conflict, when old structures have been blown to pieces, problems can be reconsidered in the suddenly transformed context. If one does not boldly make use of the propitious moment, fixed positions are taken and harden, both sides swear oaths, and then it becomes no longer possible to free oneself from them. One side naturally plans to win back what it has just lost, while the other, because of recent memories of former danger, feels it must cling to what it calls its stake—visible privileges the perpetuation of which will supply the enemy of yesterday with additional reasons for revenge.

Certainly a nation oppressed, decimated, or unjustly attacked, can hope to free itself only by a great, passionate awakening; there are acts of violence and evil which cry out for vengeance and revolt. At such times the temptation of those who are directing the battle is to appeal to the most primitive, elemental, nationalist feelings. They set up peoples, one against the other, as though they were entities endowed with innate characteristics, irreducible and irreconcilable. They denounce the so-called vices and defects of the ancient oppressors, or simply their neighbors, instead of denouncing only the criminal policies of their leaders. This mentality, these actions, are in a word just variants of racism. For racism, which consists of looking at someone who is *distinct* as *fundamentally different* and as an *enemy,* is today one of the great evils which endangers humanity.

Thus heads of government in this way finally find themselves prisoners of the popular passions which they often have themselves let loose. It then takes uncommon courage for them or their successors to work towards understanding and pacification.

I slept a little as we flew over Greece, which is also a country where there is great suffering, yet a hundred and fifty years ago it was the symbol of the aspiration for freedom. Here the plans of the imperialists and the interests of the armaments merchants are supporting the most detestable dictatorship.

In a feat of modern technology, we have flown nonstop from New Delhi to Rome. Rome is still and again man's eternal appeal to dignity and peace. In the first days of a new year when resolutions rise irresistibly from the heart, may one wish that the most disinherited may find tranquility, security, and the right to work freely for their advancement and the construction of their future? Peace to Vietnam, peace to the Middle East, peace to India, and peace to Pakistan.

I am not one of those who wish to see the world governed in a sovereign way by a few great powers; each nation, small or large, like each human being, must have the right and full independence to seek the means for its growth and happiness. What distinguishes the large nations from the others is their particular obligation and duty not to misuse their influence and arms to embitter and aggravate so-called local hostilities and tensions. Countries which have the atomic bomb are, for the time being, in the position of being deprived of the possibility of going to war; yet the small countries still today, to a certain extent, can among themselves take the risk or bear its threat. In this way their great friends and protectors can act and maneuver through proxies (that is to say, victims). That is precisely what has been happening for dozens and dozens of years in the Middle East, and what has just reoccurred only a few weeks ago on the Indian subcontinent. Neither the superpowers nor France—without mentioning several others—are beyond reproach in this regard.

And what if the small and medium-sized countries should one day free themselves from outside intervention, take their own interests in hand, and settle their affairs and conflicts themselves?

It is only a dream of course. But I believe in these dreams which, from generation to generation, if they have soothed human misery have also given rise to human progress. History has shown that small resolute peoples, bearing witness to the world their will to decide freely for themselves, imposing self-discipline, and self-sacrifice if needed, possess overpowering advantages in the long run, and also that it is possible for them to increase their power by regrouping by means of formal agreements. Yet they must then be capable of suppressing their rivalries and their hostilities in the interest of their genuine universal independence.

I believe that justice and peace will certainly prepare a way for themselves and will assert themselves in the long run. In the meantime we live, we can live, despite so many failures, because deep inside we feel that men's struggles bring them a little closer each day to the moment when "all men on earth will reach out to one another."

Here we are already back in Paris. Our trip around the world has ended.

Thursday, 20th January

Everyone is asking me about my journey. Since this morning I have already had twenty interviews on China and Japan over the telephone.

But are people here aware of what is at stake there?

The European nations and their governments for a long time monopolized the centers of decision and, in one form or another, have guided the entire world's evolution. Their influence was decisive in all spheres—economic, monetary, political, military, and cultural. We are living in a period which will eventually probably be considered a period of great change. After the storms which laid Europe waste, it is experiencing a kind of quiet, a style of life, and system of internal relations which demand a stabilization, the maintainance, at least for a while, of the *status quo.* I would almost say that it has become conservative in the primary sense of the word. Now it no longer seeks, at least not as much as in the nineteenth century, to influence other parts of the world.

But at the same time the latter are experiencing a period of emancipation and upheaval. Thrusts forward, sometimes sharp and sweeping, occur there, and this is true of both Japan and China, though obviously in very different ways.

How will the influence, expansion, or even explosions of these high-pressure zones affect the regions which are still unformed and undecided? Their effects on South America, India, Africa, the Arab countries (and on Europe itself) are difficult to foresee but, in any case, they will be considerable.

If we do not very soon become aware of them, if we do not reach the necessary conclusions about them, we will soon experience potentially formidable counterthrusts. Will Europe, after remaining in the forefront for so long, be late for the rendezvous with contemporary history?

1. The island was returned to Japan on May 15, 1972.
2. As of January, 1974, the General National Assembly still had not been convened.
3. *Ibid.*
4. Fukuda was succeeded not by Sato but by Kakuei Tanaka.